EPHEMERAL BY NATURE

BOOKS BY
Stephen Lyn Bales

NATURAL HISTORIES
Stories from the Tennessee Valley

GHOST BIRDS
Jim Tanner and the Quest for the Ivory-billed Woodpecker, 1935–1941

For a deeper look and color photos of some of the adventures and stories in this book, go online to: ephemeralbynature.blogspot.com, or my author's blog, stephenlynbales.blogspot.com.

STEPHEN LYN BALES

Foreword by Joel Greenberg

Ephemeral BY NATURE

Exploring the Exceptional with a Tennessee Naturalist

The University of Tennessee Press / *Knoxville*

All illustrations by the author.

LIBRARY OF CONGRESS CATALOGING-IN-PUBLICATION DATA
Names: Bales, Stephen Lyn. author.
Title: Ephemeral by nature: exploring the exceptional with a Tennessee
    naturalist / Stephen Lyn Bales; foreword by Joel Greenberg.
Description: First edition. | Knoxville: The University of Tennessee Press,
    [2017] | Includes bibliographical references and index.
Identifiers: LCCN 2017004063 (print) | LCCN 2017005383 (ebook)
    | ISBN 9781621903543 (pbk.) | ISBN 9781621903550 (Kindle)
    | ISBN 9781621903567 (PDF)
Subjects: LCSH: Natural history—Southern States. | Animals—Southern States.
    | Plants—Southern States.
Classification: LCC QH104.5.S59 B35 2017 (print) | LCC QH104.5.S59 (ebook) |
    DDC 508.75—dc23
LC record available at https://lccn.loc.gov/2017004063

To Mary Helen Bales, née Latham,
"Mama Bear," my beloved mother,
whose time on earth ended in 2015.
She taught me to walk and talk and love birds,
and in the end, what more did I need?

CONTENTS

Ijams Nature Center in Knoxville is an amazing place. Boasting first rate exhibits and superb staff, the facility offers a variety of programming designed to foster an understanding and appreciation of nature among the broadest array of visitors. I first became familiar with Ijams through an acquaintance with former executive director Paul James, who shares my passion for passenger pigeons. He graciously invited me to Ijams to present a talk on the species to help mark the 100th anniversary of the bird's extinction. While there I met Stephen Lyn Bales, senior naturalist at the center. Lyn and I were able to spend some time together, and we talked about the natural history books we had written. Lyn was working on a new book, he informed me. I was excited when just six weeks or so ago he sent me a copy. I loved it.

Ephemeral by Nature is a wonderful book akin to a field trip led by an engaging naturalist, both passionate and erudite, as he tours the byways of East Tennessee. For many, it is easy to become complacent regarding the places with which they are most familiar. Surely there are no mysteries to solve or gems to uncover. A good naturalist, however, points out things we may not have noticed or sheds light on a common bird or plant that transforms it into something remarkable. Lyn follows local connections to such disparate and fascinating topics as red pandas, freshwater jellyfish, jack-in-the-pulpits, pine beetles, lake sturgeon, and green-breasted mangos. (I was fortunate to have seen the very individual of this Mexican species that Lyn mentions as having lingered in Beloit, Wisconsin.)

People enjoy stories, and it is through story telling that interest and appreciation can be kindled and stoked. Lyn's mastery of this art lies in his field experience, love of the subject, delight in research, and his ability to use language that clearly explicates and sometimes takes flight like the short-eared owls he tries to show a good friend as a birthday present.

Joel Greenberg
September 2016

There is this rock. It's been at my house for fifteen to eighteen years. I found it somewhere in the Tennessee Valley, probably along a river or near a lake. Who knows? I often go wandering and bring home interesting rocks or other bits of nature. The rock weighs 5.64 pounds, just a chunk of greywacke, a dark, coarse sandstone, of unknown origin. The coarseness comes from very visible grains of quartz and feldspar. The weird rock is rounded, what geologists call a cobble, and the only way nature can make a cobble is to put a rock in a river and roll it around, tumbling it for a while and bumping off all of its sharp edges.

But the odd thing about this rock is that it has a couple of deep grooves. That's what intrigued me. How did nature make the grooves? That's why I noticed it and brought it home, puzzled. For the past eight to ten years, the rock has lain in the middle of my birdbath. Songbirds would come and go, standing on the rock to get a drink of water. The birdbath is heated in the winter, and last February, I noticed that the rounded, grooved rock was covered with a slimy green algae, so I moved it onto a nearby table in the sun where I feed the birds—especially mourning doves, because I like their cooing. A few nights later, a raccoon climbed on the table to eat leftover seeds and knocked the rock off. BAM! The sound woke me. Finding that the rock had once more been tumbled, I brought it indoors and looked, yet again, at the strange grooves.

"Dr. Charlie needs to see this," I thought. Could the grooves be manmade?

I often bump into retired University of Tennessee anthropologist and professor emeritus, Dr. Charles Faulkner. He might have an answer to the question posed by my weird rock.

"Oh, yeah. It's a hand tool," he said when I showed it to him. "Native American people used the grooves to straighten and smooth their arrow shafts. It's like a big piece of sandpaper. As a tool, it would date back three thousand to five thousand years ago."

And it had been in my birdbath for nearly a decade!

The rock itself is perhaps millions of years old, but the people who once used it as part of their handyman's toolkit have come and gone. Compared to the chunk of greywacke, their lives were ephemeral.

Shakespeare's Macbeth realized it in his final days. He knew that life is but a brief candle, flickering in the wind. It struts, it frets, it struggles across the worldly stage of natural history. Some species leave a profound mark, while others are mere whispers in the night. Some we see, some we do not, some we glimpse albeit but briefly, while others are just shadows left in stone.

Within this splendid pageant, across this aged stage, there is rich diversity, enough of a Wonderland, dear Alice, to enthrall an aging naturalist his entire life.

As author Thor Hanson writes in his book *Feathers,* "I'm never at a loss for things to study or topics to write about: everything in the natural world is fair game. If I'm not intrigued and excited every time I step outside, it just means I'm not paying attention."

In *Ephemeral by Nature,* we explore some of nature's brief candles, lives that burn and go dim, burn and go dim, and so on and so on, ad infinitum, to the last syllable of recorded time.

Stephen Lyn Bales
June 23, 2016

ACKNOWLEDGMENTS

With love to Karen Sue Webster and Rachael, two women who have read more books than are housed in many libraries and who watched me grind out two. Thank you for your continued love, support, and understanding.

Thank you, Dr. Charles Faulkner, my exercise buddy at the University of Tennessee, for your interest and insight into my weird rock and to Dr. Colin Sumrall, assistant professor of paleobiology for insight into just what kind of rock it was.

Thank you, freshwater jellyfish expert Dr. Terry Peard of Indiana University of Pennsylvania now retired for reading that chapter and providing input.

Thank you, friend and fellow "craniac" Vickie Henderson who became chair of the board of directors for Operation Migration for reviewing the whooping crane chapter and all of our great times in pursuit of cranes.

Thank you, Sarah Glass, curator of red pandas and special exhibits at the Knoxville Zoo and Coordinator of the Association of Zoos and Aquariums North American Red Panda Species Survival Plan, for chatting with me about red pandas in general and letting me feed one in particular.

Thank you, Dr. Steven Wallace, Curator East Tennessee State University Museum of Natural History and Professor Department of Geosciences for talking to me and giving me a wonderful behind the scenes tour of the museum. Wow! I'm a graduate of ETSU, so this was something of a homecoming and one of the most memorable afternoons I have spent since the Miocene.

Thank you, Joyce Coombs, Research Associate with the University of Tennessee Forestry, Wildlife and Fisheries, and Thom Benson, Senior Marketing and Communications manager for the Tennessee Aquarium for you assistance on the chapter about lake sturgeons.

I am grateful to my dear Ijams's friend Charlie Morgan. She has urged me for years to complete this project and volunteered repeatedly to read the initial manuscript and was the first to do so, offering many meaningful suggestions. What can I say, Charlie? You are brave.

Thank you, my friends Laura Twilley, Linda Claussen, and Karen Claussen-Bishop, for your continuing encouragement.

Thank you, Dr. Guy Smoak, my family physician and dear friend, for your continued encouragement and keeping me healthy and alive long enough to write another book. And to Dr. Raj Baljepally, cardiologist on call at the University of Tennessee Medical Center that weekend in August 2012 when things went bad for me. Thank you for saving my life. It would have been hard to complete this project if I weren't alive . . . well actually impossible. Although this book had divine guidance, that would have been quite a stretch. And thank you to the regular staff at UT's Cardiac Rehab: Tammy, Maija, Judy, Cindy, Rebecca, and Felicia for helping keep me heart healthy and fit.

Thank you, to my dear friends and staff at Ijams Nature Center: Bo, Amber, Ben, Dr. Louise, Lauren, Cindy, Sarah, Jill, Sharon, Rex, Charlie, Jake, Ashlind, Christie, Parker, Jake, Elizabeth, Brenda, and especially to my supportive supervisor and Georgia Bulldog, Jennifer.

Books are difficult beasts to wrestle into submission. Forget that, they are monsters. The notion is ephemeral in itself. This one began over six years ago but went on hiatus because of my own health issues and then time spent caring for my beloved mother. She lived with me her last three years, a time I will forever cherish, but during that time, the fervor for *Ephemeral by Nature* flickered out. The spark is an impermanent thing and inertia is a wearisome barricade to overcome. I will always be grateful to the University of Tennessee Press Acquisitions Editor Thomas Wells for reigniting the flame last January (2016) and to Manuscript Editor Gene Adair for the same expertise he used on my first two books and to Director Scot Danforth for believing there was a fire in me in the first place. Also, thank you to the rest of the staff: Tom, Lisa, Linsey, Kelly, Stephanie, Jon, and Jake. Keep up the good work.

adjective

fleeting, short-lived, transitory, brief, fugitive, short, temporary, transient, volatile, episodic, evanescent, flitting, fugacious, impermanent, unenduring

Life itself

EPHEMERAL BY NATURE

Short-eared Owl
Asio flammeus

"All is in flux, nothing stays still."
—Heraclitus of Ephesus

IT WAS BLEAK, early January. For her twenty-fourth birthday, I decided to give Rachael Eliot an avian twofer: two Life Birds in one afternoon, two species she had never seen before. But their reported locations were miles apart. We would have to be quick and lucky. The clock was against us.

Rachael's middle name should have been "Chutzpah," and in this case, I mean nerve. A student at the University of Tennessee, she attacks her classes with pluck and steely-eyed resolve. She has true grit, what some would call moxie. When a class in something like differential equations—that is, "equations that involve derivatives of a function"—knocks her down, she gets right back up and charges at it with renewed vigor. (Don't ask me about differential equations; it's advanced math that doesn't use numbers, only Native American petroglyphs and signs of the zodiac.) She's tenacious. She has the doggedness of a middle linebacker, like famed Baltimore Raven Ray Lewis. Missing a tackle only makes her even more determined to make the next one. She stays pensive like a jaguar. Rachael Eliot is also a darn serious birder with laser-beam focus and the perfect skillset: sensitive hearing, encyclopedic memory, and attention to detail. To be searching for a bird, a particular bird, is to be totally in the moment, totally alive, immersed in the fabric, the warp and weft of life.

Serious birders—a term preferred over "bird-watcher" by serious birders—keep "Life Lists," noting the time and place they see each new species. Dollyann Myers and Ron Hoff, an East Tennessee couple, are not bird-watchers. They are serious enthusiasts: birders.

"They have each seen and cataloged more than 8,000 different species of birds. That's about 80 percent of the bird species on Earth," wrote WBIR *Live at Five at Four* reporter Emily Stroud. "They're in an elite group." Stroud is a savvy newswoman, specializing in human-interest features. She's been with the Knoxville NBC affiliate since 2006 and thinks fast on her feet, adjusting her questions to go with the flow. Stroud's "Life Bird" story took her to Anderson County and the home of Myers and Hoff in January 2016.

"I never want to lose my sense of wonder. And birds do that for me," said Hoff, who has photographed over forty-one hundred of the species he has seen.

"We're right up at the top because we like to travel, so therefore we see a lot of birds," Myers said. "It's a hobby you can do anywhere, anytime. Walking down the street, in the woods. There are always birds."

Rachael Eliot is just starting, a talented novice. If it becomes an overriding passion, she'll have to travel the globe in search of faraway birds as did famed birder Phoebe Snetsinger, née Burnett. In 1961, it was the sight of a Blackburnian warbler that clicked on her zeal. By 1995, Snetsinger had logged 8,000 of the 10,534 species recognized by the International Ornithological Congress today. But that's a moving target, as the number will surely grow by the time you read this; new species are being discovered all the time. Snetsinger's bid to reach 8,500 was cut short at age sixty-eight, when she died in a vehicle accident in Madagascar in 1999. She was there to find yet more birds.

Birding is a lifetime pursuit, a sailing of the seven seas in search of treasure: a fleeting glimpse of something rare and exotic. So a Life List is precious. It requires a lot of planning and road trips. A good list is something that has to be cultivated and worked. Forget the subtlety; it's an obsession.

For Rachael Eliot's twenty-fourth birthday, the rumored merlin *(Falco columbarius)* that was reported to be wintering at Lakeshore Park in west Knoxville presented itself quickly. The medium-sized falcon was perched on a bare branch in the afternoon sun for all to see. That was a bit of good fortune. It gave us extra time to skedaddle to Cades Cove and Hyatt Lane in the Great Smokies, well over an hour away.

Cades Cove is an anomaly. It's villatic—former flat, grassy farmland surrounded by the rugged mountains. Local geologists like Harry Moore call it a "limestone window," and the weathering limestone created deep, fertile, grass-loving soil, making the exposed basin attractive to early settlers.

The day before, I heard from local birder Jimmy Tucker that short-eared owls *(Asio flammeus)* were wintering there, something they periodically do—not every winter, just some winters. Short-eareds primarily nest in Canada, venturing south during the colder months, but not always as far as Tennessee. I also knew that they present themselves if you are in the right place at the right time. The so-called "ghosts of the grasslands" are crepuscular. They begin to feed by flying low over open fields in half-light, the afterglow of a dying day or predawn.

We were in position an hour before sunset, patrolling the well-traveled dirt road of Hyatt Lane on foot, fifty to one hundred yards apart in the cold, watching both sides. The wide meadows were windblown and tawny with native grasses. There was a beauty to the starkness, the isolation, the long shadows, the fading sunlight, the close of day: January 11, 2016. For over an hour we watched and waited, waited and watched. Northern harriers cruised over the broad expanse, as did a lone kestrel, all hunting for that one final meal before a frozen nightfall.

The eager anticipation of the hunt, the rush of adrenaline that had kept us warm in the twenty-degree afternoon, began to ebb away, to be replaced by numbing cold.

At last, through my binoculars, I found two moving shapes in the twilight and what seemed an odd flash of color, but the distance was too great and details scant. The birds looked right in their circular movements low over the ground, wings rounded, light undercarriage, but yet too far away to be absolutely sure, and only I saw them. If you're searching for a Life Bird you want a satisfying look, not a fleeting glimpse. You want to savor the satisfaction like a good glass of Cabernet Sauvignon. By the time Rachael and I were back together, darkness had set in, and the shadowy phantoms had vanished. We had been tantalizingly close, but that didn't count. But you do not expect to find a ghost every time you look.

FEATHERED GHOSTS, SILENT AND SPOOKY

Owls are mysterious to us. They are phantoms of the night, there but unseen. Far more common in most places than people realize, they exist, practically invisible, at the edge of our awareness, but they are there, watching. Owls by their very nature are secretive and stoic. By and large they are nocturnal, active when we are asleep, so their movements go undetected, their shadowy existence unknown to us. Owls are built for sensory input. Their enormously large eyes give them an unmistakable allure somewhat like the famed, albeit kitschy "Big Eyes" paintings of Margaret Keane that once decorated motel rooms in the 1960s. But an owl's eye size in comparison to its head size is real, unlike the soulful stares of Keane's waifs. If a great horned owl's head were the same size as a human's, its eyes would be as large as oranges, and its eyes are not spherical.

"Their eyes are long and tubular," said Dr. Cheryl Greenacre, an avian veterinarian at the University of Tennessee Teaching Hospital, located on the Tennessee River near the university's main campus. Dr. Greenacre sketched the shape of an owl's eye on a piece of paper to show me their unusual shape, long and much wider at the back. We were outside in the cold, counting birds with Rachael Eliot for the Audubon Christmas Bird Count at the time.

"They're really tube shaped," said Dr. Greenacre, "long unmovable sclerotic tubes. That's why owls have fixed stares." Whereas owls themselves are really quite handsome, their flat-faced, large-eye-socketed skulls are rather grotesque, like the loathsome Gollum in Peter Jackson's adaption of J. R. R. Tolkien's *Lord of the Rings* trilogy.

They are forward-facing with fixed-stares, unable to glance out of the corner of their eyes like you and I. There's a misconception that an owl can spin its head all the way around, 360 degrees. In fact, they can only turn their heads up to 270 degrees because an owl's neck has fourteen vertebrae, twice as many as humans, so there are more swivel points.

The back of an owl's eye is packed with rods that allow them to see detail, discern light from dark. We humans have a lot more cones, the eye structures that distinguish color. We see a colorful world; an owl sees the world in high definition, even at night, relying less on color and more on detail. An owl's eyes are one hundred times more sensitive to light than our own eyes. The visual input must be overwhelming.

"Why are the owl's eyes so big?" wrote Dr. Alan Van Norman, a neurosurgeon at Medcenter One in Bismarck, North Dakota. "Well, the owl needs to be able to see a mouse scratching his nose 50 yards away on a dark cloudy night. That is how the owl makes its living. If the owl can't do that, it will starve."

To imagine an owl's vision, a comparison is in order. Dr. Van Norman noted that an owl could read the bottom line of an optometrist's eye chart on the wall across a basketball court, in very low light. A regulation college court is fifty feet wide. We, on the other hand, can see the scoreboard from that distance but may not even notice the eye chart itself, let alone the bottom line of letters (P E Z O L C F T D, in case you are wondering). And like humans, their flattened faces and forward-looking eyes give owls binocular vision, excellent depth perception. But as you might expect, they are extremely farsighted and have trouble seeing something nearby, like the mouse they are about to eat. For up-close work, an owl relies on its sense of touch, namely hair-like feathers called filoplumes, that are found near the feet, beak, and eyes.

Folklore teaches us that owls are wise. That's not really true. Pondering is not their forte. I've worked with a number of owls over the years; they're gentle, soft creatures with massively strong feet and sharp talons, but not deep thinkers. An owl can sit on a perch for hours, staring straight ahead, just waiting for something to happen. They never seem restless or bored, but if any tiny little thing moves, they notice it.

Neurosurgeon Van Norman is also an avid birder, having seen birds in more than seventy-five countries. He noted, "In our brains, a relatively small portion is involved in actually creating a mental image from the light our eyes detect, while a relatively large portion is used to interpret that image and decide what to do about it. In owls, just the opposite is true. Most of their brainpower is used in recreating a visual image from the fantastic amount of information they take in. Very little brain is left over to make decisions." This would make their occipital lobe the most dominant portion of their brains.

Owls don't think; they react, responding to the mental images their brains have assembled. If it's moving, that probably means it's edible. If it's not moving, it's inert and not worth the bother.

"An owl's decision-making process is limited to attack or fly away, keep watching or ignore. That's about it," added Van Norman. "An owl can't think about tomorrow or reminisce about last week." Super vision, not wisdom, is the hallmark of any owl.

And as if that is not enough, most owls, especially ones that hunt in darkness, have superhuman hearing. Their ear canals are forward facing and do not have a human-like pinnae, or fleshy funnels that direct sound into the ear openings. Owls do not need such because they have specialized feathers that do the same thing. Behind the ear canals there are modified, dense feathers that in tandem form a facial ruff, which creates forward-facing concave walls that cup the sound into their ears. It could be said that with their flattened faces surrounded by the circular ruff of feathers, an owl's head is shaped like a satellite disk or parabolic mirror with two enormous eyes in the center. If you need someone to guard your property at night, hire an owl.

Additionally, you and I have brow ridges that shade our eyes from the overhead sun, making it easier for us to see. Many owls have essentially the same thing, which runs north to south between the eyes, shading at least one eye from the low-lying sun at dusk when their activity begins. Thus these avian predators have evolved the perfect face for sensory input.

But wait; there's more. Our ears are symmetrical, level with our eyes, one on each side of the head. An owl's ears are asymmetrical, one located higher on the skull than the other, so sounds from above reach the right ear first and sounds from below reach the left ear first. This offset placement allows the owl to pinpoint the location of its prey by sound. With its ears set at different heights, an owl is able to determine quickly the direction from which a sound is coming—left or right, high or low—by the tiny time difference that it takes for the sound waves to penetrate the right and left ears, even when that differential is as little as thirty millionths of a second. All the owl has to do is rotate its head, again like a satellite disk, until the sound enters both ears at the same nanosecond. Once that happens, the sound maker is directly ahead.

Owls may not be wise, but their ability to sense their world and the minuscule movements within it, in very low light, can be likened to the superhuman abilities found in comic books. Clark Kent's alter ego would no doubt agree.

Our culture has become enamored by superheroes, in part because our problems seem so big, so unsolvable, that we need super help. Kal-El, where are you? If, this weekend, you have the desire to go to your local cineplex to see the latest Ironman, Superman, or Spider-Man movie, you might want to consider going to the closest woodland and watch for owls instead, although invisibility is another one of their special gifts. Oh, and take a mouse with you. It could prove interesting.

"The owl is going to fly at the mouse, through the dark, without hitting anything, at 30 mph and catch it with pinpoint accuracy on a dead run," wrote Dr. Van Norman.

In addition to hypersensitive awareness, an owl's flight can be utterly silent. Serrated edges along the leading edge of most owls' flight feathers muffle the sound of their wing beats. Some fish-eating owls lack this adaptation because it has no evolutionary advantage. Fish can't hear the approaching wing beats anyway.

Using their talons and bills, owls tear their prey into large chunks that are easier to swallow. Their muscular stomachs, or gizzards, do the chewing, squeezing out all the nutrients. Roughly ten to twelve hours after the meal, the owl regurgitates a large, compacted, wet pellet made up of the parts of the meal they cannot digest. Depending on the species' preferred diet, a pellet can include the exoskeletons of insects, indigestible plant matter, bones, fur, feathers, bills, claws, and teeth.

"The same thing can happen in people," said Dr. Guy Smoak, a family physician in the University of Tennessee system. "They're called bezoars." Always quick with a quirky story, he promptly found Internet photos on his laptop to show me. Not to be gross, but look it up, if you have the stomach for it, witticism intended. They are solid masses of indigestible bits and pieces that can accumulate in your digestive tract, potentially causing a blockage. They can stay in place for years before eventually being passed. Owls, however, simply upchuck their bezoars routinely.

Ijams Nature Center is located in south Knoxville. Its roots go back to 1910 when Harry Pearle (H.P.) and Alice Ijams bought twenty acres along the river across the sluice from Dickinson Island. In time they had four daughters that were involved in the early days of the scouting in the area. The entire family was outdoorsy. They hiked the Smokies and canoed the river. Girl Scouts began coming to the Ijams home site in 1923 for badge workshops. Soon Boy Scouts began to visit followed by the general public, all wanting to learn about nature and walk the trails in the essentially private Ijams sanctuary. H.P. passed away in 1954, Alice in 1964. Not wanting to lose the refuge just upstream from the city, the Knoxville Garden Club rallied to raise money to buy the twenty acres and create a nature center to honor their memory and keep the educational tradition in place. In 1968 it opened to the public. Since then thousands of people both young and old have attended a program, a talk, or a walk with an interruptive naturalist as a guide. And Girl Scouts still routinely come for badge workshops over nine decades later. Ijams Nature Center is a nonprofit. Budgets are always tight, funding a continuing issue, but the environmental and nature education established by H.P. and Alice goes on.

As senior naturalist for Ijams for the past seventeen years, I've had the best job in town: each week a different group both young and old, and a different topic.

One of the most popular programs I host is "Owl-ology 101." (I also do Frog-ology, Duck-ology and Spider-ology, etc.) All are designed to be fun and entertaining for kids and adults. In Owl-ology, we get to dissect owl pellets. Most contain the small tibias, fibulas, femurs, and vertebrae that make up the framework of all rodentia. Of course, there's always the hope of finding an intact skull.

The pellets have been sanitized, and the dissectors wear surgical gloves. They use wooden toothpicks as tools to carefully disassemble the avian fur balls. In October 2015, a twelve-year-old girl named Daphne was on the front row with her grandmother. Both were new to Ijams.

After a few minutes the nascent biologist shouted out, "I found a skull!"

"Well then, you get the prize," I announced to all.

"What's the prize?" she asked.

"You get to keep the skull," I responded, handing her a Ziploc sandwich bag to protect her find.

Daphne was excited. And her grandmother was thrilled because Daphne was thrilled. But Mom, on the other hand . . . I'm not so sure. At least a mouse skull in a sandwich bag is an interesting conversation starter. I once found a cat's skull beside the road and kept it hidden under my bed, as if it were a magical talisman, until Mom found it and my lucky charm disappeared.

I grew up in Gatlinburg, Tennessee, with a national park nearby. Bringing home skulls, crayfish claws, and snail shells was all part of a kid's workday. We got dirty, living up to the South Korean proverb, *Shin to bul ee,* or "Body and soil are one." Yet children today do not get to spend much time outdoors. Teenagers do so even less—only about 10 percent spend any time at *all* outside. Introducing urban kids to nature has been a large part of my vocation for the past two decades. Studies have shown that if you can light the spark in a nature-lover early in life, the fire burns for years like mine. Too many children today never get the chance, especially in urban areas. The actual world often takes a backseat to technology and the virtual world.

For twelve-year-old Daphne, finding a mouse's skull inside the regurgitated contents of an owl's stomach was captivatingly gross. And most kids love gross—in fact, the grosser the better. They love to learn that a bird's poop and pee come out at the same time; just one big white splat. (A British study discovered that birds prefer to drop their wastes on red cars more than on cars of any other color.)

Birds, unlike mammals, do not even produce urine.

"Their kidneys extract nitrogenous wastes from the bloodstream like other animals' do, but instead of releasing it as urea dissolved in urine, birds excrete it in the form of uric acid," reported Matt Soniak for *Mental Floss* magazine. "It comes out as a white sort of goo with minimal water loss."

Kids are somewhat relieved to learn that an owl's pellet comes out of the north end of the bird rather than the south. Rejectamenta is somehow more hands-on than excrement. One summer at the nature center, I was watching a barred owl outside when it coughed up a pellet. I walked over and picked it up, still warm and wet from the up-chucker's stomach. It was strangely green and metallic looking, made up almost entirely of cicadas' exoskeletons. Pretty gross. But nature is not always pretty; sometimes it's pretty gross, yet kid friendly.

"There are some who cannot resist picking up an owl pellet with its bits of bone, fur, teeth, and feathers and taking it on as a puzzle. Each pellet is a mystery, and behind it is the drama of a predator lurking in the night," wrote biologist and nature writer Bernd Heinrich.

Lynne McCoy, a local wildlife rehabilitator, provided the sanitized pellets we dissected at that Owl-ology 101 class. Each fur-ball like pellet had been baked in an oven at 325 degrees for forty minutes. McCoy cares for hundreds—yes, hundreds—of orphaned or injured birds and mammals every year. Receiving no state or federal funding, she's a one-woman nonprofit with an emphasis on the "non." In 2015, she cared for 1,051 animals that included 242 rabbits, 144 squirrels, 11 screech-owls, 61 robins, 9 deer mice, 1 bobcat, and 2 turkeys. Most were nursed back to health and returned to the wild. She's also a good source for owl pellets. Two non-releasable great horned owls named Grumpy and Scarthy are not good education birds but excellent at regurgitating.

"Great horned owls are born pissed off," said McCoy, "And they remain that way all their lives." They are intense. I've held them. Her words ring true.

"I don't know what we'd do without Lynne," said UT's Dr. Greenacre. "She's big hearted and never says no."

Lynne also provided the grand finale of that Owl-ology workshop: an albino barred owl named Sugar that she took in to care for in the fall of 2015. When she walks into the room with Sugar on her gloved hand, a hush falls over the class and out come the cameras. It was like seeing Theda Bara, the pallid silent movie starlet surrounded by the paparazzi. The pure white owl is jaw-droppingly beautiful but far too delicate to ever survive in the wild. Albinism in biology is the congenital absence of any pigmentation or coloration. The animal is extremely vulnerable; it lacks camouflage and has a weaker immune system and poorer eyesight.

DECEITFUL WITCHES OR WISE OWLS OF ATHENA?

According to historian James Mooney, the native Cherokee knew the same three owl species that live in our woods year round: the great horned owl they called *tskili,* the same word they used for a witch or a bad-medicine person; the hooting or barred owl they called *uguku';* and the Eastern screech-owl they called *wa`huhu'.* Whether they knew of the short-eared owl—the winter migrant—is unclear.

"Cherokee Indians believed owls and other birds that called at night were embodied ghosts and disguised witches," wrote Marcia Davis for the *Knoxville News Sentinel.*

The Cherokee apparently did not hunt owls for food. They weren't worth the time it took to stalk them. They were a poor source of meat with very little flesh on their bodies—heads yes, but their bodies no. An adult male barred owl weighs less than two pounds, while an adult male wild turkey can weigh up to twenty-four pounds. Owls look big and fluffy, but under all those feathers they are wiry, mere skin and bones. To spread the word to young hunters eager to prove themselves, the Cherokee passed along a myth of how the hooting owl became scrawny through heartache. He pined away over his lost love, a young Cherokee woman. She had scorned him after discovering he was not the skillful young hunter she thought she'd married, but rather a deceitful owl, supporting a second object lesson: it pays to be truthful up front.

So, if the Native Americans who lived in the Southeast saw owls as being deceitful witches, where did the notion of the wise old owl come from? Surely it wasn't that self-appointed authority on everything, Howland Owl, who lived with Pogo Possum in the Okefenokee Swamp of South Georgia. No, that was only a comic strip.

Our European immigrant ancestors brought the concept of the wise old owl with them. And it's firmly rooted in Greek mythology.

As the story goes, Athena, the Goddess of Wisdom, having just banished the mischievous crow from her presence, probably for good reason, was so impressed by the owl, its great eyes and solemn appearance, that she honored the nocturnal bird by making it her favorite among feathered creatures.

Athena's species of choice was the little owl *(Athene noctua),* and all little owls were protected, inhabiting the Acropolis in great numbers. It was believed that a magical "inner light" gave owls night vision. So an owl became the companion for the Goddess of Wisdom. We have already learned that the special inner light is the result of remarkable eye design and an oversized occipital lobe in the brain.

The "Owl of Athena" has been used as a symbol of wisdom, knowledge, perspicacity (keen vision), and higher learning throughout the Western world. The actual species little owl *(Athene noctua)* is still very much with us, while Ancient Greece is not. It's a small species, weighing about six ounces, and is very similar in size to our own screech-owl. The Greek species is found along the Mediterranean Sea east to Korea. It's widespread and not endangered in any way, which suggests that it still falls under the watchful eye of Athena. The owl's generic name *Athene* honors the goddess who protected it.

As the symbol of Athena, the little owl served as a protector as well, accompanying Greek armies into war, and provided inspiration for the soldiers' daily lives. Seeing an owl before a battle was taken as a sign of victory; seeing an owl after battle proved you were fortunate enough to have survived it.

OWLS OF THE SOUTHEAST

In my region, the same three owl species the native Cherokee knew are still the most common: great horned, barred, and eastern screech-owl. In the past two decades, I have worked with all three species at the nature center. All the birds had different personalities, if I can use that word without anthropomorphizing them. Giving human characteristics to animals has become more acceptable of late. Humans are indeed animals, and we share a wonderfully wide range of characteristics and behaviors with all sorts of animals. Avian behavioral biologists are now even writing a lot about bird divorce, a parting of the ways once reserved for only humans. And we now also know that all sorts of animals make tools, once believed to be a cultural behavior that was found only in humans.

Over the years, the owls of Ijams have all been injured birds, rescued, and rehabbed but ultimately determined to be non-releasable. Generally, the injury is damage to a wing; but two have had vision issues, and an owl without two good eyes would starve in the wild. Nature centers like Ijams have permits to take in disabled animals, which otherwise would probably be euthanized. At Ijams they are part of the education department and are used in programs for all ages.

In a word, owls are stoic. If I use a second word, it is generally "soft." Yes, they are bigheaded; and like the Cherokee myth, they are scrawny, puffed up with billowy feathers.

At the nature center, screech-owls, like Athena's little owl, garner the most *oohs* and *ahs*. It's something about their petiteness—they're about the size of a can of Coca-Cola—that amazes most. They are little darlings, but that's not a word anyone should use describing a bird of prey. Screech-owls primarily eat rodents. Studies have shown that they make up to 42 percent of the little owl's diet. These pint-sized birds—and in this case the descriptor is true—are opportunistic carnivores.

"Screech-owls hunt fish, frogs, crayfish, and even tadpoles, adding to the 138 vertebrate species that have been found in their cast pellets," wrote Julie Zickefoose for *Bird Watchers Digest*. Screeches have been documented to eat animals as small as pill bugs and snails or as large as blue jays and mourning doves. If it moves in the night, it's on the buffet. They simple are not picky eaters.

Ijams recently took in a male barred owl *(Strix varia)* with soulful black eyes that are a bit deceiving. An unknown accident left him blind in one eye and with only partial vision in the other. His first two months at the nature center, the handsome night bird had to be caught twice a day and held immobile while eyes drops were put into each eye, principally to reduce inflammation and risk of infection. In the end, both eyes were saved. He's a powerful flyer with two good wings, just poor vision. Dr. Louise Conrad is the veterinarian who oversees all the animals—turtles, snakes, birds, mudpuppies, opossums—at the nature center. She routinely has to diagnose a sick animal with a minimum number of clues; after all, the patient cannot tell her "where it hurts."

Barred owls routinely nest in the woodland behind the visitor center at Ijams. Since they eat a considerable amount of cold-blooded animals—frogs, salamanders, and crayfish—their preferred habitat is woods near water. Retiree and volunteer staff member Rex McDaniel has taken dozens of photos of the wild barred owls found around the original Ijams home-site pond and down the wetland to the Tennessee River. He pays close enough attention to track them to their nesting site if possible.

We once cared for an elderly great horned owl, which for the sake of this narrative we'll call Gramps. He had one injured wing, which was virtually useless. Consequently, he also had poor balance. It was difficult for him to stand on a gloved hand for long periods. He was a favorite of Dr. Conrad's, who would carry Gramps around, cradled like a newborn in her arms—a large, yellow-eyed, fluffy newborn with talons. Early naturalists described great horned owls as the "winged tigers," but unlike others, Gramps was reasonably docile. Perhaps it was his age.

In the wild, both barred and great horned owls eat a considerable amount of rodents. And don't forget that gray squirrels are the rodentia that climb trees. Each mature female squirrel produces a brood of one to four pups, although up to eight pups is possible in late winter. But if the mast crop—acorns, hickory nuts, and beechnuts—is bountiful, each may produce a second brood in late summer. Thus, each female has the potential of adding eight to sixteen new squirrel pups to any given forest. If the gray squirrels were left alone, we would be hip deep in them after only a few years. Yet, this does not seem to happen. Why not? Great horned owls are most adroit at catching and eating gray squirrels.

If a pair of great horned owls only catch and eat one squirrel each per week (a very reasonable assumption), that's a net loss of 104 of the arboreal rodents per year. When I was young growing up in the Smoky Mountains, we often ate squirrel in the fall. They are quite tasty, although Mom knew the best way to cook them. But the point is this: owls and squirrels both live high in the trees, and nature finds a balance with great horned owls, the winged tigers, being at the top of the food chain.

THE WINTERTIME WANDERER

The three owl species I've described are relatively common in the Tennessee Valley, even in the urban environs that surround Knoxville. I routinely hear all three in the woods behind my house near UT Medical Center. If you add the barn owl, which is found more in the farmland surrounding the city—historically, before the arrival of barns, they nested in caves—and the northern saw-whet owl, which nests in the highest elevations of the Smokies, that would be the list of the permanent residents of this part of the country.

Yet, in winter, a sixth and even a seventh species can sometimes be found, an erratic migrant that doesn't need to come this far south every winter. Both are mysterious, ephemeral. When word gets out about their presence, birders cloister to its location at sunset, hoping for the chance to see one.

Snowy owls *(Bubo scandiacus)* or the species made famous by a young British wizard, Mr. Harry Potter, occasionally make appearances this far south if prey farther north is scarce. A snowy was observed at Spring Hill, Tennessee, in 2009 and another near Louisville, Kentucky, in 2013. Author and historian Donald E. Davis recalled, "I even observed one as a child in north Georgia during the mid-sixties. The owl made such an impression on me that over the next several years, when my siblings or elders asked what I wanted to be when I grew up, my immediate response was, 'a big white bird!'"

Owls leave such impressions. That's why I was searching for one in Cades Cove for Rachael Eliot. If there are plenty of rodents in the meadows of Pennsylvania and the Ohio Valley, short-eared owls avoid crossing the Mason-Dixon all together. And unlike our woodland triad, short-eareds are birds of the grasslands, with a penchant for hunting over open fields at twilight when there's still just enough light left to see them. It's as unpredictable as freshwater jellyfish (which we'll meet later).

Owls in the genus *Asio* are also known as the "eared" owls because they have tufts of feathers resembling a mammal's ears. But they are not ears, just clusters of longer feathers that look like ears, which may or may not be visible.

As the name suggests, the short-eared owls' ear tufts aren't very long, virtually nonexistent, but they're there. *Asio flammeus* will display its tufts only when in a defensive posture. But what they lack in head adornment, they make up with a flash of color on their wing beats. Their specific name *flammeus* is from the Latin for "flaming, or the color of fire." Even in low light, they flap with an unmistakable flash of orange-yellow created by markings on the underside of their longest primaries at the tips of the wings.

"The short-eared owl is one of the most cosmopolitan of birds, as it is found in every continent except Australia. In its habits it differs from most owls in preferring open plains, marshes, and sand dunes to thick forests, where it is almost never seen," wrote Charles Wendell Townsend in 1938. He was a leading contributor to A. C. Bent's encyclopedic *Life Histories of North American Birds.*

The worldwide range map shows that they nest at the top of the world and the bottom, migrating to the middle during each hemisphere's respective winters.

It is reported that short-eareds are now more common in the northern portion of their breeding range, but their historic populations fluctuate greatly, along with prey population cycles. Rodents are good at making more rodents; sometimes they get carried away. When the field rodent population explodes, as they are wont to do from time to time, short-eared owls come to partake. There are several records going back to the sixteenth century of such "plagues" of vermin, with parliaments of owls flocking to exterminate the hordes of mice.

One such rodent explosion was recorded south of Camrose in central Alberta in the fall of 1931. An unprecedented number of mice appeared in the fields of grain. Then, in October and November, unusual numbers of short-eared owls were observed patrolling the fields, hunting for mice.

As reported in Bent's *Life Histories,* an observer named Frank L. Farley noted, "The number of mice that this vast army of owls destroyed must have reached enormous proportions, and the birds may have prevented what otherwise would have resulted in a serious plague. An invaluable service was rendered at a time of emergency, and at no cost whatever to the people."

But how did the short-eareds know to come to the rescue?

According to the North American Breeding Bird Survey, the overall short-eared worldwide population declined by 2.5 percent per year between 1966 and 2010, resulting in a cumulative decline of 67 percent. This is somewhat alarming, yet the conservation group Partners in Flight estimates a global breeding population of three million, with 14 percent spending some part of the year in the United States. That "part of the year" is winter since the bulk of their North American breeding happens in Canada.

If you do the math, that means that over four hundred thousand "shorties" spend some time in America, and although most of those are in Alaska, a few still venture as far south as Tennessee some winters. Rachael Eliot and I only wanted to find one of the diminishing things. Just one.

Their fluttering flight has been compared to that of a moth or bat, or maybe even a flapping flag. That's what we were looking for on our return trip to isolated Hyatt Lane; after all, I had to finish that birthday present I had started twenty-seven days earlier. On-again/off-again snow and ice and conflicting schedules had delayed our second attempt, but in the meantime others had found a shorty in the same general location. I later learned that Kari Everett, a nurse at the University of Tennessee Medical Center, made four trips to Cades Cove during the month and saw short-eared owls twice. So they were there, but would one still be there waiting in the twilight for us?

Driving back to the Smokies late that Saturday, we fortified ourselves, sharpening our senses with mocha java chillers from a Sonic Drive-In. Again we arrived at the south end of Hyatt Lane about an hour before sunset. It was cold but not unbearable; long shadows hugged the ground pointing east. We were soon met by an early sign of spring. A brief few days of record warmth had encouraged local chorus frogs to fill a muddy roadside puddle with eggs destined to be frozen solid by a return of arctic air and snow forecast for midweek.

"April is the cruellest month, breeding / Lilacs out of the dead land," wrote Rachael Eliot's namesake. Tell that to these frog larvae that will never survive until April, their water-filled embryotic sacs ruptured by stiletto crystals of ice. The change of any season is cruel to those caught too early or too late in its unveiling.

We found the meadows on both sides of Hyatt Lane as before: tawny to bright gold, windswept and beautifully stark. There was surprisingly little activity before the sun slipped behind Gregory's Bald to the west. Then, in the growing cold darkness, three shapes emerged to patrol the grassland, but none were shorties. All proved to be ultra-pale northern harrier males known as "gray ghosts," as indeed they appeared to be in the failing light. All were handsome in their sleekness, divine in their economy of motion like fighter jets on one last strafing run. We were surprised to see all three suddenly drop in unison to disappear in the tall grass, not to be seen again. Why would such magnificent raptors choose to roost on the ground, huddled together. Was it warmer?

"Do you hear that?" whispered Rachael, bundled, her blond tresses stuffed deep inside a brightly patterned toboggan, Bushnell binoculars at the ready.

"It's a woodcock!" The chunky upland shorebird is one of her favorites. And after a few distant *peents,* he became airborne, flying directly over our heads in his practice mating flight display.

"Wow!"

Yet another early sign of spring. But that was it.

No short-eared owl again that night. We were in the right place, at the right time of day, but the owl, if it was still in Cades Cove, was elsewhere, or gone, winging its way back to breeding grounds much farther north. To paraphrase Frost, the question that framed me in all but words was, "what to make of a diminished thing." With the poet's oven bird, it was the approaching fall, and perhaps with our wintering owl, it was the coming spring.

Jack-in-the-Pulpit
Arisaema triphyllum

Contemplating our ephemerality
can be a profound experience.

—James Atlas

LATE WINTER AND early spring is a favorite time of the year for many people. The early woodland wildflowers thrill their souls. My hometown of Gatlinburg hosts the "Wildflower Pilgrimage" every April and it has done so since 1951. It's a festival that pays tribute to these early blooming beauties. Often called spring ephemerals, these fleeting flowers, spring's first gentle whisper across the land, appear and disappear in a matter of weeks. They have to grow, bloom, and produce seeds quickly before the forest canopy leafs out and covers their homeland with shade.

As the stormy weeks of late March give way to flamboyant April, woodland wildflowers like bloodroot, toothwort, hepatica, spring beauty, squirrel corn, Dutchman's britches, twinleaf, trout lily, Virginia bluebells, jack-in-the-pulpit, and several species of trillium will come and go. Poof. By late June, you are hard pressed to find where they grew and lived out their days in the sun. But weep not, for most are perennials; they'll be back next spring, in the same place.

The explosion of wildflowers across the late-winter hillsides could be seen as an analogy of the appearance of the flowering plants on planet Earth in the first place. It has always been a puzzlement that perplexed even the great evolutionist Charles Darwin himself. He called it "an abominable mystery."

"What worried Darwin was that the very earliest samples in the fossil record all dated back to the middle of the Cretaceous period, around 100 million years ago, and they came in a bewilderingly wide variety of shapes and sizes. This suggested flowering plants had experienced an explosive burst of diversity very shortly after their origins," wrote Colin Barras for the BBC.

So, even in the early 1800s, naturalists were flummoxed because they knew that at some point in the Cretaceous period of geologic time—that's 145 million to 66 million years ago—flowering plants appeared for the first time on planet Earth and within a very short amount of time exploded into a rich diversity of species. Like friends of a lottery winner, they appeared out of nowhere quickly.

For a point of reference, dinosaurs still roamed the planet, not the Jurassic dinosaurs of Hollywood but the ones that came later in the Cretaceous. (Just between you and me, so it's our secret, *Tyrannosaurus rex* was a Cretaceous dinosaur. They were not even here during the older Jurassic period. So the movie and the novel that preceded it should have been called "Cretaceous Park.")

Thus, when dinosaurs ruled the Earth, but late in their reign, the terrible lizards were sharing their domain with flowers. The heavily plated Jurassic *Stegosaurus* probably ate nonflowering plants no taller than about three feet in height, mostly ferns, cycads, and conifers, tough chewy things. Then millions of years later the Cretaceous *T. rex* was a meat-eater that ate his bloody fresh kills in the presence of flowers like a centerpiece on the dining room table. *Stegosaurus* and *T. rex* never knew each other, much to the slow-moving former one's good fortune.

The planet itself looked different. If we could climb into H. G. Wells's 1895 time machine and go back to circle the globe 145 million years ago, the first thing we would notice was that the continents were a jumble, like a hotel room after a rock band has spent the night. The major landmasses would look something like they do today, although misshapen and much closer together. North America was in three major pieces, each separated from the other by shallow seas.

Plants themselves have been on the planet for at least 480 million years— some researchers now say at least 700 million years—but the earliest plants did not produce flowers or fruits. Botanists classify these nonflowering seed producers as gymnosperms, from the Greek *gymnos,* meaning "naked" and *sperma,* meaning "seed" or "naked seeds," after the unenclosed condition of their seeds; flower producing plants, meanwhile, are angiosperms, from the Greek *angeion,* or "casing," and again *sperma,* meaning "seed" or "enclosed seeds," because of the enclosed condition of the seeds inside fleshy fruits.

The ancient ferns, cycads, and conifers that *Stegosaurus* ate reproduced by spores or were nonflowering, yet seed-producing gymnosperms like today's conifers. And that's just the way it was for eons. The isolated horsetails or Equisetum that grow by the ponds at Ijams are living fossils.

Likewise, Darwin suspected that perhaps flowering plants had first appeared long before the Cretaceous in isolated locations, only waiting to sally forth in abundance when conditions were amiable. But where? Soft-tissue plants are not very good at leaving behind any fossil evidence.

Flash-forward over a century after Darwin to New Caledonia, a small island east of Australia, and you'll find another living fossil, *Amborella trichopoda,* or *Amborella* for short. It's very rare—found nowhere else, one of those odd things living at the edge of our awareness. *Amborella* is an evergreen understory shrub that produces small, creamy-white, inconspicuous flowers. Its DNA suggests that, hereditarily speaking, it's at the base of the flowering plant family tree. "Careful study over the last century has shown it to be the sole survivor of one of the very earliest branches of the angiosperm evolutionary tree," continued Colin Barras.

Flowering plants must have evolved from nonflowering plants. But how? A close look at the complete genetic makeup of *Amborella* suggests that at some point its entire genome was doubled. "Genome doubling occurs when an organism mistakenly gains an extra copy of every one of its genes during the cell division that occurs as part of sexual reproduction. The extra genetic material gives genome doubled organisms the potential to evolve new traits that can provide a competitive advantage," added Barras.

The new trait that *Amborella* apparently created out of its expanded toolbox was small white flowers that needed to be pollinated. Then some flying insect had to venture forth to figure out how to be a pollinator, not unlike haberdasher Harry Truman had to learn how to be a politician and then president. As new flowering plants presented themselves, new pollinators had to come into being as well because each flowering species tends to attract a specific pollinator. In some orchids, only a single species of insect has the right *je ne sais quoi* to serve as pollinator. With the emergence of thousands of unique new flowers, thousands of new pollinating insects (and the ruby-throated hummingbird we'll meet later) had to evolve as partners to progress hand in hand through the millennia.

SPRING OOZES WITH SENSUALITY

Okay. Let's be candid here, we're all adults. These newly evolved flowers are the flashy reproductive organs of flowering plants. They are, in many cases, enticing and sensual, the most remarkable feature distinguishing them from the naked seed gymnosperms. Flowers provided angiosperms with the means to have a more species-specific breeding system, with an intermediary—the specific pollinator—and consequently a way to evolve more readily into a host of different species without the risk of crossing back with related species and remain genetically stymied.

Flowers were a big deal. As a group, the magnolias have been on the planet millions of years, and they tend to produce large, voluptuous blooms that are really modified leaves. The next time you are staring at a sweet bay magnolia blossom, you should blush. Am I being tawdry? Well, yes, maybe a little. But flowers are openly sexual. I once had an office at the nature center with a sweet bay planted just outside. When it was in bloom, I felt I should close the curtains to give it some privacy.

With this mechanism for rapid speciation, the new flowering plants could exploit changes in the environment and move into new habitats, ultimately outcompeting the nonflowering plants, and the data back up that claim. Today, estimates vary, but they generally coalesce around these numbers. There are 400,000 plants that produce flowers and 38,800 plants that do not (1,050 conifers, 15,000 ferns and horsetails, and 22,750 mosses). Even though nonflowering plants have been around millions of years longer, the in-your-face flowering plants truly dominate.

"The richness of the biological world is the most wonderful feature of the biosphere," noted British natural historian Richard Fortey, "and every story is worth the telling no matter how humble, or indeed insular, is the organism concerned."

Putting that to the test, let's look at one of the springtime ephemerals that grows throughout the East. It's my favorite woodland wildflower: jack-in-the-pulpit *(Arisaema triphyllum)*. Humble they are not, with their erect stature and sculpted spathe, which forms the "pulpit." The spathe can be yellowish, chartreuse, or sometimes fully green, with brownish or maroon stripes and an overhanging flap or drape that rather coquettishly hides the sexual organs inside. The long shaft, or "jack," which the spathe protects, is called a spadix. At its base it's covered with very tiny flowers virtually too small to see. So jack-in-the-pulpits are spectacular, even bodacious, which means we cannot say they're humble. Artist Georgia O'Keeffe's series of jack-in-the-pulpit paintings border on being erotic.

But insular, meaning "detached, standing alone, isolated," they surely are. You really only find one here and there, seemingly shunning the colonial lifestyle of bloodroot, trout lilies, and trilliums. Celandine poppies like the company of other celandine poppies, while the curiously named squirrel corn likes to hang out with other squirrel corn. For these flowers, their strategy of pollination suits a colony. Each flower wants to attract a specific insect pollinator that will move quickly from flower to flower to flower, spreading pollen all along the way. Yet, jack-in-the-pulpits—unlike most flowers, which are androgynous, or bisexual, having both male and female flower parts on the same plant—are diclinous, or unisexual, meaning there are male plants and female plants that live separately. And they tend to be loners.

It's even curious that the jack-in-the-pulpit's flower structure does not readily encourage pollination. They are inviting and not inviting at the same time. The overhanging flap, or hood, that protects the rest of the tubular spathe would seem to be too difficult for butterflies or even robust bees to maneuver their way into.

So just what does pollinate such demure damsels?

Gnats.

Yes. Fungus gnats, those insects that buzz around your face on hot afternoons in the summer. There are thousands of living things around us throughout the year, yet most go unnoticed, too trifling and transient to gain our attention. Yet, all have a role to play, some more than others. I could hum from the *Lion King*'s "Circle of Life" here, something like "There's far too much to take in here, More to find than can ever be found," but that might be too Broadway for such an infinitesimally little thing.

And fungus gnats are small—two to five millimeters long, depending on the species. That's one-sixteenth to three-sixteenths of an inch, so it would take sixteen of the little ones, lined up end-to-end to make an inch. They are related to houseflies, only much smaller. Both are in the insect order Diptera, which means two wings. Fungus gnat larvae help with decomposition by feeding on plant roots and fungi, hence the name.

They are short-lived, producing several generations each year. The overwintering larvae can either tolerate freezing or avoid freezing. Some even have antifreeze proteins in their cells, a neat trick for something so small. The winged adults of spring have evolved to have an important role: helping male and female jack-in-the-pulpits reproduce.

Here's where it gets interesting: To attract the gnats, the jacks produce a fragrance, a plant pheromone that smells like a mushroom. It's an odd scent for such a glamorous flower, but they are in the same family as calla lilies and skunk cabbage, both noted for being deceptive.

The fungi-sniffing gnats and even tiny flying insects called thirps take the bait. Because of their size, the petite bugs are able to fly into the flower's opening with ease; it's the escaping part that's difficult. The inside of the spathe, or pulpit, is too slick to climb. If it's a male flower, the base of the spadix is covered with tiny male reproductive organs called stamens, part of which are the pollen-producing anthers. The trapped gnat repeatedly climbs the spadix, getting coated with pollen on every trip, only to slip and fall back to the bottom of the pulpit.

It might seem like a Chinese bamboo finger trap—the harder you struggle, the more difficult the escape—and to a degree it is. The gnat has to stop the struggle to prevail. Eventually the winged prisoner falls to the bottom exhausted, only to discover a small opening just big enough for anything gnat-sized to crawl through. The pollen-drenched insect then flies away.

You might think the escapee had learned its lesson, but its brain is indescribably tiny and perhaps soon it sniffs the wafting of another fungus aroma. This time, if the fates are in align, a female jack, which for the sake of clarity we'll call a jill, is producing the pheromone. The process is then repeated, with the gnat getting trapped and spreading the jack's pollen onto the jill's reproduction organs, called pistils, and then onto the ovaries to complete fertilization. As before, the gnat struggles to free itself. But the jill is a true *femme fatale* because she has no escape opening at the base of her pulpit. The gnat falls to the bottom of its tomb and this time dies, its mission complete. And I suspect that the decaying dead gnats provide nutrients to the now seed-producing female.

"Gnats often become exhausted by the rigors of escape and fall to the flower floor, and if you peel open one of the jack's pulpits you will sometimes find the victims," wrote gardener and author Peter Loewer.

"A cruel deception," noted retired biologist Beatriz Moisset.

Even Henry David Thoreau knew that some jills were likely tombs, as he noted in his journal on May 11, 1859: "To Flint's Pond *Arum triphyllum* out. Almost every one has a little fly or two concealed within. One of the handsomest-formed plants when in flower."

THE NATIVE AMERICAN APOTHECARY

The *femme fatale* has another secret. Like a botanical Lucrezia Borgia, the plant possesses poison. Legend has it that the lovely Lucrezia, the daughter of Pope Alexander VI, kept her poison in a ring and used it on lovers she no longer desired. Jill and jack-in-the-pulpits keep their poison throughout the plant, but primarily, it's in their corms, their potato-like underground tubers. The toxin is calcium oxalate, a calcium salt of oxalic acid that in plants exists as needle-shaped crystals, known as raphides. Ouch!

Swallowing the crystals can produce sores and numbing or, even worse, death. The wildflower is a member of the plant family Arum, Arabic for "fire."

The calcium oxalate crystals are bitter, causing a violent burning sensation. The microscopic needles stab the mouth and throat causing blisters and swelling and, ultimately, if enough is eaten, choking and suffocation.

Native Americans did not have a Walgreens. (We didn't have one ourselves until 1901.) Their pharmaceuticals were herbal medicines they collected in the woods around where they lived, and it seems they had a use for everything.

There's a wonderful master's thesis in the University of Tennessee's Hodges Library. Submitted by William H. Banks Jr. in 1953, it's titled, "Ethnobotany of the Cherokee Indians." Dr. Aaron J. Sharp was Banks's botany master's professor, while noted UT anthropologist Madeline Kneberg approved the work for acceptance. Both are noted prominent past professors at the University of Tennessee.

While conducting the research, Banks lived on the reservation in North Carolina in 1952, interviewing the native Cherokee. Some were reluctant to give out many of their secrets, fearing the plants would lose their power; others were less taciturn. The document is a wonderful window into Cherokee culture's use of the herbal apothecary in the woods around them. And even though the bulbs of jack-in-the-pulpit are toxic, handled properly they had their uses. Mollie Sequoyah remembered that by beating the root and creating a poultice, it could be used to treat boils before they began to ooze. Will West Long added that after being roasted for a few seconds, pieces of the root were rolled into small balls the size of possum grapes and taken for kidney trouble. And Aggie Lossiah from Yellow Hill noted, "The root was made into a poultice which is used for a headache."

Many Native American tribes treated a variety of medical conditions using the powdered root in small doses. Mohegans developed a liniment oil and throat soother from the powder, while the Chippewa used it for sore eyes. It was also used to treat croup and a variety of other respiratory illnesses.

NO GENDER BIAS HERE

This may seem like a major digression, but bear with me. In the 2003 animated movie *Finding Nemo,* one of the central characters is a clownfish named Marlin (voiced by Albert Brooks), who sets out on a great adventure to find his kidnapped son, Nemo. The story opens on the Great Barrier Reef in the Coral Sea off the coast of Queensland, Australia. The orange and white ocellaris clownfish are coral reef fish that in the wild have a strict dominance hierarchy. The largest and most aggressive female is found at the top. It's her group, and only two clownfish, a male and a female, in that group get to reproduce through external fertilization. The young are all males, and when they mature and grow bigger, they become females through a process called sequential hermaphroditism.

If something happens to the dominant female clownfish, then the largest, most dominant male will often change genders and replace her. This also means that by now, little Nemo has perhaps grown up to be a dominant female.

The point here is that one's gender is not always set in stone, primarily with some fish, snails, slugs, and plants. Some species are like clownfish: they start out as males, and as they age, they become females. In other species the females become males. As a general rule, size matters. While mammals are an exception, nature's males tend to be smaller because you do not have to be big to produce and carry a lot of small sperm cells. Females need to be bigger to carry the larger eggs.

This brings us back to our jill- and jack-in-the-pulpits. The male plants are shorter, with only one leaf made up of three leaflets, while the females are taller and have two leaves, each with three leaflets. However, their sex and size often change from one growing season to the next.

David Policansky, with the Gray Herbarium at Harvard University, did a detailed three-year study of 2,038 jacks and jills in Estabrook Woods, Concord, Massachusetts, and determined that 380 millimeters (14.9 inches) is the dividing line. Plants shorter were mostly male, while plants taller were mostly females. So, as a plant ages and grows bigger each successive year, it eventually becomes a fruit-bearing female. But there's a caveat. Some years, the former robust female may come back the following year as a shorter male.

Why?

Here is where it gets interesting again. Growing conditions may change—say, less water or more shade, for whatever reason—and inhibit growth. But the most fascinating reason may have to do with energy reserves. Male plants, once the fungus gnats have spread their pollen, are finished. They die away usually by early summer. Only the corm remains to soak up nutrients and grow underground. But female plants must stay viable until October, pumping nutrients into their cluster of bright red fruits. The more fruits, the more energy is required. Once the fruits are dispersed, the female plant dies away as well, her energy stores depleted.

Thus, it may simply be easier for her to take a year off next season and only be a male to replenish her reserves. It then is entirely possible to encounter a thirty-year-old jack-in-the-pulpit in the woods that had spent several growing seasons as a male and several as a female.

Fans of science fiction may be reminded of Ursula K. Le Guin's 1969 award-winning *Left Hand of Darkness*. The novel is set in the "Hainish" universe on a perpetually cold planet named Gethen and examines our own sexual roles through the lives of the Gethenians, the planet's inhabitants, who are "ambisexual," or androgynous.

"They only adopt sexual attributes once a month, during a period of sexual receptiveness and high fertility, called *kemmer,* in which individuals can assume male or female attributes, depending on context and relationships," according to English professor Charlotte Spivack in her college class on Le Guin. "Many mothers are at differing periods fathers."

So, as it turns out, that seasoned thirty-year-old jack-in-the-pulpit in your forest may be the mother to part of the younger jacks and father to still others.

A WILDFLOWER PILGRIMAGE

Lynne and Bob Davis are simpatico. Both are in the Knoxville Choral Society and both are pilots who fly out of Island Home Airport near downtown Knoxville. So both are quite comfortable with highs and lows; Lynne is an alto, Bob's a bass. They are also at ease aloft in small aircraft but equally content on terra firma pursuing one of their other passions: wildflowers. As it is with any good plant aficionados, spring is a favorite time of the year.

The Davises lead an annual wildflower walk for Ijams, generally in April. In 2016, it was the last Saturday of the month, which dawned with a threatening forecast. And just as the registered guests were gathering in the parking lot, a heavy rain set in to soak the group. Bob made a quick call to move everyone indoors for an impromptu class on how to identify hard-to-identify wildflowers. Many people feel flustered while trying to affix a name on a quickly moving bird, but plants are sedentary and yet can be even more perplexing. Leaf shapes include basal, whorled, opposite, alternate, ovate, elliptic, spatulate, pinnate, palmate, lobed—the list goes on. Flowers themselves can be single, composite, or spadix, or be borne on spikes, panicles, racemes, or umbels with florets.

When the rain stopped, we moved on to our outdoor walkabout at William Hastie Natural Area near the nature center, part of the Knoxville Urban Wilderness. The seventy-five-acre, heavily forested parcel was sodden from the rainfall; the trees were still dripping, giving the protected area a lush tropical feel, sopping and sensual. At times I think that you are never more primal, more close to the womb or to Eden, than in the woodland after or during a rain, preferably during. And about twenty minutes into our walk, one last shower soaked us yet again.

Like any good avocational botanists, Lynne and Bob know the trilliums and mayapples, and bloodroot; that's a given. But the Davises have a particular penchant for the humble and insular, or as Bob likes to say the "inconspicuous" wildflowers—the ones that often do not appear in flashy field guides simply because they are small and understated. These flowers generally go unnoticed because they bloom modestly beside the much showier celandine poppies or wild phlox.

Lynne and Bob seek out these vascular plants with flowers that are, well, underwhelming, oddball plants with even odder names like Cumberland spurge, Carolina cranesbill, rattlesnake orchid, spreading chervil, crane-fly orchid (a.k.a. crippled cranefly), hoary puccoon, adder's-tongue (a fern with leaves like an orchid), small-flower crowsfoot, sweet cicely, little brown jugs, and cursed buttercup, or as the Danish are apt to say, *tiggeranunkel,* which means "beggar's buttercup." And you simply do not get a name like little brown jugs or beggar's buttercup without having a story attached to it, and Lynne or Bob can generally supply the story.

In the case of the latter, it is said that there was a time when folks who were down on their luck and forced to beg were known to put the toxic plant sap from this buttercup on their skin. The sap induced eczema and unsightly rashes that made them look even more wretched. They hoped their pitiful appearance would increase the size of the handouts dropped in their beggar bags.

Nick Stahlman, a volunteer naturalist at Ijams was one of the walkabout group that day. He asked Lynne, "Do you have a particularly memorable find that stands out in your mind?"

"Three-birds orchid," she quickly replied. "I had read that they are hard to find, rarely bloom, or bloom only after a sudden change of weather or thunderstorm. We were at Tremont in the Smokies, just after a passing thunderstorm and looked down to find an entire cluster in bloom."

Three-birds is small. It's an orchid, which makes it sound spectacular. It's not. Its impermanent offering gets its name because it often has a triad of nodding blooms that look like petite flying doves. It sallies forth from July through September but is infamous for its elusive nature, with fleeting flowers that last for only several hours on a few days of the year. To complicate observation even more, it has been reported that populations across a region synchronize blooming to specific days. As Lynne found out, being in the right place at the right time is paramount, or you miss the show.

As you might suspect, on this particular pilgrimage, I had a secret agenda and Lynne knew it: to find a jack-in-the-pulpit. The group left the parking lot at the end of Margaret Road on View Park Trail and climbed steadily up the side of a ridge.

"We won't find any here, " said Lynne. "This is a dry, south-facing slope, but soon we'll be on a wetter, northern slope and they should be there. Jacks like the damp."

We did find one wildflower completely new to me: yellow pimpernel, similar to the European version *(Anagallis arvensis),* with a name reminiscent of the Scarlet Pimpernel, a fictional character in a 1905 novel based on a very popular English stage play. The storyline is set during the time of the Reign of Terror in France and revolves around a chivalrous, albeit foppish Englishman named Sir Percy Blakeney. With his secret coterie of gentlemen—the League of the Scarlet Pimpernel—Sir Percy rescues aristocrats before the violent government in revolutionary France can guillotine them. The fictional Pimpernel, a master of disguise, succeeds by skillfully blending into his surroundings much like his symbol, the simple, inconspicuous European flower of the same name.

The American pimpernel is as skillful at going as unnoticed as the fictional English one. After the initial green-up of spring, the delicate umbels of tiny saffron flowers last through the heat of summer.

"They look like exploding yellow fireworks," said Stahlman.

"William Hastie is the only place we've ever found it," said Bob.

After we rounded a switchback and moved onto a shadowy north slope, we found a colony of foamflower still in bloom and then several of the treasured jack-in-the pulpits growing together, cloistered like Carthusian monks, many with chartreuse robes but some with festive purple-striped hoods. In a word, they were magnificent, although their cloister largely goes unseen—as perhaps it should, sequestered beneath their umbrellas of leaves, a world within a world within a world, as hidden as anyone within a monastic order tucked away on a mountainside. All were fairly low to the ground, suggesting that they were males, which begs the question, "How many males per each female does one forest have or need?" I seriously doubt if the ratio is one to one. Nothing in nature is really that simple.

It seems then that Richard Fortey was correct. In nature "every story is worth the telling no matter how humble, or indeed insular, is the organism concerned." And on this particular day, Lynne and Bob were happy to provide those stories.

Appalachian Pandas
Pristinailurus bristoli / Ailurus fulgens

"On this dynamic earth, nothing stays still:
neither climate, nor life, nor the oceans and continents,
although they all move to different rhythms."

—Richard Fortey, *Horseshoe Crabs and Velvet Worms*

FOSSIL.

Say the word. What mental images come to mind?

Do you see broken pieces of bone turned to stone in faraway dusty places? Are the images of dinosaurs in arid Wyoming, Colorado, or the Black Hills of South Dakota, or perhaps early hominids in Olduvai Gorge in Tanzania or Hadar in Ethiopia?

When you think of the lush, green Appalachian Mountains, you don't think of fossils. But they are there, just covered with vegetation and the bedrock is generally much older, hundreds of millions of years old, too aged for dinosaurs. The fossils that are generally found—crinoids and brachiopods—are of small creatures that lived in marine environs long before life got serious, grew legs, and started walking around on old Mother Earth.

That's why May 31, 2000, was remarkable. Larry Bolt, a geologist with the Tennessee Department of Transportation (TDOT), and three others had been sent to Gray, Tennessee, just west of Johnson City to investigate a puzzling layer of dark gray clay. The mud-like deposit was unearthed at the site of a road-improvement project: the straightening and flattening of a section of Fulkerson Road where it intersects State Route 75 near Daniel Boone High School. Work crews using heavy equipment had already removed roughly twenty feet of hillside before they encountered the mysterious muddy layer. The soft clay soil presented a problem to establishing a firm foundation for the new road, and TDOT needed to figure out a solution.

With Bolt that day were three other geologists, Peter Lemiszki, Martin Kohl, and Bob Price, all with the Tennessee Department of Environment and Conservation. What happened next is something they will never forget. While watching a backhoe remove the curious thin layers of soft black and gray clays, they started noticing pieces of bone: jawbones, teeth, and other peculiarly shaped fragments. "Everybody was suddenly picking up bones," Bolt recalled. For the four geologists, it was like Christmas morning and Santa had left some interesting things under the tree. Their discovery brought a quick end to the road project.

Fulkerson Road no longer intersects S.R. 75; indeed, that state highway was diverted to bypass the location and a brand new $8 million Natural History Museum, visitor center, paleontology lab, and educational facility was built at the site instead. Nearby East Tennessee State University (ETSU), my alma mater, hired a young vertebrate paleontologist, Dr. Steven Wallace, to study the site and write papers about what is found. In addition to teaching geosciences at the university, he is now the curator at the museum. Dr. Wallace likes to be called "Wally," because, as he said, "geologists are a very informal group."

Dr. Wallace has a *full* beard that is old-school. It's a statement like Mount Rushmore, as bold as a whiskered nineteenth-century president, we're talking Grant or Hayes or Garfield or maybe like Andrew, one of the Smith Brothers on the box of cough drops, a cold remedy that has been packaged since 1872. But Wallace is a paleontologist, an old-school profession. Yet, that is not to say he is staid. When he talks about geology, rocks, or fossils he enthuses with boyish exuberance.

"We're basically twelve-year-olds that get very excited by what we find digging in the dirt," he said. Even though their subjects—rocks and fossils—are inanimate, geologists simply are not. They are also down to earth, and that is a bit of wordplay that is spot-on. Wallace has already been working the site for fifteen years, and it will take his entire career to write about just some of the things unearthed at Gray.

ONE OF THE RICHEST FOSSIL SITES ON THE PLANET

In a word, the Gray Fossil Site is colossal. The size and depth of the deposit makes it one of the most extraordinary, even opulent, in the world. Most other fossil deposits are a few inches or maybe a foot or two thick. Core samples at Gray have determined that the silty, organic, fossil-rich sediments cover four to five acres up to 130 feet deep. That's a mountain of preserved biota (the animals, plants, fungi, and so on, of a region or period), and they have only begun to scratch the surface. To date perhaps only one or two percent of the location has been excavated, yet thousands of fossils have been discovered, too many pieces to even begin to categorize from tiny snake vertebra to skulls as big as microwaves. Image if you took one thousand boxes of jigsaw puzzles and dumped them out in a hole and covered it with dirt. Paleontologists will probably still be working on the location hundreds years from now. Originally it was believed that a long-ago cave collapsed, causing a sinkhole and subsequent pond that plants and animals fell into and later died there. However, the notion suggesting Gray is a death trap like the La Brea Tar Pits in California or Cerro de los Batallones in Spain has now been modified. "The evidence does not back it up here," said Wallace. "In a true trap, when an animal falls in it whines, it makes noise and that attracts carnivores that fall in too. At La Brea the carnivores are ten times more common than the herbivores. But we are finding very few carnivores here."

At Gray, Wallace believes that the sinkhole plugged itself. It's rare, but it does happen. This created a water-filled basin or lake where animals came to drink. And like all such bodies of water, "it eventually filled in with sediments. But that may have taken fifteen thousand years. Well, if only one animal fell in per year, that's fifteen thousand dead animals piled up in one spot; perfect conditions for creating fossils," added Wallace.

From the fossils recovered so far, researchers date the deposit somewhere between 4.5 and 7 million years old, but as fossils are recovered and identified that window of time will narrow. The lake would not have existed 2.5 million years, so it's a sliver of time that falls somewhere between those two points, a period of geologic time known as the late Miocene and early Pliocene—Greek for "less recent" and "more recent," respectively. The terms were coined by Sir Charles Lyell, the most-noted geologist of the nineteenth century and author of *Principles of Geology: being an attempt to explain the former changes of the Earth's surface, by reference to causes now in operation.* (Book titles were much longer in his day.)

During the Miocene, if we could climb into Doc Brown's *Back to the Future* time machine, a stainless steel DeLorean DMC-12 with flux capacitor, and go back and circle the globe five million years ago, we would notice that the continents looked more like they do today but were still very close together, in some cases only separated by narrow interstitial waterways. Central America and Florida were still under the sea and the subcontinent of India had moved north, colliding into Asia and beginning to push up the Himalayan Mountains. This is still happening, as evidenced by the 7.8 magnitude earthquake centered in Nepal on April 25, 2015, which killed over eight thousand people. The quake shifted Kathmandu, the capitol of Nepal, ten feet to the south in a matter of just thirty seconds and demonstrated that planet Earth is a dynamic place.

The Miocene was a time of warmer, drier weather, when grasslands and grazing animals dominated. The earliest known camel originated in North America. But from the plant fossils in the deposit, the Gray site itself appears to have been temperate woodland. So as a fossil filled location it is unusual because it preserved a long ago forested ecosystem with a watering hole for animals wandering in from the surrounding open spaces.

"This is rare in the fossil world, as most fossil sites preserve either bones or plants, but not both," wrote Judy Lundquist for *Smoky Mountain Living* magazine.

Macrofossils of acorns and hickory nuts and pollen grains that have been found belong to oaks, hickories, hackberries, elms, birches, ashes, and willows, much like the forests of the lower elevations of the Appalachians today. There were also cypresses, suggestive of environs more like south Georgia today. Plus, they have found alligator parts. Yes, alligators.

Gray is an unfolding anomaly. The Miocene is known as the "Age of Horses," and horse evolution occurred mainly in North America, with many early, now-extinct forms such as *Parahippus, Miohippus, Anchitherium, Hypohippus, Pliohippu, Merychippus,* and *Dinohippus* all present. If you could see any one of these alive today, you'd easily recognize it as a horse or, at least, as horse-like, although some were quite small. It is believed that all modern equines—horses, zebras, and donkeys—evolved from *Dinohippus.* This group somehow survived the vicissitudes of the past five million years while the others did not. Browsing and grazing horse types were so widespread then that fossilized equines generally dominate Miocene sites of this age, but so far, only a few three-toed horse parts from the extinct genus *Miohippus* have been found at Gray.

During the late Miocene, somewhere on the planet, you could also find very recognizable early beavers, deer, camels, raccoons, wolves, and birds like plovers, dabbling ducks, cockatoos, and typical owls, such as the ancestral owl. By the end of the Miocene, it is believed that almost all the modern bird families were present, although individual species were still evolving.

Since the first bones were found Gray, a treasure trove of fauna material has been discovered at the fossil site, although many are of animals you would never expect to find in East Tennessee. In addition to the alligator parts, by the summer of 2006, fieldworkers had finished uncovering the near complete skeletons of some rhinoceroses, and there have been other oddities, mostly bits and pieces: a short-faced bear, a camel, a peccary, a shovel-nosed elephant, and a saber-toothed cat. The presence of fossilized frogs, fish, shrews, snakes, turtles, and salamanders suggests that this was basically a watering hole. Not a sinkhole trap, but rather an aquatic, inviting environment and tapirs love watery places. Lots and lots of tapir parts have been unearthed so far. The most numerous animal found to date has been tapirs, at least one hundred fifty individuals. Tapirs are built like pigs with short prehensile snouts. Modern day tapirs spend a great amount of time in or under water, even walking along the bottom of a pond or wetland where they eat soft vegetation.

"In reality, the other animals we are finding are rare, because they were just passing through pausing at the watering hole and occasionally dying, perhaps even of natural causes," said Wallace. "But the tapirs were living here. This is why we are finding so many more of them."

But how do we know about that environment?

"As tooth enamel is highly resilient and is not substantially altered after the death of the animal, we can therefore analyze the carbon ratios locked; in the fossil teeth to determine if an animal consumed leafy vegetation and/ or warm season grasses," wrote Wallace for a symposium on the ten-year anniversary of the site discovery. "Similarly, oxygen isotopes that occur in water are a function of temperature and precipitation."

Digging in the dirt looking for fossils is a very old-school science, but analyzing what you find is quite high-tech. The stable carbon and oxygen isotope analysis at different locations on the same tooth can infer canopy density and if the foods were seasonal or available year-round. To date, most of the fossilized animals appear to have consumed vegetation consistent with a canopied forest with little seasonal change.

In the fall of 2016, Dr. Wallace and the staff were very excited about the four-tusked elephant parts being unearthed at the time. They are just beginning to work on them and think the skeleton may be relatively complete. When I visited Wallace in the museum's lab, several workspaces were being devoted to assembling various sized pieces together. It was going to be a beast of an elephant. At one table a preparator was working on just one of the four tusks that may be when pieced together ten to twelve feet long. It could turn out to be a new species and a new genus, longer legged than an African elephant but barrel-chested like a mammoth. If it were up to me, I'd call it *Kingus kongi*, but that name may be already taken.

"It's so big. Every time we get another bone out, it's absurd how big it is," Wallace said as we looked down on the tusk being patiently assembled. No one knows at this point just how huge this beast will ultimately be. Time will tell.

Nature abhors a vacuum, or, as stated in the sixteenth century by French scholar François Rabelais, *Natura abhorret vacuum.* Originally, the observation applied to physics, but as modern-day astrophysicist Neil de-Grasse Tyson correctly noted, the universe does not abhor a vacuum: it's everywhere. Today, the comment perhaps applies more accurately to describe nature's rush to fill a void or empty niche within a habitat: opportunist species quickly rush in claim the larder. When the sinkhole at Gray created a new lake, aquatic animals like turtles, frogs, alligators, and tapirs rushed in to fill it. In this case, quite literally filling it with their dead bodies. One day an incredible beast of an elephant ventured in for a drink and somehow added its body to the pile. Needless to say, Gray is far from revealing all of its holdings.

Habitats are ephemeral. Habitat specific species come and go as well, which leads us to an early, unexpected fossil discovered at Gray.

BEING IN THE RIGHT PLACE AT THE RIGHT TIME

"I just happened to look down at the right place and at the right time," said Larry Bristol, geology professor at ETSU. It was in the fall of 2003.

How Bristol even noticed the tiny tooth as small as a kernel of un-popped popcorn is a wonder in itself. When Dr. Wallace showed me the nubbin of a thing, I was taken aback by its minuteness. But indeed it was a tooth, and paleontologists know teeth. It's the body part that most often survives as this odd one truly had. Bristol knew it was a molar, but what kind was a mystery. Back at the university, it reminded Dr. Wallace of a raccoon's tooth, but even that wasn't quite right. After photographing it, Wallace emailed the image to a list of other fossil experts. He heard back quickly from the revered vertebrate paleontologist Dr. Xiaoming Wang, curator at the Natural History Museum of Los Angeles County.

"This looks like a really weird raccoon to me," said Wallace.

And Wang replied, "Actually, it's a panda."

Wallace wasn't "super shocked." A panda fossil had been found in Washington State in 1977. He was sort of in the ballpark. He knew it was raccoon-like and the two groups are closely related. Wallace just wasn't expecting it at Gray. But like the four-tusked elephant, you never know quite what to expect there. In time, he realized that a canine he had found in 2002 was also from a panda. Canine teeth are a little harder to classify than the upper first molar that Bristol had discovered. Looking back on it now that more is known about the Gray site it makes sense.

"Forested ecosystems are real common around the Northern Hemisphere," said Wallace. "Pandas are real common in Europe and Asia in the fossil record, but they are mainly known from tooth and jaw fragments. We have the best material in the whole world. It's like having chocolate cake with even more chocolate poured on top of it."

YES, PANDAS IN TENNESSEE

On Saturday, May 6, 2006, I led a group of Ijams members that included former Executive Director Paul James and member Nancy Tanner on a trip to Gray. We had never been to a real dig site. At 1:00 p.m., we met Bristol at the back gate of the chain-link fence that surrounded the property. He had set up a small table outside in the gravel parking lot to display a few of the fossils that had been uncovered so far. He was eager to show us around. Down below, near the road, was the location of the planned museum about to be built. (It opened in August of the following year.) Walking along a trail below a crumbing clay slope, we came to the dig site covered with canvas.

Bristol continued his story of that fortuitous find. The tooth was from the lesser panda group, very much like the red pandas of Asia. In the September 2004 issue of the science journal *Nature,* Wallace and Wang published a paper about a new badger species and the unique tooth, giving the panda the name *Pristinailurus bristoli.* The generic name roughly translates as "former for the living genus," and the specific name honors Larry Bristol for his serendipitous discovery. Its common name is Bristol's Appalachian panda.

"The tooth represents the first occurrence of a panda in Eastern North America, and only the second occurrence of a panda in the Western Hemisphere; the only other find in Washington State some years ago is of a specimen that is significantly younger than ours," said Bristol. "More importantly, ours is the oldest and most primitive panda ever found anywhere in the world. It was not only a new species, but a new genus as well."

Does it mean that the small pandas originated in Asia and dispersed to this part of the world? Or is it the reverse? Whether the little panda moved west-to-east or east-to-west is a puzzle for future paleontologists. The consensus is the latter, but the jury is still out until a new clue is found. That's the way science works.

"However, it is likely that the Gray-site panda was able to subsist on non-bamboo leaves while passing through an arctic arboreal corridor and ultimately found more habitable land in the eastern deciduous forest of the southern Appalachians," wrote Wallace in *Nature.* Since modern pandas eat bamboo, current speculation is that Bristol's panda may have eaten river cane, a member of the bamboo family found throughout the Appalachian lowlands. (See my UT Press book *Natural Histories.*) But the small panda is also an omnivore and will eat about anything.

Since Bristol's initial 2003 find, fieldworkers at the Gray Fossil Site in 2010 and 2012 recovered numerous teeth and bones, plus two nearly complete skeletons of *Pristinailurus bristoli,* the oldest known panda.

"It's like panning for gold. It's not what we find, it's what we might find. That's what makes it fun," said Wallace. We were standing in the lab with broad windows that looked out on the dig sites. "That's what keeps us out there. We dig most days because who knows what we might uncover. We have a really cool list of things that we have found and a list of what we expect to find, but then there's this whole other third list, the mystery column, and who knows what might turn up because it's Gray and everything here has been weird so far. The four-tusked elephant was completely unexpected."

JUST WHAT IS A PANDA?

The mystery of the tooth Bristol found was solved with the lightning speed of the Internet. But the ambiguity of just what a panda is remains a subject of some debate, a conundrum not completely solved for almost two centuries, although modern DNA tests are clearing up some of the murkiness.

In 1821, Major General Thomas Hardwicke, an Englishman in the Indian Civil Service, spoke of a mysterious animal of "beautiful fulvous brown color" that lived along rivers and mountain torrents. At the November meeting of the Linnaean Society of London that same year, he showed a red furry pelt at a presentation titled, "Description of a new Genus of the Class Mammalia, from the Himalaya Chain of Hills Between Nepaul [*sic*] and the Snowy Mountains." (Even talks had longer titles back then.) But Hardwicke didn't assign the new mammal a name, planning to do that in a juried paper to follow. He planned on calling the new mammal a "wah," a name used by the Nepalese locals.

The scientific community itself was experiencing something of an overhaul. Naturalists were scampering to affix a label to every living thing. Swedish botanist and zoologist Carolus Linnaeus had adopted a new system of naming all plants and animals. Prior to him, the names of species were wordy polynomials—that is, long descriptive paragraphs. Linnaeus's *Systema Naturae,* published in the late 1700s, provided a new, simpler method. It was known then as Linnaean taxonomy; today we call it binomial nomenclature or simply binomials. Henceforth, every living thing was given a unique two-part scientific name, generally in Latin. The first word designated its genus, the second its species. And we formally became *Homo sapiens,* or wise humans.

The reddish pelt Hardwicke was describing was collected by botanist Nathaniel Wallich, who also supplied specimens to Alfred du Vaucel of the

Museum of Natural History in Paris. It was there that it caught the eye of famed French zoologist and paleontologist Frédéric Cuvier, who wasted no time including it in a book he was writing about the natural history of mammals, *Histoire naturelle des mammifères,* published in four volumes. Using the pelt and skeleton he was supplied, Cuvier described the new mammal as a "fire-colored cat." The binomial he assigned it was *Ailurus fulgens,* from the ancient Greek word αἴλουρος (ailouros), meaning "cat" and *fulgens,* from the Latin for "shining, bright." Thus Cuvier's published name appeared in 1825, two years before Hardwicke's paper. The Frenchman's binomial is the one still used today.

Cuvier wrote that the new animal was a "beautiful species, one of the handsomest of known quadrupeds." He also called it "Bright Panda" and even though the generic name he used means cat, he placed it in the raccoon family, the Procyonidae, noting its raccoon-like teeth.

Thus the word "panda" entered our lexicon, and not Hardwicke's "wah," but where the French zoologist got panda is something of a mystery itself. Many believe it came from the Nepalese names *nigayla-poonya* or *nyala-ponga,* which mean "eater of bamboo," a logical assumption.

Placing them with the raccoons makes the oddity a member of the biological order Carnivora. That makes it a herbivorous carnivore; unlike their fellow carnivorans, they are primarily vegetarians that eat mostly bamboo leaves, fruits, and flowers, but they do eat meat if they can catch it.

It wasn't until May 22, 1869, that a live, but sickly, red bearcat was shipped to the London Zoo (two others died in transit). The puny panda fell under the watchful eye of Abraham Bartlett, who had no idea the poor thing ate bamboo, but through trial and error nursed the panda back to a degree of health, at least for a while. That same year, the Western world learned that there was yet another remarkable bamboo eater living in that same general region. The Chinese called it *beishung* or white bear, because, after all, it looked like a bear. The West simply called it the giant panda, and the original red panda became known as the lesser panda much to the chagrin of today's mammalogists that work with the original.

"Is the giant panda a bear? Are the red and giant pandas closely related? These two questions have been debated for over a century. Anatomists, behaviorists, paleontologists, and molecular biologists have led the fascinating inquiry into the evolutionary relationships of these species with ingenuity and persistence, yet they continue to derive different conclusions on the basis of different evidence, and they still pursue the elusive answers," wrote George B. Schaller, considered the world's preeminent field biologist, in his book *The Last Panda.*

Are the two pandas closely related? Are they bear-kin? Or raccoon-kin? In a roomful of biologists, you might not get a consensus, although you might detect a regional bias.

"Most likely the giant pandas and red pandas had a common ancestor in the Miocene [the same timeframe as Bristol's found tooth]. Where should the two pandas then be placed, with the bear or with the raccoon family? Even though the giant panda is most closely related to the bears, I think that it is not just a bear," wrote Schaller.

"Red pandas and giant pandas are inextricably linked," he adds. "They share not only a name but also many physical similarities. Skull, teeth, and forepaws in each are similar, evolved to process bamboo. They even grip bamboo in much the same manner, except that the red panda lacks the functional sixth digit or pseudothumb so useful to the giant panda for manipulating stems. No one questions that the two pandas resemble each other. But are they really related?" Did they coevolve to fill similar niches? Are they pandas in name only?

"Science will overcome this paradox and perversity of evolution and ultimately assign each panda a final taxonomic home," wrote Schaller in 1993. "But as yet this game of taxonomic Ping-Pong has no winners."

Standing in the lobby of the museum in Gray twenty-three years later, I had a conversation with Dr. Wallace about who is who and what is what. Now that we can do thorough DNA studies on these animals, his college professor side came out. He sketched out the relationships on an imaginary blackboard using his finger like a piece of chalk. Under the order Carnivora there's the family Mustelidae, the weasels, and close to them is the family Procyonidae, the raccoons, then next is the family Ailuridae, the original pandas ,and the family Mephitidae, the skunks. These four families tend to be grouped together. So our panda emphatically *is* closely related to the raccoons.

"And what about the giant panda," I asked.

Wallace quickly replied, "Oh, they are bears." Period. End of story. "And lesser pandas aren't lesser, they are the original panda."

From a genetic prospective, the cute-faced red bearcats are more like skunks and raccoons than giant pandas, but since the red panda had the panda moniker first, it's the black-and-white pseudo-panda that should go searching for another appellation. We could use the Chinese beishung, or white bear.

Today, wild red pandas, the true original pandas, are found at elevations between 7,218 and 15,749 feet in the temperate forests of the Himalayas and high mountains of western China and Burma. Their home range was once an arc from Nepal east to the Chinese provinces of Yunnan and Sichunan, but today their population is much diminished because of deforestation and hunting. Their red fur is highly desirable. They exist in isolated forest fragments, mostly on mountaintops in danger of becoming inbred. Typical red panda habitat is made up of hemlock, spruce oaks, chestnuts, maples, rhododendron, and bamboo, the panda's favorite source of food. That biota sounds like the southern Appalachians, except the chestnuts are all gone and river cane grows along the streams instead of the closely related bamboo.

So how do today's red panda and its progenitor Bristol's panda differ? The red panda is much smaller, with both males and females averaging eleven pounds, while the older panda seems to have had a much greater difference between the sexes, with females weighing roughly seventeen pounds and males weighing thirty-three pounds.

"The skull of Bristol's Panda is not as domed and it lacks a sagittal crest suggesting a weaker bite," wrote Aaron Woodruff, a paleontology graduate student at ETSU. Its complete denture suggests that the Miocene panda ate a wider range of foods and wasn't as dependent on plant material as today's red panda.

Larry Bristol's panda molar discovery is a summons to action for all naturalists. The next time you feel the call of the wild, go outside and look around. You never know what wonders await.

THE WONDER COMES HOME AGAIN

Whatever goes around comes around. Call it karma. The philosophical concept of "eternal return" posits that our universe and all existence and energy is recurring, and will continue to recur in a self-similar form an infinite number of times across infinite time or space. German philosopher Friedrich Nietzsche wrote of "eternal recurrence," the idea that with infinite time, events will recur again and again infinitely. The concept is found in Indian philosophy and in ancient Egypt. Even the long ago Mayans and Aztecs had similar views.

On October 19, 2016, my sister, Darlene Brett and I recurred in Gray as we had in the mid-1970s. Sis and I both graduated from East Tennessee State University, and she lived in Gray, just northwest of Johnson City, her last three years at the university. She majored in music and taught in middle schools for thirty-six years. But this recurrence in Gray was to visit the Natural History Museum. Who knows? If she had gone on a long walk in January 1974, she could have discovered a molar as well and today the species might have been known as Darlene's Appalachian panda.

On that recent visit, we stopped at the General Shale brick building located along the road I had driven a decade earlier on my first visit with Larry

Bristol. The facility is unique in that there is a fully functional lab and museum right on the dig site. Once a big fossil is discovered, it's encased in plaster (called a jacket) and wheeled in through double doors at the back of the lab. And as it did on my first visit with Bristol, the active fossil dig continues on the hillside behind. My sister and I visited the Ivory Pit being worked that day where they had unearthed bits of a panda tail the previous August.

Behind glass in the museum itself was the shattered yet reassembled skull of a female Appalachian panda from specimen number ETMNH 3596. Even though only the skull was on display, it is part of a female skeleton discovered in the summer of 2010 and is roughly 95 percent complete. The dental wear indicates the panda was of advanced age. Also on display at the entrance of the exhibit hall was a complete Appalachian panda skeleton model—a best guess at the time before a lot was known about Bristol's panda.

Afterwards, my sister and I revisited the university and all the dorms, apartments, and old houses we had lived in while at school. It had been over four decades since we had walked across the heart of the university's picturesque campus together.

"This is still the prettiest campus I have ever visited," she said.

The landscape sculpture by Ron Bennett was still in front of Reece Museum. I was there the day it was installed and remember Bennett polishing its shiny brass surface, now rich with green patina.

Everything looked the same yet somehow different. The buildings we had known, spent so much time in, were still there, but their uses had evolved. There's Nietzsche's eternal recurrence again, like we were guests in a parallel universe. Sis visited her dorm next to the student center that is no longer the student center on the street that's no longer a street across from the library that is no longer the library.

In this recurrence paradigm, time is not linear but cyclical. Things repeat themselves, only slightly different. Some would say, we start from home—our safe place, our womb—and ultimately return to a feeling of a "spiritual home" and even if dislodged, like J.R.R Tolkien's Bilbo Baggins, eventually we come back to find peace in our Hobbit-hole. In the same vain, the red panda lineage returned to its ancestral Appalachian homeland in 1977. That's when the first modern day pair of Asian shining bright cats: *Ailurus fulgens* arrived at the Knoxville Zoo, only ninety-seven miles southwest of the Gray Fossil Site where the progenitor panda once lived millions of years before. Recurrence. The first two were named Dave and Dierdre, and they were the forerunner to many more to follow.

Something about the environs suited the new arrivals because only a decade later, the Appalachian location's breeding program was second only to the National Zoo in the number of successful births in this country. Globally, the Rotterdam Zoo in the Netherlands led the way until the 1990s. But the early captive breeding success at the Knoxville Zoo brought it media attention.

"It's very difficult to work with this species," said Dr. John Gittleman, a research assistant professor of zoology at the University of Tennessee at the time. "It's a very complex and fascinating problem."

"Red pandas will go extinct if they're not preserved" Gittleman said in an article in the *Knoxville Journal* in 1987. Their hold on life is fleetingly fugacious at best. Their native habitat was being destroyed, and they weren't reproducing with much success.

"We can do more with our panda here than anywhere else in the world," said associate zoo director at the time, Randy Wolfe. Were the hot summers, quick cool autumns, and mountain air a key?

Both the red and giant panda puzzle scientists because of their very limited bamboo diet, poor breeding rate, and low birth weights. Why weren't they already extinct? The theory at the time was that predators like lions and tigers had forced the gentle-natured red pandas into hiding in thick bamboo forests where there was little to eat but the bamboo itself. With their dentition and short gut, they are built like carnivores but are forced to eat like herbivores. The shape and surface of any animal's teeth is directly related to its diet. Carnivores need sharp canines to kill prey and tear its flesh. Herbivores need flat molars for chewing and grinding. Red pandas and people are omnivores and have a combination of both.

Just a decade into the zoo's captive breeding program, it was estimated that only about one thousand red pandas still existed in the wild and fewer than two hundred in captivity. Of these, thirty-two had been born and reared at the Knoxville Zoo, which had noticeably more limited resources than the National Zoo. But, number thirty-two proved to be difficult.

The poor birth rate is a huge challenge. In 1987, panda number thirty-two, a cub named Spandeau, had to be hand-raised because her mother Kelly wasn't able to produce enough milk. At birth the tiny thing weighed only eighty-seven grams or a smidge more than three ounces. (A golf ball weighs one ounce.) Initially, Spandeau had to be fed every two hours. It was labor intensive with a feeding tube being inserted down her throat and milk formula injected with a syringe. Seven people divided the feeding chores. Three people: senior small-mammal keeper Karen Webster, keeper Midge McGill, and tech Carol Newsom, "lost a lot of sleep," said Wolfe. Webster is a smart, shy strawberry blonde. She is endlessly reading and is the only person I know who routinely reads both the *New York Times* and translated Russian newspapers just to keep informed.

Baby panda number thirty-two, Spandeau, was born on July 31. After the early critical weeks passed, she could be fed less often with a traditional nursing bottle but it was determined by October that she needed a playmate to grow up with. Wolfe and Webster went to Washington and picked up Wicket. For a writer it's a fortunate piece of alliteration; for a young panda, it's was a necessary step in her maturation because Wicket was a month older. Spandeau could follow his lead.

"I remember that the National Zoo's panda breeding facility was much more elaborate than ours, yet we were having just as much success," said Webster. "Spandeau and Wicket became instant playmates. We raised them together," she added, fondly remembering the three breeding pairs she routinely cared for, especially Rodney and Kelly.

"Back then, I knew I had a special job. I'd drive to work thinking, wow, no one in Tennessee is going to work right now to feed red pandas," recalled Webster. "They'd see me coming up the trail and start pacing back and forth. They'd be manic by the time I opened up to feed them. I'd go in rain, snow, or sleet to take care of them. In the winter, I remember shoveling the snow off my little Honda, just to go in and check on them. They become part of you."

Perhaps it was the ancestral memory of the Appalachians: the hot summers and cool autumn nights; the oaks, maples, and hickories; the sense of home. Whatever the reason, the Knoxville Zoo began to lead the way in red panda captive breeding and, in particular, the hand-raising of young red pandas who needed the help. Spandeau and Wicket were the first of many. Today, some times young cubs that are born in other zoos and need to be fed by hand are sent to Knoxville.

By 2009, Sarah Glass, curator of red pandas and special exhibits was appointed as coordinator of the Association of Zoos and Aquariums (AZA) North American Red Panda Species Survival Plan (SSP). That's a long moniker but its responsibilities are weighty. The future conservation of the species is in the hands of the SSP partners. Their agenda items include population and genetic management, which adult pandas go to which zoos and who mates with whom, plus they oversee research and education while keeping an eye on the wild population in Asia. Currently red pandas are housed in roughly eighty zoos, before each new cub is born, its ultimate home has to be predetermined and, in time, its breeding partners. The latter is a matter of its genetic makeup. Who is related to whom and how closely are they related? Mary Noell, Animal Records Manager at the Cincinnati Zoo, one of the red panda's SSP partners keeps a very detailed studbook with all the red pandas' pedigrees.

Glass has been working with the red pandas at what is marketed today as Zoo Knoxville for twenty-four years. Originally she volunteered while taking comparative animal behavior classes at the University of Tennessee. The zoo hired her in 1993 as a research assistant and she has worked her way up through the ranks from a keeper to curator to coordinator of the red panda North American survival plan.

Being a caregiver for any living creature is a weighty responsibility, caring for one on the verge of extinction ratchets up the worrisome nights. Your mind is always on your vulnerable charges. As Webster said, "They become a part of you."

By the time I wrote these words, Zoo Knoxville had birthed and raised one-hundred-eight of the—it's hard *not* to use the word "adorable"—pandas. The last two were memorable because they were twin males sired by an aging father named Madan. The twins had a young mother named Scarlett, but they were born on their father's sixteenth birthday. That's a bit of a surprise since a red panda's average lifespan is around ten years. Madan's age did not hamper the young, the mothers do all of the parenting.

On a mild October afternoon, Ijams volunteer coordinator Lauren Bird and I met with Glass at the zoo's Red Panda Village. Bird is organized and efficient. She was there as an extra pair of ears for me, plus she wanted to see the sweet-faced pandas. Who wouldn't? Glass is one of those instantly likable people, warm and welcoming. She's a good panda mom, and this was her arboreal panda world she had helped to create. She was at home. The zoo will mark its fortieth anniversary of the red panda program in 2017, and Glass has been there for sixty percent of it.

The cool nights of autumn had finally arrived in the Tennessee Valley, and the tree-loving mammals relished the change of season. It is more like the temperatures of their mountainous Asian homes: cool, damp, misty.

"They can tolerate our hot summers," said Glass. "But this is what they like. They would probably be even happier on the top of the Smokies."

As Glass explained, in the case of any species maintained in captivity under an SSP, there are two things you look at: the Inbreeding Coefficient ,or how inbred an animal is, and the Mean Kinship, or how related an animal is to the rest of the population. An individual with a high Mean Kinship has a lot of first cousins, second cousins, third cousins, brothers, sisters, aunts, and uncles. An individual's Inbreeding Coefficient is set, it cannot change, but the Mean kinship can decrease as an individual red panda's relations die off.

"What you want to breed are your low Mean Kinship and low Inbreed Coefficient animals," said Glass. Those genes need to be preserved. "And the goal of every SSP is to maintain a population diversity in captivity that is the same as in the wild."

The long-range goal is to return captive-bred red pandas to the wild, but with their natural Asian mountainside habitat still in decline that will not happen anytime soon.

We stood outside an enclosure with a male red panda named Zhu in a tree behind us looking on, rather laid-backed, even blasé. It seemed perhaps insensitive for us to even discuss how breeding partners were chosen with Zhu overhearing our conversation, yet individual female choice still governed the process. Maybe Zhu learned something.

Red pandas are loners. Females keep individual territories. They will tolerate another female nearby but only so close. Males also keep individual territories that may overlap the territories of potential mates but a female in estrous will only accept a male with "proper manners."

In the past keepers used index cards. Every individual panda had a card and keepers would spread the cards out on a table and sort them to determine the best possible matches. Today there is a computer program that does the matchmaking. Yet, the female still has the final say. Politeness counts.

"Some pairs prove to be incompatible," Glass added. "They are solitary in the wild. So the males have to have a certain set of manners. If he goes into her territory and she chases him off. He needs to go away and not push her around."

"How apropos for this date and time," I thought. Here we were in the final two weeks of the 2016 presidential election, and one of the issues that had bubbled to the surface was the interaction between human males and females and the question: Were we as a nation ready to accept and respect a female Commander in Chief?

Curious, I asked Glass about the two hand-raised red pandas from 1987: Spandeau and Wicket. Sadly, the female born to Deirdre at the Knoxville Zoo had only lived three years and did not produce any offspring. But the young male that Wolfe and Webster retrieved from the National Zoo to be Spandeau's playmate ultimately ended up at the Cheyenne Mountain Zoo. Billed as America's only mountainside zoo, it is located in Colorado Springs, Colorado, at an elevation of 6,800 feet above sea level. It was a sweet spot for a red panda, very similar to his high-elevation ancestral homeland in the temperate forests of the Himalayas of Nepal. Wicket lived a bountiful life of twelve years.

"His full name was L. P. Wicket Esquire," said Glass. And with a name like that, you know he created a legacy. Glass produced a printout— as long as she was tall—of Master Wicket's pedigree chart with the seven generations that have followed him. In human terms, his descendants to date include twelve children, nineteen grandchildren, twenty-five great-grandchildren, fifty-one great-great-grandchildren, one hundred-eight great-great-great-grandchildren, seventy-six great-great-great-great-grandchildren and thirty great-great-great-great-great-grandchildren. That's a total of 321 direct descendants, and that number is still growing, even though Wicket has long since passed way. Lauren and I were witnesses to two bearing his genes. Two-year-old Zhu, who had watched over our conversation with Glass from an above tree, was Wicket's great-great-great-grandson, and we were about to meet another descendant.

After our outside interview ended, Glass welcomed us into the keeper's room where the food was prepared. After showing us the proper way to feed long thin wedges of apple, we were escorted into the enclosure of Lincoln (his name honors Lincoln, Nebraska, where he was born). He was the great-great-great-great-grandson of Wicket and likes a snack in mid-afternoon, particularly apples.

Inside his enclosure, Lincoln descended from the trees to stand on a rock at eye level with us. That was his comfort zone. He was in control and could quickly scamper back up into his arboreal world if he wanted to escape us. We were reminded not to touch him and even though I wanted to pick up Lincoln, coddle him like a stuffed animal won at the county fair, I refrained. He looked amiable, but he was still wild with sharp claws and teeth. Following Glass's lead we took turns feeding him.

"Look at that face!" gasped Lauren.

"Those plump round cheeks are the muscles that operate his jaw," said Glass. "He has a strong bite to chomp tough bamboo." They also have recurved claws like a cat that are four or five times bigger than they should be considering the size of the animal, a holdover from their larger Appalachian panda ancestors. This enables them to climb down a tree headfirst.

I told myself that I could not use the word "cute" to describe him, it was too cliché, but you lose all internal composure when you are eye-to-eye, two-feet away from such an unbelievably *cute* creature. The recurrence surfaced again. I became a kid on my fourth birthday, and I was staring at a living Teddy bear. I didn't jump up and down, but I wanted to. As I looked into his face and watched him enjoy his afternoon snack, I couldn't help but think about the Appalachian panda that once lived only a few miles up the road, many thousand, thousand generations removed. That ancestral panda was two to three times bigger than the panda I was currently pondering. But that's so human of me to mull over space and time and how short-lived everything truly is. Contemplating such things takes away the playfulness of the moment.

Lincoln? He only had the sweet taste of the apple on his mind.

6 JULY 2016

Cerulean Warbler
Setophaga cerulea

Almost nothing where birds are concerned is set in stone.
They are creatures of change, creatures of air, their only charge
to adapt to a capricious environment in the best way they can . . .
their distribution and behavior are much more fluid than we realize.

—Julie Zickefoose

CERTAINLY, birds do not stay still. They are built for movement. And in this case think blue, sky-blue.

East Tennessee's Royal Blue Unit is not named in honor of the cerulean warbler, but it's appropriate to think so. The parcel is part of the North Cumberlands Wildlife Management Area (WMA) and it's one of the few places the sky-blue passerines still nest in North America. One of the very few. The cerulean is the fastest declining neotropical migrant songbird, with its overall population dropping more quickly than that of any other warbler species in this country. In 2006, its numbers were fewer than one-fifth of what they were forty years before.

April 22, 2013, was a Monday. I tagged along with Tiffany Beachy and Lee Bryant to Royal Blue, specifically to four twenty-hectare plots Beachy had monitored from 2005 to 2007 as part of her cerulean warbler field research under the tutelage of Dr. David Buehler at the University of Tennessee. The plots were located on ridge tops and mid-slopes above 1,476 feet in elevation. Today, Beachy, the citizen science coordinator at the Great Smoky Mountains Institute at Tremont, is currently monitoring Louisiana waterthrush in Walker Valley as part of a citizen science project, but before that it was ceruleans. She's a superb birder with an ear for nuance; she hears the way a mother hears the sighs and moans of her infant in the crib two rooms away. Her fieldwork on the cerulean is over, but she still likes to keep in touch with the Royal Blue. You do not spend three years of your life with your mind wrapped around another living thing and not develop a strong bond.

Beachy's thesis research had several objectives, but a principal one was to assess what, if any, human activities had affected the abundance and occurrence of ceruleans at Royal Blue and, comparatively, Sundquist WMA nearby. Despite the scars from logging and coal mining, the Cumberlands are beautiful the way a rumpled, unmade bed is inviting and cozy. And the most beautiful things in the rolling mountains are the lively, colorful pixie birds: the redstarts, the ceruleans, and hoodeds—warblers all—to name a few.

The North Cumberland Wildlife Management Area comprises 140,000 acres located in the Cumberland Mountains in Scott, Campbell, Anderson, and Morgan Counties in East to Middle Tennessee; principally, it's west of the Tennessee Valley. The Royal Blue is located there, off I-75 at the end of Stinking Creek Road north of Caryville.

On that Monday, getting to the preferred habitat of the enigmatic canopy-loving warbler was an adventure in itself. The old logging roads in the tract are roads in name only. They're more like bumpy, rutted washouts eroded from years of rain and big wheels, with exposed rocks as large as mama sows lying in mud, and just as obstinate. We bounced up a slope in a beast of a truck of our own. It's the only way unless you are prepared to walk all the way to the crest.

Large-flowered bellwort, blue cohosh, and yellow-, white-, and red-flowered trillium were just beginning to open their blossoms along the way. With the zany yellow-green of spring in the valley left behind, we soon found that the ridge tops still looked more like winter. Bare branched. Yet, some of her ceruleans were already back.

"Yes! You are so beautiful!" Beachy exclaimed when she heard a male sing its buzzy song, the first she had heard in months. The male cerulean—at least the experienced, fast males—had already returned to claim the best territories. She was pleased to find three male ceruleans claiming various portions of one special ridge in a plot she had labeled "3" several years earlier. The female ceruleans will have to make choices of their own as soon as they return, and each will choose the available male with the best territory and the most beautiful sky-blue plumage.

BLUE, THE MOST HEAVENLY COLOR

"Why is the sky blue?" goes the childhood riddle.

The response: "Because it isn't green."

The real answer is a little more complicated. According to NASA, the space experts, "Sunlight reaches Earth's atmosphere and is scattered in all directions by all the gases and particles in the air. . . . Blue is scattered more than other colors because it travels as shorter, smaller waves. This is why we see a blue sky most of the time."

That may capture the reason but not the emotion of staring deeply into the celestial dome. Poet Robert Frost felt the color was no less than heaven presenting itself: "Why make so much of fragmentary blue / In here and there a bird, or butterfly / Or flower, or wearing stone, or open eye / When heaven presents in sheets of the solid hue." But, Frost was not the first to equate the color sky-blue, or *bleu celeste,* with heaven, as in "celestial," which pertains to visible heaven or celestial bliss; all are rooted in the Latin word *caelestis,* meaning "heavenly," while "cerulean" comes from the Latin *caelum,* meaning "heaven."

Completed in May 1890, just two months before he died and late in his stay in the asylum at Saint-Rémy, the artist Van Gogh described the full canvas sky in his painting of a flowering almond branch as *"bleu celeste"*—heavenly blue. Perhaps the troubled Vincent already knew what lie ahead.

And to find a cerulean warbler, you need to look towards heaven, as did Alexander Wilson in 1810. Wilson is considered the father of American ornithology for his work in identifying species in this new country when James Madison was president. But on that day over a century and a half ago, he was packing heat, a shotgun loaded with tiny lead pellets. And what he brought down was no less than a bit of Robert Frost's fragmentary blue, a little chip of heaven itself.

"This delicate little species is now, for the first time, introduced to public notice. Except my friend, Mr. [Charles Wilson] Peale, I know of no other naturalist who seems to have hitherto known of its existence," wrote Alexander Wilson, describing the bird he found and shot—bam!—in the summer of 1810. Holding it in his hand, turning it over and over, the precious little thing must have seemed delicate.

"At what time it arrives from the south I cannot say, as I never met with it in spring, but have several times found it during summer," Wilson continued. "On the borders of streams and marshes, among the branches of the poplar, it is sometimes to be found. It has many of the habits of the Flycatcher, though, like the preceding, from the formation of its bill, we must arrange it with the Warblers. It is one of our scarce birds in Pennsylvania, and its nest has hitherto eluded my search."

Wilson was the forerunner to the more flamboyant naturalist/artist John James Audubon. Like the talented Frenchman some years later, Wilson had set a lofty goal for himself: finding and drawing every species of birds that lived in America, a total number that neither Wilson nor Audubon knew when they embarked on their undertaking. Neither man quite reached the exact total, but Audubon's oeuvre came the closest. He found and drew 497 species; the Cornell Lab of Ornithology lists over 716, but that includes birds from Hawaii, an archipelago not even considered to be part of North America during Audubon's era.

Wilson's art was cruder, a simple rendering splayed out in the scientific method of the day to document the outward appearance of a bird. Lacking artistic flair, it was straightforward. Audubon sought to capture the personality of the species, the intangible quality, its quintessence.

Wilson went on to describe the "delicate little species" as being four and a half inches in length with a dazzling upper head of a fine verditer blue. Wilson the artist knew that verditer was a light blue or bluish-green pigment, typically prepared by adding chalk or whiting to a solution of copper nitrate. The mixture yielded a blue the color of sky with a hint of the forest canopy, or *verd de terre,* from the Old French, meaning, "the green of earth." Yet, even though that descriptor captures the bird's union of heaven and earth, the label that stuck, giving the bird its sobriquet still in use today, is cerulean—that is, azure, sky-blue.

It was Wilson who also gave the bird its first scientific name, *Sylvia cerulea,* meaning "of the woodland, azure blue." Later, to group it with other wood warblers, it was changed to *Dendroica cerulea,* which translates to "tree-dwelling, azure blue." And it stayed that way for over one hundred years until, as if to underscore the absolute malleability of scientific nomenclature itself, the name was changed yet again in 2011 to the less poetic *Setophaga cerulea,* (see-toff-ah-gah see-rule-ee-ah), or "moth-eating, azure blue." That is itself a bit of a misnomer; the small birds eat a wide range of insects, including bees, wasps, caterpillars, and weevils, which they find at the base of leaves of many different tree species.

Blue has been the only constant descriptor, and that color plumage in a bird is in itself something of an anomaly. Red and yellow plumage comes from the red and yellow pigments in the foods eaten by the bird. The bright red of a male cardinal is a sign of proper nutrition, the brighter the red, the better the diet. But blue pigments found in foods break down during digestion. So where do blue feathers come from? For years, researchers scratched their noggins over this mystery. The solution according to ornithology professor Richard Prum at Yale University is that blue feathers are simply structured differently. Inside each growing feather cell, molecules of keratin—a stringy tough protein—separate from the naturally occurring water. When the cells die (feathers, like fingernails, are made up of dead cells), the water evaporates, leaving a structure that looks like Swiss cheese or ruote pasta. This pattern causes red and yellow light wavelengths to cancel each other out, but blue wavelengths are amplified and reflected back to anything with the eyes to perceive it. Blue is therefore not a pigment color absorbed through nutrition but, rather, a structural color created by the splitting and bending of white light. And different keratin patterns reflect different tones of blue. Think about bluebirds, blue jays, and indigo buntings, all blue but different shades of the color.

Here's where it gets thought-provoking. If a female cardinal or female goldfinch chooses the brightest red and yellow males available respectively, they are in theory choosing the healthiest, the ones that ate the best diets the year before. Then why does the female bluebird choose her blue mate? Is she choosing solely on beauty? Does she have an eye for aesthetics? Ornithologist Prum thinks so. He teaches a class at Yale on the "Evolution of Beauty" and thinks that physical beauty and the attraction to it evolved hand in hand. Male cerulean warblers are a beautiful sky-blue because females desire them to be such. Female red pandas choose a mate with "proper manners," but does the fact that he is also adorable have a role in her selection. In the case of ceruleans, female choice drives the species to produce bluer and bluer males. The warbler's color was oddly disparaged (well, it's really a left-handed compliment) as being "too unreal" in T. Gilbert Pearson's hefty, five-pound *Birds of America*, first published in 1917 under the auspices of the University Society: "Blue it is, strong yet dainty, not vivid, seeming even to be too unreal to be enduring . . . against the heaven's blue, he is lost to the eye."

Now, why should a bird want to be attractive to a mate yet need to disappear?

RARE EVEN IN AUDUBON'S TIME

Even in the early 1800s, Audubon noted that the bird he called "coerulean wood-warbler" was rare: "So scarce is this bird in the Middle Districts, that its discovery in the State of Pennsylvania has been made a matter of much importance. Its habits are consequently very little known, even at the present day, and it would appear that only a few individuals have been seen by our American ornithologists, one of which, a young female, has been figured by the Prince of MUSIGNANO." (The emphasis is Audubon's.)

In this case, the term "figured" means "wrote the first scientific description," and the Prince he mentions with such gusto was Charles-Lucien (Carlo) Bonaparte, French biologist and ornithologist, nephew to the French emperor

Napoleon I. Being somewhat safer and less political on *this* side of the Atlantic, Prince Carlo spent four years in America studying birds, befriending
the completely unknown, down-and-out Audubon and updating Wilson's
American Ornithology, publishing revised editions between 1825 and 1833.
The young cerulean the prince shot on the banks of the Schuylkill River on
August 1, 1825, was the first female ever collected, the "type specimen" later
sketched by famed artist Titian Ramsay Peale. In this case, a type specimen
is a single specimen expressly designated as the name-bearing original that
represents that species.

Like all naturalist artists of the day, Wilson, Audubon, Bonaparte, and
Peale knew it was easier to sketch a bird if it was shot first, a difficult mindset
for modern naturalists to accept. Rightly so. But as Henry David Thoreau
quipped, "A man is wise with the wisdom of his time only, and ignorant with
its ignorance." Talking on a cell phone while driving is stupid, even dangerous,
but many of us do it because so many other people do. We are all ignorant in
the ignorance of our day. So Wilson and Audubon shot birds, and we abhor
them for what they did.

Fact is, even with the dead birds lying in front of them, the early American
naturalists, got it wrong. Simply put: warblers are not warblers. Initially, it
was believed they were closely related to Old World Warblers, in the family
Sylvia. But New World warblers are different, they do not warble but make
vocalizations variously described as lisps, buzzes, zips, hisses, chips, or rol-
licks, with a rollick being defined as if in a carefree, frolicsome manner. By
the time their true relationship was determined, the label "warbler" was
fairly entrenched, so their designation was changed to "wood warbler" to
separate them from the Old World group. (Robins are not robins in a true
ornithological sense; they are thrushes. But that name will probably never
be corrected. Trust me, most first graders know a robin is a robin.)

Originally, most of the American wood warblers were separated into either
the genus *Setophaga* or *Dendroica.* But recent genetic testing has determined
that the two are inseparable, so both groups have been merged into one, and
Setophaga (first published in 1827) is the older of the two distinctions. The
birds themselves really do not seem to mind or even notice what label we
give them. To classify is a human, not avian, predilection.

COLORFUL TROPICAL BIRDS
IN THE NORTH, ALBE!T BRIEFLY

Wood warblers are perching birds, or passerines, considered to be the most
recently evolved birds. But this is not to say that the process is at a logical

conclusion. There is no logical conclusion, no final outcome; there's just the process of change. Generally, individual females choose the most colorful male available. This pushes each species toward male birds with brighter and brighter plumage. The dull guys get picked less often and leave behind fewer offspring, which might explain why I am childless.

Another misconception is that they are North American birds forced to migrate south in pursuit of insects during the winter. Truth is, they are only in the North a few months of the year. They are really colorful tropical birds that have, over time, advanced north in the summer to find safe, food-laden places in which to nest and raise families. Most wood warblers, like other neotropical migrants—tanagers, vireos, flycatchers—dash north to nest and beeline it back to Central or South America as soon as they can.

The American tropics are great bubbling cauldrons for creating biodiversity. "This land is one great wild, untidy luxuriant hothouse," wrote Charles Darwin in 1830. It's chockfull, so much so that bird species have pushed their way north during summer to find less crowded, secluded habitats to raise their families. Over time some have worked their way as far as northern Canada, claiming unique territorial sites to call their own. Ovenbirds nest on the ground, hooded warblers in dense understory like rhododendron thickets, waterthrushes in wet woodlands near water, and ceruleans in the treetops in mature forests, while the Connecticut, Nashville, and Tennessee warblers all nest much farther north than their namesakes. Go figure. Yet, it certainly could be argued that their true homes are south of the border; North America is only the equivalent of the maternity ward at the hospital.

Like a cummerbund around the belly of a groomsman, the tropics are a band around the Earth that surrounds the equator, between the Tropic of Cancer to the north and Tropic of Capricorn to the south. Although they have wet seasons and dry, they really do not experience winter. If I could flap my arms and fly there, I'd be on my way right now. The neotropics, or new world tropics, are an ecozone that includes Central America, northern South America, the Mexican lowlands, the Caribbean islands, and the southern tip of Florida. All of these regions share a large number of plants and animals. The neotropical migrants are the birds that fly north of the tropics for the summer breeding season. The entire coterie of neotropical wood warblers is based on extreme mobility. They are mainly small, colorful, insect-eating birds, somewhat ephemeral in their habits. There are a total of 53 species that migrate to North America—well, 52 if you leave out Bachman's warbler, which is probably extinct. Of the 52, 14 are western species and 38 are eastern birds that fly in and out of our sphere of awareness with the seasons. Some are widespread and others, like the Kirtland's warbler, are extremely localized in their breeding haunts. Another 70 or so intratropical species of wood warblers stay put in the tropics year round, so in the northern winter, all 120 (plus or minus) species vie for the available food south of North America. That's a lot of vying. (In all, over 500 species of migratory birds breed in North America.)

Despite working with many dead birds, both Wilson and Audubon described the cerulean warbler as being "scarce" in their day. Or, perhaps, darn hard to see. As American ornithologist and encyclopedic author Arthur Cleveland Bent observed, "This warbler [is] a bird of the treetops in heavy deciduous woods, where its colors make it difficult to distinguish among the lights and shadows of the lofty foliage and against the blue sky."

In Bent's day—his life's work, the twenty-one-volume *Life Histories of North American Birds,* was published between 1919 and 1968 and, like Wilson's, completed posthumously—the cerulean was considered to be widespread, occupying a rather extensive breeding range. The heavenly blue woodland species could be found west of the Alleghenies, east of the Great Plains from southern Ontario and central New York, and southward to the northern parts of the Gulf States. Yet, and this is a big caveat, it was highly localized. Tennessee and Kentucky are entirely within its known breeding range, although the bird nests only in a few isolated locales. Highest densities occur in the mountains of West Virginia, western Kentucky, and the Cumberland Mountains of East Tennessee, the mature deciduous forests of the East, with an estimated 80 percent of the population breeding there. Bent recorded that its preferred habitat was high in the treetops in heavy deciduous woods, clear of underbrush. Paul Hamel of the U.S. Forest Service reported that the birds need large tracts of mature forest, preferring woodland with structural complexity caused by small forest gaps, open spaces resulting from natural disturbances. Ceruleans rush in to take advantage of changes in the forest, particularly the canopy cover.

There just isn't enough data to estimate the cerulean's abundance or lack of it historically, but a report titled "Cerulean Warbler: Status Assessment," published in April 2000 by U.S. Fish and Wildlife stated, "Currently the birds are much less numerous in areas where formerly they were abundant." The report, prepared by Hamel, does include a modern population trend: "The North American Breeding Bird Survey suggests that, during the past 30 years, the population has declined at an average annual rate of approximately 4 percent."

Recently, those declines have been fine-tuned to 3.2 percent per year from 1966 to 2003, and 4.6 percent from 2003 to 2008. If you do the math, starting with one hundred birds in the year the perennial holiday favorite *How the*

Grinch Stole Christmas by Dr. Seuss first aired on CBS, you would only have twenty-three, or a total loss of 77 percent, by the time Indiana Jones came out of retirement to go after the Crystal Skull. As I write this, four years later, if the same downward spiral has continued, we would be down to nineteen birds, or a total forty-six-year loss of 81 percent.

"The cerulean warbler is among the highest priority landbirds for conservation in the United States," reported Terry Rich with U.S. Fish and Wildlife for Partners in Flight. It's one of the "most specialized and threatened birds of the deciduous forest and is in need of focused conservation attention throughout its range."

But why?

Fortunately, there are more than one hundred cerulean warblers left. One guesstimate, just a few years ago, set the number at half a million; but the continued gradual losses are real, and ceruleans are declining in population faster than any other warbler. A movement was started to have the sky-blue bird listed as threatened, which would have earned it federal protection. After six years of deliberation, the request was denied on November 8, 2006, because even though their decline was real, there were tens of thousands left and would be for the next one hundred years.

The U.S. Fish and Wildlife report goes on to list several possible contributing factors: predation, disease, lack of regulatory mechanisms, nest parasitism by cowbirds, and reduced survivorship during migration, but it concludes that the "primary threat to the species is the loss of habitat on the breeding and on the winter grounds. Clear documentation of this exists."

Before you can help a declining species, you have to know its needs. The UT field research of Tiffany Beachy and later Than Boves and others set out to answer some of the unknowns about the diminutive warbler's life history and habitat requirements.

COAL, CLEAR-CUTS, COFFEE, CHOCOLATE, COCAINE, AND CERULEANS

A declining species, it would seem, should shun any alteration to their habitat like fragmentation and large-scale lumbering that causes forests to be clear-cut to the ground.

Yet, Tiffany Beachy's research seemed to suggest a counterintuitive acceptance to having bites taken from their woodland sandwich. Ceruleans "were more likely to occur in areas adjacent to [coal] mines than older successional gaps and clear-cuts. How could this be? The majority of coal deposits in the Cumberland Mountains occur in prime Cerulean Warbler habitat, on ridgetops above 450 meters [1476 feet] and dominated by mixed mesophytic forest," wrote Beachy. ("Mesophytic" refers to a deciduous broadleaf mixed forest with a moderate amount of moisture.)

Surprisingly, the ceruleans tolerated the gaps left by the human activities, nesting frequently near the edges of the newly created openings. As a general rule, forest fragmentation certainly alters the landscape. Are the remaining ceruleans learning to tolerate at least some of the disturbances? Royal Blue encompasses the largest remaining mature interior forest patch in the Tennessee Cumberlands. Is it their last stronghold? The gaps and edges are minor there compared to other locations in the region. Since the ceruleans spend more time on their wintering grounds, let's look south.

Early last century, it was generally assumed that once the neotropical migrants migrated for winter, they intermingled, living here and there, higgledy-piggledy, catch-as-catch-can. The pressure was off, and there was little need to defend a territory. All could coexist as one big happy feathered tribe. Kumbaya.

As detailed studies of each individual species began to occur, this notion disintegrated. Logic dictates that competition has to be intense. More than 50 percent of all migrants are packed into 1.4 million square acres in the Bahamas, Hispaniola, Cuba, and Mexico, about one-seventh of the area they dispersed into during their summers in the United States and Canada.

Perhaps this is why the cerulean migrates farther, all the way to South America. They are certainly built for flight with extra-long wings and shorter tails. It was once believed that the cerulean generally spent its off-season in low densities across a large area of the northern Andes, but recent research indicates that the species is quite selective.

"Once in South America," wrote Scott Weidensaul, "the cerulean warbler is restricted to a thin, snakelike ribbon of misty forest in the eastern foothills of the Andes, within a very narrow band between about two thousand and forty-five hundred feet—the smallest elevational range of any migrant songbird."

They prefer specific climatic conditions—namely cooler (but not too cool) lower subtropical climes with low rainfall (but not dry) from Venezuela and Colombia south to Ecuador and Peru and possibly into portions of Bolivia. They are absent from the wettest and driest slopes. These are roughly the same conditions the species prefers during its breeding season in the North. In winter, the ceruleans like tall forest canopy, especially those with shade trees with narrow leaves called "Guamo" in the *Inga* plant family and borders with shade where local farmers traditionally grow the spice plant cardamom, cocoa (*Theobroma cacao,* the source of cocoa pods, the primary ingredient in chocolate), and coca (*Erythroxylum coca,* the major ingredient in cocaine).

Unfortunately, this also corresponds to areas of high coffee production in the Andes, in particular the intermountain valleys of central Colombia. This could hardly be a poorer choice of habitat for a tiny sky-blue songbird. Chocolate, coffee, and cocaine are all hot commodities in the civilized world, but the changes in coffee farming are the true bête noire.

Coffee is not native to Latin America. The obscure shade-loving shrub, originally called *bunn,* was discovered in the ancient land of Abyssinia—today's Ethiopia, southeast of Egypt. But over the course of a few centuries, its cultivation spread around the world, and in the mountains of South America it found a new home.

One hundred percent Colombian coffee was marketed as being richer, more flavorful, than other brands. It cost more and was worth it. For over forty years, sporting the Juan Valdez trademark, it has sold for a price twenty cents per kilo higher on average than coffee from other countries. The dominant crop grown by the *cafeteros* in Colombia was Arabica coffee *(Coffea arabica),* an understory plant that requires canopy shade, a habitat type that suits cerulean warblers.

But in recent years, market pressures and the accidental importation of a fungus, coffee leaf rust *(Hemileia vastatrix),* forced farmers to alter their methods. The fungus must have access to, and come into physical contact with, Arabica coffee in order to survive. The fungus eventually kills the leaves, denuding the shrub, and it dies—but not before it spreads to the nearby coffee plants. It was believed it flourished in the moist conditions of shade. It thrived in monoculture farms where coffee shrubs are planted in close proximity.

Leaf rust seems to have originated in Ceylon and first appeared in Brazil in 1970 and soon moved throughout Latin America. To stop its spread, farmers were encouraged to remove the tree canopy and switch to higher-yielding, "modern," full-sun coffee varieties. But to survive, the coffee plants needed babying, with lots of care, fertilizer, and agrochemicals to kill weeds and pests. By 1990, 69 percent of all Colombian coffee was being grown in closely packed rows in full sun.

"In 2006, Colombia produced more than 12 million 132-pound bags [the standard industry measure] of coffee, and set a goal of 17 million for 2014. Last year [2010] the yield was only nine million bags," wrote Elisabeth Rosenthal for the *New York Times.* "Average temperatures in Colombia's coffee regions have risen nearly one degree in 30 years, and in some mountain areas the increase has been double that, said Cenicafé, the national coffee research center. Rain in this area was more than 25 percent above average in the last few years."

"The sun coffee revolution has failed to fulfill its promise," noted Mark Pendergrast, author of *Uncommon Grounds,* a history of coffee. "Instead, it has contributed to ecological degradation and loss of important habitat."

The bitter irony? Regional climate change associated with global warming has caused Colombian coffee production to decline, and one contributing factor to global warming is deforestation. And today, much to the detriment of cerulean warblers, one important wintering stronghold has lost 80 percent of its shade canopy cover.

One of the most reliable estimates of deforestation reported that in Ecuador, Venezuela, and Colombia, between 200,000 and 600,000 hectares per year are being cut. This tops out at 2,316.612 square miles, roughly an area the size as Delaware. These kinds of numbers boggle the mind, but we have to remember that a hundred years ago there was a rush to cut the old forests in eastern North America as well.

The little suitable forests that survive in Colombia are fragmented, unprotected, and at high risk of being cut some time soon. Some experienced biologists familiar with ceruleans believe that only 40 percent and, shockingly, perhaps as little as 10 percent of their preferred forest cover survives.

Whether it was coffee in the South or lumber and coal in the North, the end result was the same.

"The Europeans happened upon ecosystems so remote and fragile that the disruption they brought caused the natural fabric of those places to unravel completely," wrote British environmentalist Tony Juniper in his book *Spix's Macaw: The Race to Save the World's Rarest Bird.*

THE COMING OF SPRING AND ZUGUNRUHE

Some studies in Colombia suggest that the cerulean is more sedentary and solitary during the tropical rainy season when insects are plentiful (October–November) and, in the dry season that follows (January–March), more gregarious, joining mixed flocks to increase foraging success. They are not clannish. In mixed winter flocks of migrants and residents, they occur at a rate of one or two per flock. "This exceptionally low density means that the cerulean warbler, as a species, needs a lot of elbow room," concluded Weidensaul.

Once any given cerulean survives into the new year, enduring the rainy season and the dry, and when the tilt of the Earth's axis makes its seasonal shift, bringing longer and longer days in the Northern Hemisphere, a stirring begins inside each sky-blue warbler. All migratory birds feel the pull, the intense desire to fly north (or south in the fall) called "zugunruhe." It's a German compound word consisting of *zug* (move, migration) and *unruhe* (anxiety, restlessness) or, simply put, migratory restlessness. The desire is so strong that a caged bird will throw itself over and over against the north side of the cage, beating itself to death as it's driven by the intense desire to fly north. And for the birds that do make the journey, it's an arduous one of thousands of miles—a mad rush to return to familiar breeding grounds and claim the best territory or best mate available. It is, as ornithologist Miyoko Chu noted, "a dangerous situation, given that some songbirds are fifteen times more likely to die during migration than at any other time of the year."

Short-distance migrants and birds of prey tend to migrate during the day; long distance migrants like ceruleans migrate at night. It's an odyssey flown in the dark that runs a gauntlet, filled with unseen perils: storms; cell phone, radio, and TV towers; glass office buildings. Each obstacle is as difficult as any faced by Homer's Odysseus on his ten-year journey home after the fall of Troy. For a bird scarcely weighing over three-tenths of an ounce—assuming you could coerce three ceruleans into one envelope you could mail them anywhere in the continental United States with a single first-class stamp—it's an unimaginably grueling journey of up to twenty-five hundred miles. They fly at night to conserve energy and avoid predators; also, after the sun sets, the earth cools and the atmosphere becomes less turbulent.

How birds migrate, know the way, is a book unto itself. Suffice it to say, they use a combination of landmarks; sun, moon, and star positions; polarized light; and the irresistible pull of the north magnetic pole. Fifty-five species of neotropical migrants take the direct six-hundred-mile route across the Gulf of Mexico, forsaking the safer overland curved route of Central America to Mexico to North America. It's like golfer Jordan Spieth choosing to blast his Titleist ProV1x golf ball over the pond rather than work methodically around the hazard.

It's risky, so why chance it?

The over-the-gulf route is days faster, and the race is on to claim the best breeding territory. A race for turf that an experienced male knows is worth the risk. It could make all the difference between whether your genetic material is passed on to a new generation or not. With luck and a fortuitous tailwind, a songbird can cross the gulf in a single night, while going around the gulf could take five or six nights. In April and May, winds over the gulf shift from easterly to northerly. Leaving at sunset, with a favorable tailwind of fifteen miles per hour, a flock of songbirds can arrive in midmorning on the American Gulf Coast, exhausted after their flight of eighteen hours or more.

The early arriving males that Beachy, Bryant and I found in the spring of 2013 on the ridges of Royal Blue had survived the ordeal. They arrived back on the ridge tops before the leaves were even on the trees. Migrants can add up to 50 percent to their body weight before the trip and burn much of it crossing the gulf. Ornithologist Paul Kerlinger calculated that each gram of additional fat can yield about 125 miles of flight. A single Kentucky warbler can burn four or five grams of fat on its 600-mile, eighteen-hour flight, landing 35 percent lighter than when it took off. That would be like me going from here (Knoxville, Tennessee) to Fort Smith, Arkansas, shedding sixty-six pounds along the way. Oh, if I could only fly.

Encountering a strong headwind, a late-season storm front flowing down from Canada, an early tropical storm, or a hurricane is like running into the one-eyed Cyclops Polyphemus blocking the way home. But as we know, Polyphemus was drunk, and Odysseus was able to outsmart him. For a tiny warbler, its desire to get back to its nesting home is as strong as the Greek hero.

A migrating bird's flight northward across the open water saps its energy. After it uses all its fat reserves, it's forced to start burning muscle mass. If it loses the struggle, it falls into the gulf to flounder and drown. Thousands perish this way, thrashing around in the salty water, too weak to proceed. Their race is over on the very first day, their genetic material lost to the world. Only the hardy and lucky survive.

Fighting a headwind, some complete the journey but make landfall completely spent, barely able to walk or perch.

"Truly emaciated birds, those whose bodies ran out of fat on the crossing and began to catabolize muscle tissue in a desperate bid to stay aloft face a much longer period of recuperation. Some will not be in shape to breed," wrote Scott Weidensaul, "especially the older individuals who have made the grueling trip three or four times before. They won't make it at all." Their race is run.

"If you care greatly for these birds, as we do, there's a special sadness in that. Even though you know it's natural, even though you know all these birds eventually reach the end of their days, that makes it no easier to accept," lamented the late Bob Sargent, a bird bander and migration expert.

The fact that any make it across the churning seas of the gulf seems a miracle, but huge flocks manage the impossible every spring, knowing that food awaits in the mangroves of Louisiana and the forests inland across the South.

Not a lot is known about the spring migration of ceruleans. Data suggest that they move in large flocks from South America overland to the middle of Central America and then across the gulf to the southern United States. Stopover locations have been found in Belize, Honduras, and Guatemala. But records of stopovers are so scarce that others believe they fly nonstop between the northern coast of South America and the southern United States.

IN PERIL: CERULEANS IN AMERICA

Notably, the amount of forest cover in the eastern United States has increased over the past one hundred years. It's second growth, but it's still woodland. Is it quality habitat? Well, yes and no, or not just yet. Once the original trees were harvested, the woods came back. The regrowth of the Appalachians have led to an increase in such mature forest species as the northern parula and Blackburnian warblers. But, here's the bugaboo about ceruleans: they like disturbances. It's a boon to them when woodland gets messed up a bit, naturally by fire, weather-related tree fall, or simply when a forest ages and older trees begin to die off (senescence) and come tumbling down. Ceruleans move in after the ruckus is over to claim nest sites in tall trees near the openings. These bits of feathered fragmentary blue thrive. They take advantage of the disruption in the status quo—out with the old and in with the new.

Yet, if ceruleans take advantage of change, moving into disturbed areas, and there's more forest today than one hundred years ago, why is the species in decline? Is there not enough natural disruption? And is there something that can be done to improve their chances, at least in the American East, their breeding ground? Is there something missing? Some key tree species? Is there some key bit of diversity that's lacking in contemporary second-growth forests? Or are the impacts to their wintering grounds the sole problem?

Why a species goes into decline is a tough nut to crack. We lost passenger pigeons because they were overhunted, but the same is not true for Carolina parakeets. We lost the dusky seaside sparrow because of habitat loss, and the same may be true for the ivory-billed woodpecker. Are we losing the cerulean wood warbler by altering their preferred habitat? Ecological traps are scenarios in which rapid environmental change leads organisms to prefer to settle into "poor-quality habitats." The concept stems from the idea that organisms that are actively selecting habitat must rely on environmental cues to help them identify high-quality habitat.

In 2011, following the research of Beachy, University of Tennessee PhD candidate Than Boves completed a four-year study of cerulean warblers in the Cumberlands. His doctoral dissertation, "Multiple Responses by Cerulean Warblers to Experimental Forest Disturbance in the Appalachian Mountains," was the culmination of his fieldwork.

Originally from a southwest suburb of Chicago, Boves attended the University of Illinois at Urbana-Champaign, where he worked as a field assistant on avian ecology and conservation research projects in the tropical forests of Belize and in restored oak savannahs in the Windy City area. He was lured to Tennessee and the cerulean study by Dr. David Buehler, who became his mentor and faculty advisor. Boves had several assistants who helped him collect data in the field, but perhaps none was more important than his wife and soul mate, Emily, who shared his passion for birds. "She was also the greatest field assistant I could ever imagine, personally responsible for finding over 100 cerulean warbler nests, and I could not have done it without her," wrote Boves.

Conservation plans to save a declining species begin by determining exactly what it needs to survive. Such research really began in the 1930s with James T. Tanner's Audubon-funded fieldwork on the ivory-billed woodpecker in the cypress swamps of the Gulf Coast states. (See my UT Press book *Ghost Birds*.)

In the cerulean study, Boves explored the effects of emulating natural disturbances by altering forest stands to varying degrees and assessing how ceruleans responded. Can we imitate the natural ebb and flow of a forest? And can we create appropriate habitat where they can reproduce successfully? And could the techniques be used on a larger scale to improve the species' chances of long-term survival?

Habitat loss or degradation is the number-one problem a threatened species has to overcome. Fortunately today, with recent developments in ecology theorem, wildlife managers have more tools in their toolbox than Tanner had eighty years ago.

For Boves, seven study sites within the known cerulean range were chosen: two in Tennessee, three in West Virginia, and one each in Kentucky and Ohio. Each site was embedded within a mature forest, with an elevation of between 820 and 2,800 feet. Plant composition varied only slightly. Common canopy trees included tulip tree, sugar maple, northern red oak, and various hickories, plus white and chestnut oaks.

Each site was divided into four quadrants with each being disturbed to varying degrees: light, intermediate, and heavy. One plot was left as an undisturbed control. Timber was cut to imitate natural disturbance. The plots with light treatments mimicked an area with multiple tree-fall gaps with a loss of approximately 20 percent canopy cover; the intermediate-treatment plots mimicked a more severe natural disturbance such as a fire or blow-down with a 40 percent loss in canopy cover; and the heavy-treatment plots were designed to mimic a severe natural disturbance like a landside, ice storm, or major fire that resulted in a 75 percent loss in canopy cover.

In all plots, cerulean warbler nests were located and monitored, April through June, 2008–2010. Nests were found by first finding a male defending his territory. Their territorial song is generally described as zhee zhee zizizizi zzzeet, zee zee zee zizizizi zeet, with capitalization indicating heavily stressed syllables.

On May 29, 2010, Ijams Education Director Jennifer Roder and husband Wayne visited one of Boves's study plots in the Cumberlands with Than and Emily. To prepare, Jennifer had made the song of a cerulean her cellphone ringtone. She knew it well and kept thinking her phone was ringing as they bounced up the old logging road.

To fully monitor the individual birds, identities had to be established. To that end, they had to be caught and banded with numbered metal bracelets placed on their legs.

"Than had set up mist nets to capture and band male ceruleans," remembered Jennifer. "He used a recorded song and decoys to lure the birds into the nets and had learned they only challenged an intruder if the decoy was dinged up a bit. Less than perfect." This is curious, a perfect decoy got a pass. Did the real males not want to take on a bird they perceived as being equals, or betters?

Boves's fieldwork ultimately yielded some surprising conclusions. Mature male ceruleans "consistently selected territories located relatively close to canopy gaps, resulting in increased breeding densities in disturbed habitats." Beachy's research indicated the same. But Boves's research went one step further and looked at reproduction success, finding that it "was significantly depressed on all disturbances."

The males choose their territories, but they were choosing poorly—for whatever reason—with a net outcome of much fewer successful nests. They were, in effect, nesting in harm's way. Sharp edges between mature forests and manmade gaps offer high-visibility access points for natural predators of nestlings: rat snakes, raccoons, crows, Cooper's hawks. They were ecological traps, a concept introduced in 1972 by Wayne Dwernychuk and David Boag. And the many studies that have followed suggest that this trap phenomenon may be widespread because of human-related habitat change.

A male bird chooses a habitat in part because of the perceived availability of food for rearing young, but there's little way for him to determine future predator issues. Female birds select a mate for a host of reasons, but his claimed territory ranks high on her list. His real estate matters.

In 1988, H. Ronald Pulliam, director of the University of Georgia Institute of Ecology, published the beautifully simple, ten-page article "Sources, Sinks, and Population Regulation" in the journal *American Naturalist*. It presented the concept that species can be lured to habitats that are good, labeled "source" or poor, labeled "sink." To help a declining species, ample source habitat needs to be provided. After his fieldwork, Boves recommended that only the southern region of the Cumberland Mountains could function as good source habitat—that is, safe for nesting. Other sites Boves looked at were attractive to the male but too vulnerable because of nest predation opportunities.

A graduate student's thesis or dissertation is infinitely fascinating for the mounds of ancillary information it contains, gleaned from direct observances in the field. Such detailed studies can be traced back to the doctoral thesis of Arthur Allen, completed in 1911 for Cornell University. Allen went on to found the Cornell Lab of Ornithology, but before that his fieldwork, "The Red-winged Blackbird: a Study in the Ecology of a Cattail Marsh," was groundbreaking (see my book *Ghost Birds*). It set the stage for researchers like Boves. Before Allen's blackbird study most ornithologists worked in the lab with specimens.

Boves and his team learned that each male and female cerulean on average fed their young eight times an hour; that's one to five insects per trip. In addition to determining how often the ceruleans fed the nestlings, the researchers also found that both parents performed the duty of removing fecal sacs from the nest. The fathers, especially the younger ones, brought marginally larger loads, while the mothers spent more time on the nest protecting the nestlings, especially during the first eight days after hatching. As you might surmise, "males in better condition spent markedly more time attending nests, possibly because they were more efficient foragers." And keep in mind, females choose their mates. She knows she needs a good partner. Not surprisingly, the females also made more feeding trips when their clutch sizes were greater. Unusually, the males made more feeding trips, yet carried smaller food loads when understory cover increased, as is the case near disturbed areas. More food trips also may trigger greater predation because of increased visibility, although Boves's research seems to suggest that when predation does occur, it happens at night, when the predators are raccoons, rat snakes, and owls, and not during the day, when crows and Cooper's hawks are active.

Boves wrote that "nest failure was greater in disturbed habitats. If parents are unable to accurately assess predation risk in specific habitats, they may act in maladaptive ways that attract predators." Even though ceruleans nest higher than fifty-nine feet above the ground, they seem to be keenly aware if humans are watching from the ground unless the observers are concealed in a blind. They just may not be as aware if predators are watching as well.

So where does that leave us? Again, what to make of the diminished thing? We know the habitat type they need. How do we get them to choose it?

CERULEAN AS METAPHOR

By pure coincidence or Jungian synchronicity, in late summer 2010, just a few months after Boves concluded his work in the field, the cerulean warbler became the feathered literary poster child representing all woodland birds in decline when American author Jonathan Franzen published his best-selling novel *Freedom*. The sky-blue songbird graced the book's cover.

"But so why the cerulean warbler? I like the bird. It's a pretty little bird. Weighs less than the first joint of my thumb and flies all the way to South America and back every year. That's a beautiful thing right there," wrote Franzen.

"Each year, they arrived to find more of their former homes paved over for parking lots or highways, or logged over for pallet wood, or developed into subdivisions, or stripped bare for oil drilling or coal mining, or fragmented for shopping centers, or plowed under of ethanol production, or miscellaneously denatured for ski runs and bike trails and golf courses," wrote Franzen.

How can anything as small as a cerulean warbler possible survive this juggernaut? The needs of Western civilization are intense. A few critics of the novel thought the author's environmental worries were too heavy-handed. It's simply more comfortable to be in a state of denial. In this case, the heavenly blue cerulean becomes a metaphor for everything in nature that is fragile and needs protecting. Speaking of Franzen's metaphor, literary agent Russell Galen explained, "It's a beautiful bird, but there are many beautiful birds. The color is a faint, almost intangible blue, not the brilliant incandescent blue of the blue jay. There's something about the cerulean color that makes you want to protect this bird. If it were a woman you would want to take care of her."

Let's put the obvious Blanche DuBois reference and gender bias aside and end with a nod to Franklin Delano Roosevelt, who was president when Tanner did his fieldwork on the ivorybill. FDR sincerely believed that those who can should take care of those in peril. You simply cannot just look the other way.

Ghost Plant

Monotropa uniflora

But then, as she knew too well, the more fondly we imagine
something will last forever, the more ephemeral it often proves to be.

—Iian Banks

ghost ['gōst] n
1: a disembodied soul.
2: a mere shadow or semblance; a trace.

ROBERT L. RIPLEY collected odd and unusual items from all over the world.
Beginning in the *New York Globe* in 1918, his illustrated panels showcasing
his discoveries appeared in newspapers for most of the last century. In each
installment, he featured two or three true-life oddities, be it animal, vegetable,
or person born with four eyes. He was the P. T. Barnum of his day—a great
American showman whose famous tagline read, "Believe it or not." Yet, despite the fact that he gave you the option of doubting his stories, they were
always supposedly quite true. Ripley died in 1949, but his syndicated passion
for aberrancy lives on in books and in twenty-seven museums located in ten
countries that still exhibit—for all to see—the world of the weird, bizarre,
and, dare we say, the somewhat unbelievable.

This, then, is a story curious enough to intrigue even Ripley himself. It's
about a plant found in the Southeast—a vascular wisp of flora that is not green
and grows like a phantom in shaded woods, not really needing the sun or large
light-collecting leaves to get by because purportedly it can grow even in the
dark. Its existence seems so transient, so ephemeral; it's practically a ghost.

"I was in the woods next to my house," reported Robin Hill several years
ago, "and found what I thought was a rooster's tail." At the time, Hill was
chairman of the Planning Commission in Farragut, Tennessee. An active
member of the local Sierra Club, Hill has a fondness for trees and green

spaces. And, indeed, what was found tucked away in the shadows of the woods near Hill's home looked like a white leghorn had buried itself in the barnyard leaving only its caboose above terra firma. The odd-looking thing, as described in an email to me, was dead white with ghost white stems about three- or four-inches long. On a second visit, Hill noticed a bee visiting the pale oddity and figured it must be a flower rather than a fungus because "no self-respecting bee would fool with a mold spore growth." Indeed not, it was Indian pipe, a vascular plant with metaphorical ice in its veins. I stopped by Hill's home a few days after the discovery, and we walked out into the wooded lot to visit the curious thing. By then it was beginning to lose its vigor, but its strangeness still made the sunny, early fall outing memorable. Indian pipe gets one of its common names from the peoples that lived in North America before the Europeans arrived.

THE LURE AND THE LORE

The Cherokee used the sites and natural history of the Tennessee Valley as an inspiration for their myths. They were great storytellers, and the often-repeated legends served as links to their past, both historical and parabolical. The Cherokee didn't have formal schools; the world was their classroom. They told stories of mythical animals like *Dakwa'*, the great fish of the Tennessee River that could swallow a man, and *Tla'nuwâ'i*, a large hawk that lived on a high cliff in today's Blount County. Some of the stories were about legendary places like *Atagâ'hi*, the enchanted lake somewhere in the wildest depths of the Smoky Mountains; *Kana'sta*, an old lost settlement on the French Broad and *Un'tiguhi'*, the so called "Suck," a dangerous whirlpool in the Tennessee River eight miles below present-day Chattanooga.

Their parables, or morality lessons, were taught to adolescents using the plants and animals around them as metaphors. Mary Chiltoskey related a story about stubbornness and the ghostly plant found near Hill's home:

> A long time ago—the Cherokee people were happy sharing their hunting and fishing places with their neighbors. All this changed when Selfishness came into the world and men began to quarrel. The Cherokee quarreled with the tribes to the east. Finally the chiefs of several tribes met in council to settle the dispute. They smoked the pipe and continued to quarrel for seven days and nights. This displeased the Great Spirit because people are not supposed to smoke the pipe until they make peace. As he looked upon the old men with heads bowed, he decided to do something to remind people to smoke the pipe only at the time they make peace.

The Great Spirit turned the old men into grayish flowers we now call Indian Pipe and made them grow where friends and relatives have quarreled. He made the smoke hang over these mountains until all people all over the world learn to live together in peace.

This is a pleasing sort of ghost story, one with a moral. When you come across a cluster of Indian pipe in the forest pushing its way up through the decaying leaf litter, it's easy to envision a group of stubborn old men sitting in a smoky council house, their heads bowed in disgrace.

Frozen Head Mountain in Morgan County is 3,324 feet tall, which makes it one of the highest in the Cumberland Mountains in East Tennessee. Frozen Head gets its name because during the winter months its summit is frequently frosty or frozen.

There are several trails that lead to the top. In 2012, Karen Webster and I chose Panther Branch Trail, which gently ascends the southern flank of Old Mac Mountain, a spur of Frozen Head. We soon reached an area near a waterfall that must have once seen a lot of Native American quarreling. Their pale and gray ghosts sat hunkered down all along the trail.

"'T is whiter than an Indian pipe, / 'T is dimmer than a lace; / No stature has it, like a fog, / When you approach the place," wrote poet Emily Dickinson. The plant is so forlorn, its location almost sacrosanct, that you often wonder: what is this apparition? Indian pipe is such a pallid thing with stems, leaves, flowers, petals, indeed all its parts, being a translucent, waxy white. At first glance you might think it was a mushroom or even a dead or dying thing. But it is not. It's a true living, respiring organism.

Indian pipe has had many regional folk names. Because of its general lack of any color, other than an occasional bluish or even salmon-pink tint, it has been called "ghost plant." Its spindly stems and downturned flowers reminded others of the dead reaching out of their graves. Add to this the plant's waxy appearance and the cool, clammy texture, and you can understand another descriptive name, "corpse plant."

Yes, corpse plant, a living ghost. At this point Ripley might have said, "Believe it or not."

In 1899, Alice Lounsberry wrote, "Few plants are uncanny, we therefore shiver slightly when we take hold of the ghost-flower, which is so clammy and white. It further annoys us by turning black and decomposing almost instantly after having been touched."

The habit of melting away in your hand led to another folk name, "American ice plant." Today, most wildflower books, if they include it at all, call it

Indian pipe. Its Latin name, *Monotropa uniflora,* means "once-turned, single-flowered," a reference to the downward bowed, almost mournful flowers.

In addition to being a source of legend, Indian pipe was used as a medicinal plant by Native Americans. In 1892, Dr. Charles Millspaugh reported that the aborigines valued a mixture of the plant's juices and water as a soothing and curative measure. Indian pipe's oozy fluids were used to treat warts, bunions, and inflamed eyes. A tea was brewed to ease the misery of the common cold, and a drink made from the roots was prepared as a sedative to treat convulsions, fits, and epilepsy. European settlers moving to this country learned of the plant's curative properties and how to brew Indian pipe tea to treat irritability, restlessness, and other nervous disorders. This led to another list of folk names: fitroot, convulsion weed, and eyebright. This last one comes from a Cherokee remedy for sore eyes. The plant was picked and soaked in cold water. The resulting mixture was applied with a damp cloth to the inflamed eye.

When a Cherokee shaman entered the woods to gather a medicinal plant, a certain ritual had to be followed. The shaman brought beads along on the search. The colors had significance. Red symbolized success and triumph, and white embodied peace and happiness. A blue bead would have brought defeat and trouble, while black represented death. The shaman only approached the desired plant from a certain direction. When located, the medicine man would circle the plant right to left, repeating a traditional prayer. When the plant was pulled from the ground, a bead was dropped into the resulting hole, and the depression was then filled in with loose earth. The ritual was intended to maintain harmony: the bead was thought to compensate the earth for the loss of the plant. When a medicinal plant was gathered, the shaman tied it up in a package and took it to a running stream. The parcel was then tossed into the water, while another prayer was repeated. If the package floated to the surface—and it usually did—he knew the treatment would be a success.

The European settlers in the New World learned about the medicinal plants from the Native Americans. In 1878, Richard E. Kunze, M.D., wrote a letter to the *Botanical Gazette* praising the medicinal properties of Indian pipe. He noted that he had successfully treated the eyes of patients (even as young as three days old) with Indian pipe without any ill effects and added this testimonial:

> I always keep on hand a quantity of this medicinal agent—in the form of a tincture or dried plant, and when I can obtain enough of it, the expressed juice. I will merely mention a case of ophthalmia [inflammation of the eye] cured

incidentally by *Monotropa uniflora*. Fourteen years ago, it was in the early part of July, I went woodcock-shooting with two friends near Hackensack, N.J., and while taking some luncheon in a beech grove along the course of the Saddle River, found a large patch of ground literally covered with *Monotropa uniflora* in full bloom. I have never met with such a "find" of this plant in all of my frequent rambles and excursions made in search of it. It covered a space some five feet wide by nine feet long, a beautiful sight of snow-white stems and nodding flowers. Being in need of some just then, I proceeded to fill my game-bag, and to the question, what it was used for, answered "good for sore eyes," little thinking that the party addressed was suffering from a chronic inflammation of the eyelids, the edges of which had a very fiery red appearance. No sooner said, than he proceeded to take in his game-bag a supply also, and he made a very good use of it, as I ascertained afterwards. His inflamed lids were entirely cured in four weeks' time and has had no further trouble since, by applying the fresh juice of the stems he obtained while it lasted.

Dr. Kunze's story, that of a doctor gathering plants to treat his patients, is interesting not only for his endorsement of Indian pipe but also because it gives us a look into nineteenth-century medicine. A contemporary of Kunze's, a Dr. Stewart, reported that the dried plant was an excellent substitute for opium, a narcotic used in the late 1800s to treat pain. Stewart claimed that Indian pipe was good at "easing pain, comforting the stomach and causing sleep."

This is not just a quaint, old time story. Modern day herbalists still collect the plant. So much so that there is some worry it is being overharvested. "There is even concern that the plant is in global decline," pointed out historian Donald E. Davis. United Plant Savers, a non-profit organization dedicated to the conservation of native medicinal plants and their habitats will be assessing the status of Indian pipe, perhaps even designating it as an "at-risk" species. No one wants the ghost plant to truly become a ghost.

HOW THE GHOST LIVES

From a purely botanist's point of view, Indian pipe is an unusual forb; it's not green. Plants get their verdant color from chlorophyll, a plant pigment that is primarily responsible for trapping the light energy used to trigger photosynthesis, the chain of chemical reactions by which they make their own food. Photosynthesis is one of nature's most important processes because it changes carbon dioxide and water into the carbohydrates that all plants, animals, and people rely on for food. Without photosynthesis, there would be no guacamole or salad bars, no corn chips or pears flambé.

With no chlorophyll, Indian pipe is as sickly pale as Lugosi's Dracula. Because it cannot make food for itself through photosynthesis, it does not need large leaves to catch the light and can live in deep, dark woods away from the sun; and because it doesn't really need sunlight, it only pokes itself above the ground when it's time to flower and reproduce. The rest of the time, the corpse plant is aptly named: it remains buried out of sight.

In many ways, Indian pipe pushes the boundaries of what it is to be a plant. In fact, early botanists struggled with the question: What is a plant? Initial definitions included the notion that all members of this kingdom contained chlorophyll, but if so, where did that place Indian pipe? Surprisingly, however, the pale sprig is listed as being in the wintergreen family and believed to be loosely related to some of the most robust plants in the southern forests: the heaths, evergreen laurels, and rhododendrons. Yet, how does the anemic herb survive?

Indian pipe is a sycophant, a parasite, as was Bram Stoker's bloodthirsty monster. Parasitism is an intimate association between two organisms where one lives on or in the other. The parasite steals its food like a vampire from its host; it gives nothing in return. But in the case of Indian pipe, the theft is more surreptitious. The ashen plant has formed a ménage à trois, "a household for three." It employs a third party, a liaison with a fungi that lives underground and leaches food for itself from the roots of trees.

Many trees have established a mutually beneficial relationship with underground fungi. The association is called "mycorrhiza" from a combination of two Greek words meaning fungus-root. Fungi are the decomposers in nature. The trees benefit because the fungus is very efficient at breaking down the minerals in the decaying material in soil, and the tree can absorb some of these nutrients for itself. The fungi benefits by siphoning some of the carbohydrates produced by the tree and stored in its roots. Somewhere along the line, Indian pipe managed to tap into the underground fungus and now uses it as a bridge to get at the tree's stored nutrients. Thus, Indian pipe no longer has to make its own food and over the millennia moved away from its need for chlorophyll, photosynthesis, and even sunlight. It found a way to live that wasn't being exploited. Now, that's creative.

Yet, proving that it is a true, bona fide plant, Indian pipe is a perennial that produces pollen and, later, even tiny seeds that look like fine brown sawdust and are born in dried, dark capsules. As the pod ripens, the flowers lift their heads and the minute seeds are blown about by the wind. The seeds that happen to fall on soil with the right mycorrhiza associations established underground will germinate.

Because of this parasitic association, Indian pipe does not transplant well. It also makes a poor cut flower. Once picked or even bruised, Indian pipe almost immediately begins to ooze a clear glutinous liquid; it soon oxidizes and turns black. If you try to preserve the plant in alcohol, it will turn black as well and tint the alcohol a deep reddish-violet.

IT'S HARD TO PRESERVE A GHOST

Indian pipe can be found throughout the Southeast in shady woods. It prefers groves of beech trees but can be found beneath other types of trees up to elevations of around sixty-three hundred feet. Having read that ghost plant doesn't preserve well, over a decade ago, I decided to visit the herbarium located in the James D. Hoskins Library on the campus of the University of Tennessee. Complete with gargoyles, vaulted ceilings, and the rarified air of academia, the cluster of first-floor rooms in the old stone building houses the lifework of many field botanists. The museum is home to over half a million species of plants, lichens, and fungi.

"That's a good number," said Dr. Eugene Wofford, the herbarium's curator of vascular plants at the time of my visit. "The truth is we probably have a lot more than that; there's no easy way to know." The collection was then divided into two parts: the mosses, ferns, lichens, and fungi are to the left of the entrance; vascular plants were to the right. The day I visited, he gave me a tour. Each room had row after row of tall metal cabinets filled with specimens stacked on evenly spaced shelves.

To give me an idea of the collection's "hard to know" extent, Dr. Wofford pointed upwards. On top of the mosses' lockers were boxes labeled with the names "Japan," "Mexico," and those of other faraway places. "Those are full of bryophytes collected by Dr. Sharp," said the gracious curator. The contents of this collection had been gathered from all over the planet by the late Dr. Aaron Sharp, a long-time botany professor at UT. I had known Dr. Sharp; I even took classes with him in the 1980s and pondered becoming a botanist. It was his travels that intrigued me. He often spoke of his adventures with mosses away from Tennessee. He was then a grandfather figure, and I hung on every word he uttered.

"He was world-traveled," said Dr. Wofford, "going everywhere he could to collect mosses." He then came home, piled them in a box, wrote the country's name on it, and put it away. "We probably have boxes labeled Albania to Zimbabwe." Since Dr. Sharp passed away, no one has had time to go through them and count and identify their contents. There could be and probably are thousands. Dr. Sharp wrote the mosses article in the *Encyclopedia Britannica* and the book on the mosses of Mexico: *The Moss Flora of Mexico,* volume 69 of the *Memoirs of the New York Botanical Garden.*

But I was interested in Indian pipe, a vascular plant, which was Dr. Wofford's area of expertise. Wofford himself was the author of several guidebooks on plants. He has also discovered two previously unknown plants: the federally endangered Cumberland sandwort, found only in Kentucky and Tennessee, and the bog spicebush, found along the Gulf Coast. The cabinets that contained them and thousands more were on the opposite side of the entrance.

Once collected, a specimen is placed between sheets of paper and squeezed flat in a plant press. After drying, each of the herbarium's samples is glued to a 11.5-by-16.5-inch, white, acid-free card.

"We used to mix our own glue, but it contained an ingredient that wasn't good, one to which we should avoid exposure," said Dr. Wofford. They used Elmer's Glue for a while, but now the preserved flowers, leaves, and stems are fixed onto their final resting places with Jade Adhesive, a neutral pH polyvinyl glue that's extremely flexible, fast setting, and transparent. In the back of the huge room that faces Cumberland Avenue is a large worktable with plant presses weighted down with heavy lead rings. At the time, the museum acquired around twelve thousand new specimens a year from various sources.

"This is a world-class collection," said Dr. Wofford. There are more than twenty-eight hundred species of plants that can be found in Tennessee, so the bulk of the museum's vast holdings come from places outside the Volunteer State. The herbarium keeps track of where all their Tennessee specimens were collected and every county in the state where it has been found. That information can be located on their website, which receives thousands of visits a month.

In the metal cabinets, the plants are filed by their scientific name, so we were looking for *Monotropa uniflora.* After walking past several tall, numbered, metal lockers we came to the one that housed the genus *Monotropa.* Dr. Wofford opened the door and promptly pulled out a file folder containing a stack of flattened specimens; each white card had several of the stems glued to it. One *Monotropa uniflora* sample was collected by Dr. Sharp himself on Laurel Creek near Bote Mountain on August 21, 1934. All the pressed Indian pipe stems had held their shape, but now they were flat and black as coal tar, no longer the white pasty things they were in life. The oldest Indian pipe in the collection had been gathered on August 10, 1900, somewhere in East Tennessee. The preserved plant was neatly labeled in a wonderful pen-and-ink calligraphy used in an era when handwriting was an art form.

The long-ago corpse plant was from the collection of Albert Ruth. The university had purchased the specimen in 1934. Looking at the century-old sample, I found it somehow reassuring to know that the ice plant had not completely melted away, that it had become a shadow, leaving a mark like a framed ebony silhouette in a Victorian parlor. I thanked Dr. Wofford and left feeling enriched, knowing that such a depository exists.

Bursting at the seams with flattened plant corpses of all kinds, the herbarium moved to a more spacious location on campus in 2014. Located in the recently renovated Temple Hall—there are no gargoyles or vaulted ceilings—the herbarium now occupies the entire first floor with over forty-five hundred square feet of space; plenty of room to grow.

This prompted a revisit. Walking down Andy Holt Boulevard, the ginkgos were festooned with bright yellow leaves. I felt that this was appropriate since Dr. Sharp had taught me the provenance of these ancient trees in the 1980s. Considered a living fossil, truly recognizable specimens can be found in rock that date back 270 million years. In the herbarium, again I found row after row of gray metal cabinets, all neatly organized and labeled. Soon I located the one that held my prize, the samples of *Monotropa uniflora* stacked in folders. The one Sharp had collected in 1934 was there as were over one hundred others. It was like revisiting old friends, albeit ghosts of their former selves.

IS THERE MORE HARMONY HERE THAN MEETS THE EYE?

Robert L. Ripley would have agreed that a pallid parasitic plant is something of an aberrant. When I speak of such odd things as ticks, or leeches, or mosquitoes, or botfly maggots (look it up; you won't be able to sleep tonight), I am often asked what is its purpose, as though everything living should make a contribution to humanity, the egocentric center of our world. In actuality, its purpose is to survive and reproduce by any means, any niche it can exploit. To use a metaphor rooted in the natural world, each species is but a strand in the web of life. Our species isn't the most important; it's just the most self-centered. For the first time in the history of our species, we will soon have the ability to wipe out mosquitoes, one species at a time. There are roughly thirty-five hundred species, but only one hundred or so harm humans. The *Anopheles gambiae* mosquito would be at the top of the hit list; it's the one that spreads malaria, which causes 725,000 deaths per year worldwide. We could render *A. gambiae* extinct with a revolutionary gene-editing technique called CRISPR-Cas9. The acronym stands for "clustered regularly interspaced short palindromic repeats, and the Cas9 is an enzyme." Don't fret. I don't understand it either, but I'm still playing vinyl LPs.

However, there is an ethical issue here: just because we can do it, should we? Few if any will rush to the defense of A. gambiae, but how much gene manipulation on how many species is too much playing God?

Many so-called pests or parasites may have an invisible positive effect on the whole. There are trillions of living microbes inside my body; without them, could I even write this sentence? Or have the motivation to try? Do they have purpose? Might the ghost plant have a hidden raison d'être? We once used it as a medicinal but perhaps it has a veiled bond to its ecology we do not know, an unseen strand in the fabric of life.

There is another, more famous parasitic plant living in North America. Whereas Indian pipe is associated with underground roots, mistletoe grows attached to a tree's crown, its thievery in plain sight. The Cherokee called the rakish plant, uda'li, a word that meant, "It is married," because the common plant never grows alone; it needs to be connected.

Mistletoe leads a charmed life. Although it is green, like Indian pipe it is not photosynthetic, so it doesn't make its own food either but rather steals it from its host tree. Mistletoe was a favorite plant of the Druids, who believed it had supernatural qualities. This mystique was fueled by mistletoe's apparent vigor. The plant remains green and alive all year, while its host drops its leaves and goes through the temporary death of winter. Because it stays green and bushy in winter, it's easy to find in autumn when the leaves fall off the trees. Late in the year, it's also loaded with waxy white berries. Birds spread the parasite by inadvertently carrying the sticky, bleached fruit on their bills or feet as they fly about feeding from tree to tree.

It's the birds that are important in this scenario. "A study of mistletoe in junipers concluded that more juniper berries sprout in stands where mistletoe is present, as the mistletoe attracts berry-eating birds which also eat juniper berries," reported Susan Milius in the journal Science News in 2002. "Such interactions lead to dramatic influences on diversity, as areas with greater mistletoe densities support higher diversities of animals. Thus, rather than being a pest, mistletoe can have a positive effect on biodiversity, providing high quality food and habitat for a broad range of animals in forests and woodlands worldwide."

In this symbiotic relationship, it has long been believed that mistletoe is merely a parasite; the association with the tree helps it and it alone, as mistletoe robs from the tree and gives nothing in return. Yet, the Milius study suggests a bigger picture—mistletoe's role in local ecology. Does Indian pipe have a purpose? Does it help its host or its forest in some way as yet unknown? The actual web of life, with its invisible connections, is as shadowy as the ghost plant itself.

In the case of the underground, three-way mycorrhizal relationship between Indian pipe, the fungi, and the tree, ghostly Indian pipe appears to be giving nothing, the parasite of the trio. But is there more here than meets the eye? Is there a natural balance that the Cherokee, a people who valued harmony, would have found most pleasing?

YOU CAN'T GO HOME AGAIN. OR CAN YOU?

It was Asheville novelist Thomas Wolfe who said, "You can't go home again." He meant that as soon as you leave, the place begins to change. It fills with ghosts. But as we age, almost everywhere we look, there are ghosts. We see backwards, as in 1 Corinthians, "through a glass, darkly."

On Saturday, May 28, 2016, I was invited to lead a Memorial Day weekend hike back into my ancestral fountainhead: Baskins Creek in the national park and a waterfall that is located only a few miles upstream from my boyhood home.

The Great Smoky Mountains Association (GSMA) hosted the hike and Executive Director Laurel Rematore and Marketing and Membership Associate Marti Smith went along on the adventure. Lynne Davis, the Ijams volunteer and wildflower aficionado we met in the jack-in-the-pulpit chapter, also accompanied us.

The GSMA supports the perpetual preservation of Great Smoky Mountains National Park and the national park system by promoting greater public interest and appreciation through education, interpretation, and research. Growing up in Gatlinburg with a national park as my nurturing ground had a profound effect on me. It is my heritage. The apple does not fall too far from the tree. Resent research shows that kids that grow up in nature, remain nature-minded all their lives. I am that kid and I'm always happy to return, so I guess you can go home again. You just have to be prepared for the ghosts.

Mount LeConte towered over my childhood, and the prominent mountain with four peaks is drained on its north flank by three watersheds: Roaring Fork, Baskins, and LeConte Creeks. For me, just about everywhere you look in the Roaring Fork or Baskins Creek watersheds are familial ghosts: old rock walls, wagon roads, remains of stone chimneys, cemeteries. Lives were lived there, scratching an existence out of the steep mountain terrain with little flat ground for gardens. Granddad Homer Bales often told the story of a cow that once fell out of its pasture and broke its neck.

The GSMA Memorial Day hike also coincided with Decoration Day, a time of remembrance, when mountain residents reconnect with lost loved ones. Traditionally, it was both a religious event and a celebration of life, where people reunited, albeit briefly, as a community.

"Decoration Day has been an important ritual in Sevier County for generations. Today, Southerners live in less rural areas, and Decoration Day customs are being conflated into the nationwide observance of Memorial Day," wrote Sevier County historian and friend Carroll McMahan. "The long Memorial Day weekend provides the best opportunity to remember deceased family members and veterans, since a Decoration Day observed apart from this weekend is disappearing except perhaps in parts of our southern Appalachian Mountains."

On this Memorial Day hike, by pure coincidence, we parked near the restored home site of Jim Bales, my great grandfather, and walked past the well-maintained family cemetery, where several of my ancestors are laid to rest. And in this case, that term is appropriate. A mountaineer's life was hardscrabble. The buried deceased are indeed at peace in the quiet setting, and the GSMA group stopped for a while to pay our respects.

The quiet spot is hardly level, the ground donated by my great-great-grandfather Caleb Bales. Lynne Davis pointed out that the graves all point uphill, toward the east, with the feet buried higher than the heads of the departed. It was believed that on the day of Resurrection, the Lord would come with the rising sun, and the deceased should be facing toward sunrise on that glorious day. The site is also a testament to hardship. The tombstone of Maferd Bales, who would have been my uncle, only has one date: November 22, 1923. He died the same day he was born. Harison Bales, son of Ephraim, died in 1922; as the family story was handed down, he committed suicide after his wife left him. And there was my great-grandmother Emma, who died after childbirth a long way from any doctor in 1902. And in the north corner is the small grave of the severed leg of Giles Reagan, who lost the limb in a sawmill accident. Giles wanted to give it a Christian burial so that someday he and his appendage would be reunited. Giles himself is buried several miles away in the White Oaks Flat Cemetery in Gatlinburg.

Past the hallowed ground, it was only 1.7 miles to the site of the waterfall, but mountain miles can be deceiving. Oddly, for any destination in the Smokies, it's mostly downhill going in, dropping approximately 335 feet in elevation (2,580 to 2,245 feet) from the Roaring Fork Trailhead. But, we were in no real hurry.

The Baskins Creek Falls was where my grandmother Pearl Mae Ogle Bales took showers when she was a barefoot girl, as did all the rest of her large family. In the late 1920s, great-grandfather Preston Columbus Ogle sold 124.6 acres along Baskins Creek, which included a three-room frame house, four tenant houses, two barns, a mill, two hundred apple trees, and a waterfall, all for $3,500,

Great-granddad Ogle sold the family property, as did all his neighbors, to become part of a greater good: the Great Smoky Mountains National Park. And a greater good it has become.

We had chosen a beautiful day for our hike, a "stop and smell the roses" kind of day, meaning it was leisurely. Mountain laurel was in bloom at the top of the first ridge, and the rosy purple Catawba rhododendron was just beginning to flower. Most of the ephemeral spring wildflowers had come and gone—no jack-in-the-pulpits, no lady's slippers, no trillium—but there was a bit of Jungian synchronicity just beginning to poke its head above the ground. When I write, so-called "meaningful coincidences" happen routinely. For me it's a tingling feeling as the divine flows through me. I am but a conduit, accepting it as a sign that I'm on the right path. Obi-Wan Kenobi might say, "May the force be with you."

The Swiss psychotherapist Carl Jung introduced the concept of synchronicity in the 1920s, the same decade the mountaineers were asked to sell their land. But he gave a full statement of it in a lecture for Eranos, an intellectual discussion group, in 1951, the same year I was born. Jung believed that, just as events may be connected by causality (cause and effect), they may also be connected by meaning. Jung liked to quote Lewis Carroll's White Queen, who says to Alice: "It's a poor sort of memory that only works backwards." He believed the moments of synchronicity connect us with the collective unconscious—past, present, future—the part of the unconscious mind that is derived from ancestral memory and experience and is common to all humankind. And Jung believed that when such coincidental moments happen, we should ask ourselves, "What could this mean?"

Memorial Day is a traditional time of remembrance, of reconnecting and recurrence, and as we walked along the old wagon road that my grandparents Homer and Pearl would have taken in 1923 after they buried their stillborn son, Maferd, the meaningful coincidences seemed to be there. I felt the tingle but knew its' meaning was as unknowable as the anemic ghost plant's connection to its host tree and fungi. And as if that were not enough synchronicity, only a few minutes after we left the family cemetery, in the shade of the new growth trees that towered overhead, we encountered our first cluster of the very hard-to-find, or predict, Indian pipe. Ghost plant here? And on this very day, was it an apparition or a sign? The Cherokee would have seen meaning in the happenstance encounter. Did old men once quarrel here over having to sell their land? Did my grandparents in their grief?

I felt it more as a bellwether moment, a synchronistic blessing of our journey along the rutted muddy way. I smiled knowingly and led our group farther into my ancestral heartland. We were being watched over.

Ruby-throated Hummingbird

Arichilochus colubris

Every day
I see or hear
something
that more or less
kills me
with delight . . .

—Mary Oliver, "Mindful"

ZIP. HUM. SWOOSH. And then they are gone. Poof! Did I just see that?

It's Labor Day weekend. The early morning sun is peeking through the trees, and already it's warm. Some would even say steamy, Tennessee Williams steamy. The end of summer is always hot—cat-on-a-hot-tin-roof hot, Maggie-the-cat hot. A southern humid heat feels hotter than a dry Arizona heat, so I've been told, but hot is hot.

My second-floor deck is a hubbub of activity. A swarm of bees? No, that wouldn't be as boisterous. The revelers are too big for bees, although to call ruby-throated hummingbirds "big" is like calling clouds "well defined."

The date is important. It's the peak of fall hummingbird migration through the Tennessee Valley, and there are a lot more heading south than came north last spring, most of them are newborns. I'm maintaining nine sugar-water feeders on a deck that's not quite big enough to park three cars—small cars like, perhaps, a Prius and two Civics. I grew up in a Ford family so even mentioning any other brand would be an abomination to my late father, Russell. But I drive a Focus now, so there's peace in the valley.

I refresh the feeders every morning. Today, two of the Perky Pets have been drained and the day has only just begun. The hummingbirds are too numerous and active to count. They're feisty. Dad would have said the little squirts are full of "piss and vinegar," but I'm too civilized to use such language. Besides, Dad, they drink nectar and sugar water; they couldn't be that acrid.

The hummers are chasing each other from one feeder to the next, learning a valuable lesson in survival and defending one's territory. In September, they are not protecting nesting sites; breeding is long over. Instead, they are defending food sources and fattening up for fall migration. The females are just as aggressive as the males. Besides, I'm seeing few adult males. They have already departed for the tropics. Hasta la vista, *baby!*

Ruby-throated hummingbirds, what the early French trappers called *colibri à gorge rubis,* get their names from the bright patch of red throat feathers, called a gorget, on the adult male. These feathers are a brilliant iridescent red that look dark or black when not in good light, but in full sun they glitter like jewels. The adult females have white throats, as do the young juveniles regardless of gender.

If a hummingbird could be written down as a chemical formula it would be $C_6H_2(NO_2)_3CH_3$, trinitrotoluene, TNT, tough 'n' tenacious, and the juveniles are just as volatile. Dare you think I'm being too harsh, hummingbird expert Bob Sargent observed, "Fearless and ferocious, they defend feeding sites and nesting areas with intimidating zeal. With an explosive temper and nasty attitude."

That's quite a condemnation (or commendation) for a featherweight bird, but Sargent went on: "In an instant they will harass and intimidate any intruder. From creatures as small as honeybees and butterflies to adversaries as large as hawks or house pets, no living thing is safe from a ruby-throat's wrath."

This fierce reputation is justified. Ounce for ounce— no, change that; that's too heavy. Gram for gram—no, we can't use that either; this is America. We don't use grams. No one even knows what a gram is. It's small; trust me.

Okay. We're back to ounces. Ounce for ounce, ruby-throated hummingbirds are remarkable creatures. In *The Sibley Guide to Birds,* they are listed as weighing only 0.11 ounces (3.5 grams). That means—if my math skills haven't totally left me—it would take 145 individual ruby-throats to make a pound of hummingbird. Or to use a metric comparison, take two dimes out of your pocket and look at them in your hand. That twenty cents you are holding weighs four grams, only slightly more than a ruby-throated hummingbird. Not much, right? Whether you use the metric system or not, that is incredibly lightweight. It's a remarkable bird in a tiny, tiny package, and on average, a male weighs about 10 percent less than a female, so he's a bantamweight powerhouse.

Our hearts beat roughly eighty times per minute. Through a stethoscope, each beat sounds like a muffled "lub-dub." A hummingbird's heart beats about five hundred times a minute at rest and revs up to more than a thousand beats per minute as the bird bobs and weaves around your backyard.

With all this high-speed zipping around, ruby-throats burn roughly 645 calories per hour. A typical Big Mac has about 700 calories and weighs roughly 7.6 ounces, or about seventy times more than a hummingbird—that's enough heft to effectively crush the diminutive bird. Yet the hummer burns the equivalent amount of calories in just over sixty minutes. If our human metabolism were the same as theirs, we'd need to eat three hundred pounds of hamburger each and every day, or a Big Mac the size of a coffee table. Bon appétit.

Just about everything about hummingbirds is accelerated. They have the fastest wing beat of any bird, up to ninety beats per second during normal activity and as much as two hundred flaps per second during courtship. That's where they get their hum.

To power their dynamic lifestyles, they must eat constantly, visiting as many as twenty flowers per minute. Yet, even with this entire copious intake, at any given moment in an average day, a hummingbird is perhaps only a few hours away from starvation. A flowerless, feeder-less half-day could do one in.

Many birds fly into windows. CRASH! Sometimes it breaks their necks, but sometimes it just leaves them dazed and confused, like a football player after a rough hit. Colliding into windows is the number two cause of bird deaths. Outside cats kill an estimated 1.4 to 3.7 billion birds each year, while flying into windows causes 365 to 988 million bird deaths.

On Sunday, August 14, 2016, I was checking the thirty hummingbird feeders maintained around the visitor center at Ijams when I found a male ruby-throated hummingbird on a bench below a window. It was moving but not much, and naturally I feared the worst. I've watched other avian crash victims twitch only to soon die. Plus, I had no idea when the downed hummer had last eaten.

Cradling the injured foundling gently in my hands I watched it, speaking to it in soft tones. He wiggled a bit, twisting his head back and forth, blinking bleary eyes, asking itself the obvious metaphysical questions: "Where am I? Who am I?"

Its light, two-dime body weight was readily apparent. Having one in your hand is like holding a hope and a promise. An official badminton shuttle-cock weighs twice as much but only has sixteen feathers. A hummingbird has between 1,000 and 1,500 feathers, the fewest number of feathers of any bird species in the world. Without this plumage, there's very little flesh and bone inside.

Opening my fingers, the foundling didn't fly but hopped onto my thumb. A good sign! Yet, still he didn't want to fly. Had he forgotten how? Did he only need some food? A nearby visitor brought me a sugar-water feeder. The hummer seemed to slowly come to its senses, recognizing the world and the meaning of the feeder. Self-awareness was creeping in.

It drank. Swoosh! Like a swift running back, it saw its opening and bolted away.

EACH NEEDS THE OTHER

The hummingbird-flower connection is a symbiotic relationship that's taught in most textbooks. The flowers that produce nectar do it for a reason. They do it to reward hummingbirds because they need the lithe Lilliputians to carry pollen from flower to flower, anther to stigma. It's an example of mutualism: both the hummingbird and the flower benefit from the interaction. The word nectar is derived from the Greek *néktar,* meaning "drink of the gods." It is produced in glands called nectaries and is rich with natural sugars: sucrose, glucose, fructose, and other trace minerals. But it is to the benefit of the flowers that the hummingbird visits as many plants as possible during the day to spread the pollen over a wide area, so the nectaries only produce a tiny sip of nectar at a time. If the hummers need a nice long drink, they must visit your sugar water feeder. Although sip is a poor choice of words, the avian pixies do not sip. They wick and lap with extra-long tongues covered with tube-like structures. To work it deeply into the flower, the tongue is forked much like a snake's.

There's a general misconception that hummingbirds eat nectar and sugar water alone. They do consume a full range of sucrose concentrations, as much and as often as they can find it, but according to foraging studies, their major food source is insects. It is accurate to think of ruby-throats as miniature flycatchers, said hummingbird expert Bob Sargent. They need the sugary solutions to power their quick bursts of speed, but they need the fats, proteins, and minerals found in insects.

THERE'S A LOT TO HUM ABOUT
SOUTH OF THE BORDER

All of the hummingbirds we saw at my home and the nature center in September were on the move. A few remain in the Gulf Coast states and the Outer Banks of North Carolina. Most spend their winters between southern Mexico and northern Panama and on a few Caribbean Islands because the flowers and insects are abundant there during our winter. Some have their passports stamped with places like Costa Rica, Belize, and Nicaragua. Oddly, there is enough good, insect-laden, flowery habitat along the Gulf Coast and Florida during our northern winters to provide for all the ruby-throats' needs; instead they eschew our shores and fly farther to the tropics, the species' natal homeland.

Their return south begins early. The adult males are the first to go, beginning in July, while the adult females are soon to follow. By mid-September and October, it is primarily the juveniles that must fatten up to fly south in short hops and skips. Yes, they are born here, but like the cerulean warbler we met earlier, it's wrong to think of them as *our* birds; they are tropical birds that over the course of the millennia have worked their way north to find less contested nesting sites. Most of the adult males only spend about four months in the Tennessee Valley, April through July. And the juveniles that fly south for the first time are going to places they have never been, yet somewhere in their tiny brains is a map and itinerary.

Even though there's plenty of room in the East, we only have the one species. West of the Mississippi River, Sibley lists 17 species, although some are only rarely in the United States. And to our south, Mexico has 58 species, 12 of which are endemic; they can only be found in that country. Ecuador lists 103 species, and Colombia, a favorite wintering site of the cerulean warbler, has the greatest diversity of hummingbirds of any country on earth with 171 species, 15 endemic to that country. But we have not scratched the surface. Although only found in the New World, the hummingbird family contains more species than any other. The exact number may never be settled, but Bob Sargent stated that it's somewhere between 320 and 330 species, stretching from Canada south to the windswept barrens of Tierra del Fuego on the tip of South America, with the tropics being the great hummingbird evolutionary caldron. That's a lot of hum. So rather than compete with these tropical hummers for nesting sites, our own ruby-throat simply dispersed north and brought with it the pugnacious attitude it acquired in the southern latitudes. Competing with bigger species put a chip on its shoulder.

Yet, all birds do not necessarily stay confined to their official range. They can't even read a range map. One of the Mexican species is the green-breasted mango. I know, it sounds more like a voluptuous fruit than a bird. This feathered mango is a large, iridescent green hummingbird with a slightly down-curved bill. It's about 50 percent bigger than our own ruby-throat and twice as heavy. It's normally found in Mexico and Central America. It's a bird of the open savannahs, tree-dotted pastures, orchards, and tall second-growth forests, which is often found in groves of mango trees—hence the name. The species can occasionally be found in the south Texas plains but no farther north than the Nueces River. That's about it for its "official" range, but hummingbirds are rather capricious.

The green-breasted mango has twice been reported far from its normal home. Seven years ago, in November 2000, Susan Campbell banded an immature male that she caught at a feeder in Concord, North Carolina. It was the first recorded sighting of the Mexican mango in the United States outside of Texas. How it got there is a mystery, although it's a safe bet that it flew on its own accord and did not take a bus.

Then, again in October 2007, a green-breasted mango turned up in Beloit, Wisconsin, at the home of Joan Salzberg. She just looked out, and there it was at her red strawberry-shaped feeder, lapping up sugar water. If you have ever been to the Badger State, you know it's a long, long, long way from Mexico.

Bird lovers flocked to Salzberg's yard to see the rare visitor and theorize about how it got there. Was it blown off course by a tropical storm? Or was it perhaps born with a genetic mutation that messed up its sense of direction? If the latter, would that same broken internal compass be able to get it back home? We will never know because, against the advice of hummingbird experts, it was captured and placed in a zoo.

Here in the Tennessee Valley, we often get rufous hummingbirds (Selasphorus rufus) in the winter. They are University of Tennessee orange. So it looks like they belong here, but they do not. Being a purely west coast species, they nest from Washington state north to Alaska. They winter in Central America. So why do a few turn up here almost every winter? It's a mystery.

DECODING ANOTHER MYSTERY

Ornithologists place hummingbirds and swifts in the same taxonomic order, the Apodiformes, Greek for "footless," which is certainly how these birds look most of the time, but nevertheless it's a misnomer. Hummers have feet, just very short legs like chimney swifts. Their extremely undersized limbs prevent them from walking or hopping. The best they can do is shuffle along a branch. Yet, they manage to scratch their heads and necks by raising their feet up and over their wings.

As you have already read, much of what we know about ruby-throats we owe to the research of Bob and Martha Sargent. It would be difficult to write anything of real length about ruby-throats without consulting or mentioning them. The Sargents dedicated of the past thirty years to learning as much as possible about hummingbirds. Bob's book, *Ruby-throated Hummingbird*— one of the Stackpole Wild Bird Guides, published in 1999—is the definitive source on the topic. Bob and Martha spoke at the Wonder of Hummingbirds Festival at Ijams on Saturday, July 11, 2009. They were warmly acknowledged for their knowledge and accessibility.

Bob Sargent came to birding somewhat late in life. "[He] graduated from Corner High School in 1955 and served in the U.S. Air Force from 1955–59. He later was a master electrician and had his own fabricating shop that sold electrical equipment," wrote Greg Garrison, reporter for Alabama Media Group at AL.com.

"I got him hooked on birds and hummingbirds because I had feeders out," said his wife, Martha. "We started watching hummingbirds, but we couldn't find any information about them."

There's a lesson in their story: it's never too late to redefine your life, you so-called late bloomers. Laura Ingalls Wilder didn't publish her first "Little House" book until she was sixty-five; Colonel Harlan Sanders didn't start franchising his Kentucky Fried Chicken business until he was sixty-two; Ronald Reagan didn't run for public office until he was fifty-five, and we all know where that led. (I didn't publish my first nature article until I was forty-eight.)

In 1987, with the help of Tom Imhof, author of *Alabama Birds,* the Sargents acquired a permit and started banding birds as volunteer field ornithologists.

"Frankly, we didn't know anything about birds when we started out," Martha said. In time, they captured and banded more than three hundred thousand ruby-throats in their backyard in Clay, Alabama, reported Garrison.

"We'll band a bird in our yard. He'll migrate, go to South America, survive, and the next fall, he'll come back to our yard," Bob told AL.com in 2012. "I can go back and look at the data from when we banded each one of those birds. They are passing through our yard within a day or two either side of the exact date when we captured them in the yard before. That's over the course of nine years. Amazing."

The Sargents proved that ruby-throats were loyal to hospitable sites. Once they know you have a hummer-friendly backyard, they'll visit it every year.

Starting in 1989, the Sargents assembled a crew of twelve to sixteen volunteers at Fort Morgan, each spring and again in the fall to band all migratory birds. The study site was located within Bon Secour (French for "safe harbor") National Wildlife Refuge on the coast of Alabama. From a bird's eye view, it's the tip of a narrow peninsula separating Mobile Bay from the Gulf of Mexico, a strip of land only seven hundred meters wide in places. For thousands of neotropical migrants, it's the last stop in the fall before the open water, or the first stop in the spring after the long overnight trip across the gulf.

In 1993, the Sargents founded the Hummer/Bird Study Group, a nonprofit organization that raised money for the banding efforts.

"Sargent trained most of the hummingbird banders in the eastern U.S.," said certified master bird bander Fred Bassett. "To say he had a passion for it doesn't even start to describe it. Bob and Martha wanted to share that with people, get them enthused for birds and conservation for birds."

"He's my hero," said Bassett. "He changed a lot of people's lives for the better." If this sounds like a eulogy, it is. The seventy-seven-year-old Bob Sargent passed away on September 7, 2014.

THE RETURN TRIP

For birds, ruby-throats are odd ducks. (Forgive the idiom.) Unlike most other birds, they lead solitary lives, and neither live nor migrate in flocks. An individual bird may spend the winter anywhere with favorable habitat in its southern range and probably returns to the same location each winter. Creatures of habit. They do the same on their summer range. But each is a loner. Living their lives at full throttle doesn't invite companionship. They don't take time to exchange pleasantries, while other species do. In the winter, hummers have an agenda. Lost weight must be put back on. The flight from north to south depletes their resources. They know no national borders; only our species does. They have a known range but their principal problem is that their breeding grounds and their winter home are separated by the Gulf of Mexico.

The call to return north begins as early as January, and by the last few days of February they are collecting along the northern coast of the Yucatán Peninsula. There they feast on insects and spiders and add a thick layer of fat. They'll need it. Although some follow the coastline of eastern Mexico to Texas, most apparently take the direct route straight across the gulf like the cerulean warbler, typically leaving at dusk for a nonstop flight of up to five hundred miles, which again takes eighteen to twenty-two hours, depending on the weather. Everything about this flight is hazardous. Although they may fly over water with mixed flocks of other bird species, they do not seem to fly with flocks of other hummers. Their tiny bodies heat up so they fly at night to conserve energy, leaving at dusk *if* there is a tailwind, but the determined dynamos have no idea what's waiting ahead over the stormy gulf. There may be a compass hardwired into their brain, but no Doppler radar. If you get out a map of the region and draw a line between the Yucatán and our own gulf coast, it's hard to imagine such an odyssey. I couldn't do it in a bowrider with a full tank of gas and you as my navigator.

Buffeted by winds, on bad nights hummers are lucky they're not blown to Timbuktu; still they press on. If they burn all of their body fat, they start burning muscle. If they burn too much muscle, they crash into the water. Game over. Oilrig workers out in the gulf know to put out sugar-water feeders as way stations; experienced hummers know to look for them. Individual birds may make landfall anywhere between southern Texas and central Florida. A few ruby-throats may island-hop across the Caribbean taking the easier "cruise ship route," entering the United States through the Florida Keys.

Hummingbird.net reported, "Before departing, each bird will have nearly doubled its weight, from about 3.25 grams to over 6 grams; when it reaches the U.S. Gulf coast, it may weigh only 2.5 grams," slightly more than the weight of one dime. In a normal year, it is estimated that only about 20 percent of the young produced survive the fall and spring migration and return the following year. That's just one in five. Is it any wonder?

Why even continue to reproduce against those odds? It's simple. If each female in her lifetime produces only two offspring that outlive her and her mate, the overall population of ruby-throated hummingbirds stays stable. If each happens to produce more than two that outlive her, the population grows. And by all indications, the numbers are increasing.

Just as the adult males were the first to fly south seven months earlier, they're the first to depart the Yucatán Peninsula, followed about ten days later by the first adult females. But it all doesn't happen at once, the migration is spread over a ninety-plus-day period. It's prudent and prevents catastrophic weather over the gulf from wiping out the entire species. They seem to first trickle into any given location, then flood.

For a creature that must find massive amounts of succulent flowers and their accompanying protein-rich insects every hour to survive, life is a frantic whirling dervish, a mad race with the ever-present mantra "find food quickly or die." How they accomplish the dash across the gulf is a mystery to me and everyone else who's taken the time to ponder the question. Is that extra gram of fat added before takeoff enough? It doesn't seem likely.

$E = mc^2$. Einstein's prophetic equation explains so much of our universe. Energy and mass, two separate entities are essentially two forms of the same thing. Mass, everything we see, can become pure energy under the right conditions and vice versa. They are interchangeable. Einstein was the first to figure this out, the rest of us are still grappling with what it means.

Will we ever be able to formulate equations to explain *all* the wonders of the natural world? If so, what mathematical symbol will we use to represent guts, determination, drive, willpower, endurance, *intestinal fortitude?* How do you explain Peyton Manning or Michael Jordan, great beyond the sum of their constituent parts? Or Van Gogh? Or Mozart? Or Newton, or even Einstein himself? What makes some shrinking violets and others spitfires? What puts a fire in the belly? The racehorse Seabiscuit was described as undersized, knobby-kneed, and given to sleeping and eating for long periods, but he became a champion because he had that indefinable "it." What spark drives a hummingbird, gives it grit? A badminton shuttlecock has more substance.

There's a reason why I do not write fiction. Why do so when nonfiction is so often incredibly unbelievable? As Fox Mulder of *The X-Files* was apt to say, "The truth is out there."

Spring comes on like gangbusters. So much so that it's hard to take note of it all. In a wonderful example of natural synchronicity, there are three native plants that bloom to welcome the hummers' return. All have tubular, red flowers. Once in the states, the birds migrate north at an average rate of about twenty miles per day. They seem to follow the blooming of these hummingbird flowers, perhaps the most significant of which is red buckeye. Studies have shown that the diminutive little birds follow the blooming buckeyes north. As the native tree produces flowers in any given area, the hummingbirds soon appear. Trumpet honeysuckle, also known as coral honeysuckle, is also ideally suited for the ruby-throats. It has showy, nectar-rich, red-to-coral flowers arranged in terminal clusters. The color is right, and the long, slender, tubular flowers seem especially evolved for the bird's equally long bill and tongue. Another hummingbird favorite that appears early is crossvine, a native, semi-evergreen, woody vine.

Crossvine is a climber generally found growing up a supportive tree. Like most plants that use hummingbirds as pollinators, it also has cylindrical flowers that range from red to orange to tangerine in color and a scent that's mocha-like.

Throughout early spring in the East, the ruby-throats return to their chosen locales, just as they did the year before. Banding studies show that each hummingbird most often returns every year to the same location where it hatched, even visiting the same feeders. In my part of the world, we put out our feeders the first day of April. "Crazy day to crazy day," said my friend Chris Mahoney of Chattanooga. "April Fools Day to Halloween." Chris is a self-confessed hum-a-phile and has spoken several times at the nature center about the petite sprites. Her yard is a ruby-throated Six Flags.

Canada is the northern limit of the species, but not much higher than the city of Québec. That boundary coincides with that of the yellow-bellied sapsucker. The fastest, earliest males that reach Canada before the flowers bloom raid sapsucker wells for sugar, as well as eat the bugs caught in the sap. By late May, the northward migration is complete.

And boom, it's time to nest and raise a family. Similarly to red pandas, male and female ruby-throats set up separate territories that overlap. They only come in contact with each other long enough to mate, which for birds is a scant few seconds. It takes far longer for the male to get her attention and complete their ultimate courtship.

Here's a contrast and compare: female red pandas allow themselves to be approached by amiable males with proper manners. Female hummingbirds choose their mates and "seem to select the meanest, most aggressive males they can find," wrote Bob Sargent. She is very secretive about her nest location and will already have one started or even finished before she ventures out of her territory to seek a mate in his territory. If she finds a suitor that catches her eye, she apparently lures him into neutral ground, not wanting even him to know where her nest is hidden. He's going to be of no help, so why put up with any possible harassment?

He's a little cuss and she darn well knows it.

Birds are built differently. They do not have the same reproductive body parts as we placental mammals. In the majority of species, males do not have penises. Instead, like the females, the males have a cloaca opening, also called the vent. Their reproductive organs are inside this vent and when they are ready to breed, their testes and ovaries swell, producing the sperm and ova. When it's time to mate, the male and female have to align their vents, not an easy thing to do, and briefly rub them together.

This is known as a "cloacal kiss" and involves the male balancing on the back of the female and her moving her tail out of the way. It's awkward, mercifully brief, and hopefully no one is watching. When you think about it, all mating is somewhat awkward. This momentary rubbing of vents may last less than a second, but the sperm is transferred and mating is completed. Several of these kisses may occur within a few moments.

After their brief courtship and mating, they live separate lives in their separate territories. If they encounter each other again—say, at your feeder—he will probably be aggressive towards her, but she chose him for just that trait. It bodes well for her offspring.

The female's nest is about the size of a golf ball, mostly crafted out of spider silk and plant down, camouflaged with lichen. It's a masterpiece of construction. Mom usually lays two very small white eggs, each a half inch long. She does all the incubation, which takes twelve to fourteen days, long hours on the nest unless it's a warm day. When the young hatch, they are about the size of honeybees, naked with only twin tracts of hairlike feathers down their backs. The new nestlings are totally dependent on Mom for warmth and food; they're also ravenous.

"It takes all the harried mother can do to satisfy the begging, hungry mouths of her two rapidly growing offspring," noted Sargent. "As the weight of the nestlings skyrocket, that of the female plummets by 15 to 20 percent. She hardly has time to keep herself fed."

With practically all the bird species you have around your home, the father helps with the feeding. But not the ruby-throats; Mom does it all. Luckily, the young mature rapidly. In only eighteen to twenty-two days, the nestlings have fledged and are ready to leave the nest.

During this time, sugar water and nectar just aren't enough. Growing nestlings need protein in the form of small insects, and their mothers can't find it at the feeders. In May and June, the females all but disappear, becoming secretive, supervising hidden nests. They spend more time hawking and gleaning insects because they need the protein for their growing nestlings.

Somewhat astonishingly, the mother ruby-throat is so energetic that, at some point during this period, she may slip away and start a second nest, usually very near the first one, so that she can be tending to two nests at the same time.

"At this stage, the female is often ragged, with very worn plumage," Sargent continued. "She is likely to be underweight, but it does not deter her from her mission."

When the first brood fledges, mom leads them away from the nest to perch somewhere hidden deeper in the foliage. She continues feeding them until they become completely independent in a week to ten days. During this stage, she'll seek out a mate to start the process anew. To the far north, there's no time for a second brood.

By July and into August, your sugar-water feeders become the most popular place in your yard, like the new, oh-so-chic restaurant that just opened downtown. The population of your backyard hummers has tripled, and migratory hummers that nested farther to the north begin to pass through.

HOW DO YOU ASSIGN A NUMBER TO A HUMMINGBIRD?

A lot of what is known today about an avian species's range and lifespan has been learned by placing a numbered metal band around a captured bird's leg. A simple piece of lightweight "bling" on a bird can mean so much. Than Boves did the same thing during his cerulean warbler study. When the bejeweled bearer is recaptured or found deceased later, ornithologists can determine how long it lived and how far it traveled since banded.

Mark Armstrong worked at the Knoxville Zoo for 36 years, serving as the curator of birds for most of that time. Over his career he has worked with thousands of birds both captive and wild, from leggy ostriches to virtually legless hummingbirds. As a certified Master Bander, he has also placed thousands of metal bands on captured and then released wild birds. Trained by Bob Sargent at Fort Morgan, since 2005 Armstrong has banded between six and seven thousand songbirds and roughly thirty-five hundred hummingbirds. Now retired from the zoo, he regularly nets and bands birds at Seven Islands State Birding Park.

In the summer of 2009 Armstrong held a hummingbird banding demonstration at the nature center on the back terrace. Dozens of people came to coo over the diminutive hummers seen up-close. Around that simple act of education, an annual festival coalesced. The Wonder of Hummingbird Festival held at the end of August was the brainchild of Billie Cantwell, then president of the Knoxville Chapter of the Tennessee Ornithological Society. It was created as a fundraiser for both the local bird club and the nonprofit nature center, and Cantwell worked on its organization tirelessly (although I'm sure she would agree she was often tired).

Routinely, over one thousand people attend the birding fest, which includes local vendors and a full morning of activities and speakers. But the highlight is always a hummingbird banding demonstration.

Over the years, many have asked, "How do you catch something as lively and tiny as a hummingbird?"

The late Bob Sargent perfected the protocol, and it is surprising simple. In the weeks leading up to the festival, the nature center maintains an increasing number of sugar water feeders around the visitor center and Alice Ijams Garden Demonstration site. By the end of August, there's as many as thirty, plus colorful flowers to lure the hummers to the site. The morning of the festival all are removed except for three or four. A trap that looks very much like a parakeet cage is placed around the remaining feeders. The cage door is left open but can be snapped shut when a hummer enters to drink. Once inside, a handler will ever so gently reach in to retrieve the bird and place it in a soft mesh pouch that is quickly delivered to Armstrong. Wearing a jeweler's headband magnifier that looks and fits like a pair of goggles, he then places the tiny metal leg band with an even tinier number on the hummer's right leg. With the help of his partner and wife, Jane Kading, details about its weight, gender, age, and overall condition are recorded and the bird is set free. The entire process only takes a few minutes, and while being held the captive bird remains surprisingly docile.

In 2013, the festival was held on August 24, a Saturday. That year, Armstrong and his team members, Patty Ford, Richard and Gar Secrist, Colin Leonard, and others, caught a total of forty-two hummingbirds during the practice session and the day of the festival itself. One male was caught four times. So either he didn't figure out the cage-trap or he liked being held and coddled.

Holding a hummingbird is like holding the embodiment of ephemerality. A tiny heart beats inside the feathered thing, but for how long? That's why you never hold the living smidgeon for very long. You know it's in a hurry; its time is short. Its days spent perpetually in motion, madly rushing about like the March Hare, always late. But really, Costa Rica is a long way away. Who has time for a sit down tea party? Well, maybe a young Victorian English lass, but that's a girl we'll meet soon enough.

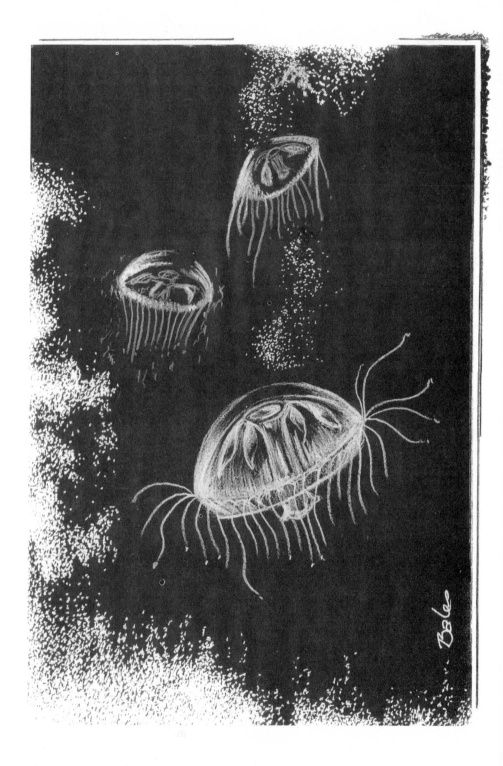

Freshwater Jellyfish

Craspedacusta sowerbii (sowerbyi)

> "Every adventure requires a first step.
> Trite, but true, even here."
>
> —Lewis Carroll

SOMETIME BEFORE ALICE stepped through the looking glass, she encountered a cat that could materialize at will. "I wish you wouldn't keep appearing and vanishing so suddenly: you make me quite giddy," she said to the vaporous feline.

"All right," responded the cat.

"And this time," wrote Lewis Carroll, "it vanished quite slowly, beginning with the end of the tail, and ending with the grin, which remained for some time after the rest of it had gone."

Of course, Alice *was* in Wonderland. You wouldn't expect that sort of tenuousness in the real world. Just like you wouldn't expect to find the other odd creatures the English girl met when she fell down the rabbit hole. However, when it comes to bizarre creatures and curious behavior, our world can be even odder than Lewis Carroll's.

In the Tennessee Valley, there's a small gelatinous creature that is virtually transparent, with only a slight hint of white or green to give its corporeal form any sort of hue. Its body is 99 percent water and has no skeleton or head or much in the way of specialized organs for respiration or excretion. The creature does have a mouth, a long tubular stomach, rudimentary sense organs and gonads—but little else.

Freshwater jellyfish are ethereal things that live a double life. For most of their existence, they're underwater polyps, so small and well camouflaged they are virtually invisible. Studying them, or even finding them, is a difficult undertaking. At times, however, on hot summer days, these polyps go through a transformation. They produce medusae that look like those of the umbrella-shaped jellyfish most of us know from trips to the beach, except the medusae of freshwater jellyfish remain small—pinhead to quarter sized, depending on their age. These milky-clear creatures rise towards the light and drift back down into the depths hunting for food, creating a shimmering effect just below the surface. Often the medusae are seen floating or swimming in clusters of hundreds, even thousands. These clusters are called "blooms." It's during these medusa outbursts that they become seeable, similar to Alice's feline, but like the Cheshire Cat, predicting when and where they'll appear borders on the impossible.

A MYSTERY, INSIDE AN ENIGMA

Like Alice's story, our account begins in England, so perhaps we should borrow a snippet from a radio broadcast made by Winston Churchill in 1939. Freshwater jellyfish are "a riddle, wrapped in a mystery, inside an enigma." He was speaking of the Russians; we're talking about near-invisible gelatinous wisps.

To begin with, these jellies are not true jellyfish. They are in a different biological class than marine jellyfish. But since the two groups look and act similarly, they both are referred to as "jellyfish." Although the genus obelia, in the class hydrozoa, are aquatic and also have polyp and medusa stages, freshwater jellyfish are classified as cnidarians in the biological phylum cnidaria. If this sounds like biology 101, bear with me. The cnidarians is a large biological group that contains over ten thousand species of animals (corals, jellyfish, hydras, anemones) found exclusively in marine or freshwater aquatic environments, although they are predominantly marine species. Their distinguishing feature is specialized stinging cells that are used mainly for capturing prey. The body of a freshwater jellyfish consists of a nonliving jelly-like substance, sandwiched between two layers of tissue that are mostly one cell thick. They have two basic body forms: swimming medusa and sessile polyps, both of which are radially symmetrical with mouths. The medusa have tentacles, the polyps do not. These cnidarians have a single body cavity and orifice that is used for digestion, elimination, and respiration. They are simple creatures, almost as simple as you can be and still be alive. In 1979, if you were lucky enough to see *Life on Earth: A Natural History by David Attenborough* presented by the BBC, you know that life on this planet comes in an astonishing array of forms. The fact that I live a six-and-a-half-hour drive from the closest seashore and am writing about local jellyfish under-scores that fact. Life finds a way to shimmy itself into every available niche.

Freshwater jellyfish seem to prefer the still water of ponds, flooded rock quarries, and impoundments behind dams, but they also can be found in slow-moving water with a slight current. According to the authority on the topic, Dr. Terry Peard of Indiana University of Pennsylvania now retired, the appearance of freshwater jellyfish is sporadic and unpredictable. Often they may appear in a body of water in small or large numbers, even though they were never reported there before. The following year they may be ab-sent and may not reappear until several years later. It is also possible for the jellyfish to appear once and never appear in that same location again. Poof! The Cheshire Cat is gone!

Another oddity: The erratic blooms of jellyfish are the only times in their lives that these creatures are sexual beings; yet, most of these occurrences apparently are all male or all female, which seems to discourage any sexual reproduction. They have gonads but rarely get to use them. This flies in the face of convention because it keeps down genetic variation. And genetic varia-tion is nature's driving force. This could explain why in North America there appeared to be only one known species of the jellies that live in freshwater, until Dr. Peard only recently began collecting information about a rare Asian species in the genus Limnocnida now appearing in our part of the world.

Peard maintains a website—freshwaterjellyfish.org—to provide informa-tion and collect data on sightings of the here-one-minute-and-gone-the-next jellies. He has been studying the short-lived cnidarians for over twenty years.

"I first became interested in freshwater jellies in the early 1990s when one of my university students brought some to my office for identification," emailed Dr. Peard. "She had collected them in a quiet river cove where she and friends frequently swim. At the time, the organism was described as rare in many accounts in the literature. So, here I was with a local supply of a 'rare' organism! That was my motivation to focus on the animal for further study."

FIRST CONTACT: THEIR DISCOVERY

This account makes the creature seem somewhat transient, as though its hold on life is precarious at best; yet, fossil records date the organism back to the Cambrian Explosion, or roughly 570 million years ago, a time when life was simple and asexual reproduction was the norm. It has the oldest pedigree of anything you'll read about in this book. Nonetheless, despite this antiquity, their here-one-minute-and-gone-the-next lifestyle left the tiny aquatic invertebrates undiscovered by scientists until, incredibly, they were first found in a water lily tank in Regent's Park Gardens in London, England, on June 10, 1880, just nine years after the publication of *Through the Looking-Glass, and What Alice Found There.*

The secretary of the Royal Botanical Society, William Sowerby, first discovered the tiny free-swimming medusas in a tank devoted to the cultivation of the large water lily, *Victoria regia.* Intrigued, he gave samples to several people, two of whom were Dr. George Allman, a zoology professor, and naturalist E. Ray Lankester. Both must have instantly recognized the significance of the find because at that time all known jellyfish lived in saltwater. Allman visited the park himself and found the tank "literally swarming with little medusae."

Both men rushed to publish an account of the unique creature. Lankester's appeared first in the journal *Nature* on June 17, 1880, only one week after the jellyfish were discovered. In it, he gave a detailed description of the creature and proposed the Latin name *Craspedacusta sowerbii,* in part, to honor the jellyfish's discoverer (from the Latin *craspedon* for "velum" and the Greek "kystis" for bladder, and *sowerbii* for William Sowerby). Lankester commented, "It is exceedingly difficult to trace the introduction of the animal into the tank in the Regent's Park, since no plants have been recently (within twelve months) added to the lily-house, and the water is run off every year." He also wondered if the warm water the jellies occurred in meant that they were originally from the tropics.

Professor Allman's account was published only one week later in the same journal, dated June 24, 1880. "They were very energetic in their movements, swimming with the characteristic systole and diastole of their umbrella, and apparently in the very conditions which contributed most completely to their well-being," wrote Allman, who also gave a complete detailed physical description of the exceptional find, remarking that the water temperature had been quite warm, 86°F, and proposed the name with nod toward the reigning queen *Limnocodium victoria.*

In the same issue of *Nature* appears a letter from Lankester, an apology, stating that he was unaware that so esteemed a zoologist as Allman was also working on the find and humbly offered to withdraw his name from contention. He remarked that there is a "certain kind of honour" between zoologists and that even though he had worked day and night getting his paper ready, the right to name the little novelty should go to his senior, Allman.

For several years an informal compromise was reached; scientists used a combination of the two names, *Limnocodium sowerbii,* when referring to the new creature. In 1907, Alfred Mayer attempted to clear up the naming issue and have the compromise name formally adopted. He petitioned the International Commission on Zoological Nomenclature. Their ruling found that the combination name violated the accepted rules of nomenclature and that the first published name had priority, that being the name supplied by naturalist Lankester; and the London medusae have been known as *Craspedacusta sowerbii* ever since, although some are quick to point out that the correct Latinized version to honor the jelly's discoverer William Sowerby, should be *sowerbyi.* Consequently, you also see *Craspedacusta sowerbyi* (lapsus) being used, with the Latin word for "error" in parentheses, correcting the original involuntary mistake made by Lankester in 1880. In the world of scientific nomenclature, there is often disagreement. Therefore, *Craspedacusta sowerbyi* is known as a synonym, separate but not interchangeable with or equal to the original, so *sowerbii* it is. If William Sowerby had been a female, the correct specific name would have been *sowerbyae.*

It is remarkable that such a unique organism—the world's first reported freshwater jellyfish—should be discovered not in a remote pristine freshwater pool but in an artificial tank in a major urban area. Life finds a way. Regent's Park is located on the north side of the English capital, only a few blocks from the Houses of Parliament and the River Thames. It only proves that you really don't have to go that far to find extraordinary things. (So put down this book right now, go outside, and look around.)

As is their habit, like the Cheshire Cat, the celebrated medusae soon disappeared from Regent's Park. Nevertheless, the story doesn't end there; tiny *C. sowerbii* would go on to prove that even more improbable surprises lay ahead.

The small jellyfish was found again, more than twenty years later, in similar circumstances—artificial tanks used to cultivate the water lily *Victoria regia*—in Lyon, France, in 1901 and in a basin at a botanical garden in Munich, Germany, in 1905.

Two years later the jellyfish quietly appeared again in a fourth location. This time, August 1907, it was across the Atlantic. A small bottle containing live medusae was sent to the office of Charles Hargitt at the Bureau of Fisheries, Woods Hole in Massachusetts. The jellyfish had been collected in Washington, D.C., in a greenhouse aquarium belonging to florist W. B. Shaw, who for many years had cultivated several species of tropical water lilies. Shaw's hothouse had six artificial tanks, each of which were twelve feet long, three feet wide, and three feet deep. All six were stocked the same way with identical sorts of plants and a species of paradise fish. The water lily *Victoria regia* was not being grown.

The tanks were used chiefly in fall, winter, and spring to carry over the delicate plants and had been used for six to eight years without significant change of water. The water that had been added was put in to replace the amount lost to evaporation. Even though all six tanks were stocked and treated the same, the small jellyfish only appeared in one of the six. Still, the connection to artificial tanks and exotic tropical plants seemed obvious to Hargitt—that is, until the proprietor of the greenhouse assured him that only seeds of water lilies were imported and propagated in the aquatic containers.

When the medusae were first found in the Washington tank, they were of considerable numbers and in a range of sizes, "some as small as a pin's head and some one-fourth inch in diameter."

The Washington medusae "disappeared as mysteriously as they came," Hargitt added, and "not a single specimen could be found where for weeks they had been abundant." Mystified, Hargitt obtained a variety of materials from the medusa tank: plants, algae slime scrapings, and other items from the sides and bottom. He was hoping to discover some clue concerning the lifecycle of the jellyfish. The samples were carefully and frequently examined over several succeeding days with "no trace" of the jellyfish ever being found. Poof! Gone again, Alice.

Curiously, in all four of these initial jellyfish discoveries, spanning twenty-seven years and four separate countries on both sides of the Atlantic, the medusae were determined to all be males. Hargitt reported that the specimens sent to his office from Washington in 1907 were indeed all males, some young and some sexually mature, "with gonads bursting with ripe spermatozoa."

Hargitt added, "Great interest was aroused at the time, chiefly by reason of the then regarded anomalousness of its habitat, but also by reason of certain other features more or less peculiar, such as the apparent absence of female medusae, and yet the occurrence of young apparently arising directly from eggs."

Hargitt refused to even speculate on the lack of females; their absence only heightened the mystery surrounding the aquatic creatures.

The next recorded occurrence of freshwater jellyfish in North America was even more baffling. Early one morning, on September 27, 1916, a "large bottle of creek water" was brought to Harrison Garman at the University of Kentucky. It contained the remainders, badly decomposed, of several small gelatinous creatures. Garman recognized them as parts of jellyfish medusas. The bottle of deceased jellyfish came from C. M. Bridgemord, who asserted that he had seen "millions" in Benson Creek near Frankfort, only twenty-five miles from Lexington.

That afternoon Garman investigated the find, traveling by motorboat with Bridgemord, Ben Marshall, and J. L. Cox down the Kentucky River and up Benson Creek. The river had been dammed below the tributary's mouth, so lake water backed up into the stream, "producing a rather narrow, deep body of water with little current," as Garman wrote in the journal *Science*. About half a mile up the backwater, they came to the point where the medusae had been collected. Garman remembered the water as being quite warm and murky; there was little breeze. To their amazement, the four men in the boat soon started to see millions of medusae shimmering just below the surface. All four men began filling containers—bottles and jars—with the small translucent creatures.

"I have worked on the aquatic animals of Kentucky waters for many years," wrote Garman, "and was not prepared to believe that medusae would ever be found within the state in such numbers." Garman took several hundred live jellyfish back to Lexington for study, reporting later that they slowly began to die "one by one." The last survived only until the afternoon of the next day, September 28. Garman published a detailed anatomical description of the medusae he collected and concluded his narrative by remarking that "where this multitude of medusae came from is a mystery."

The appearance of freshwater jellyfish in Benson Creek "far removed from any possible source of artificial introduction," wrote Charles Hargitt in 1919, "at once utterly discredited the earlier assumption of distribution by artificial means from tropical sources." There were no tropical water lilies in Benson Creek. Hagitt continued, "Those found in the Kentucky creek apparently disappeared very suddenly, as did those in the Washington aquaria . . . on the approach of cooler weather; and in neither of these localities have they reappeared, as far as known."

The next recorded jellyfish blooms happened in 1918 and again in 1919 in Boss Lake near Elkhart, Indiana. The impoundment was not a natural lake but had been constructed by J. C. Boss. It was the result of a dam built across the St. Joseph River. Boss Lake covered about four acres, was separated from the dam's backwater by a large dike, and fed by surface spring water and an artesian well. In 1918, a few medusae were spotted in the manmade lake. The following year, in August, there were ten days in which "millions" were seen. "They come to the surface on warm sunshine days," reported Boss.

Both the Kentucky and Indiana discoveries were, still yet, isolated occurrences; but they seemed to establish a correlation between the sudden

jellyfish blooms and backwater created by dams. A link between either occurrence and those in the greenhouse artificial tank in Washington or the
ones in Europe was much harder to fathom.

By 1937, freshwater jellyfish had found their way to nineteen states, mostly
in the East. They would appear and mysteriously disappear, turning up in
lots of unusual places: the Willamette River in Oregon, a concrete garden
pool in Illinois, an old gravel pit in Indiana, a goldfish pond in Virginia, the
Huron River in Michigan, Mrs. William Pappas's garden pool in Texas, the
reservoir water supply for Birmingham in Alabama, Cranberry Lake in New
Jersey, an old quarry near Gettysburg, and an indoor (yes, indoor) twenty-
gallon aquarium owned by Eloise Kuntz in Washington State. Clearly, tiny
C. sowerbii had a talent for getting around, but how? And—hold onto your
fedora—some of these gelatinous phantoms were female. Finally!

Lewis Carroll's work is classified in the genre "Literary Nonsense." It's a
mix of real and unreal, and wordplay; freshwater jellies seem to belong in
Wonderland, although they are very much real.

THE JELLIES FIND THE VOLUNTEER STATE

Tennessee joined that list in 1938. A bloom of jellyfish was discovered in
Knox County on July 15 in Andrew Jackson Lake (now called Dead Horse
Lake), a privately owned body of water about twelve miles west of downtown
Knoxville and about the same from where I write these words. Sara Betty
Fowler collected a sampling, and half a dozen live jellyfish were delivered
to the office of Edwin Powers, department of zoology at the University of
Tennessee. Powers visited the fifty- to sixty-five-acre lake that afternoon and
saw thousands of medusae swimming near the surface. He collected another
group of around three hundred and placed them in an un-aerated aquarium.
By July 18, most appeared to be nearly dead, but eleven of the more active
specimens were preserved and later identified as being all females. By the
time *C. sowerbii* made it to the Volunteer State, it had been established that
the medusae were indeed either male or female but, strangely, as far as gender
goes, they seemed to occur separately.

Harry McCann, custodian of the Knox County lake, reported that 1938
had been the third year in a row that the jellyfish had appeared in the lake
and that each occurrence had lasted about forty-five days. At the end of each
bloom, they had "more or less suddenly disappeared."

In the mid-1970s, probably August 1975, Bob Terry witnessed the "Mother
of all blooms" on Norris Lake in Union County. At the time, Terry was a

scientific aide for the Tennessee Valley Authority, working out of the Norris Aquatic Biological Laboratory. The lab got a call about a "Red Tide" on the lake at the Highway 33 Bridge. Terry and a coworker were sent to investigate. Stopping on the south side of the bridge they could see that the water mid-channel to the north shoreline had a slight pinkish cast. They crossed the bridge to get a closer look. At the time, Seymour's 33 Bridge Marina was located at the base of the bridge on the north shoreline. There they collected a gallon or more of water filled with the shimmering creatures and took them back to the lab at Norris, where they were identified as *C. sowerbii*. "We'd never seen anything like it before," said Terry. Amazed, they all watched the creatures moving up and down in a bell jar.

Close to thirty years later, Terry and I drove back to the Highway 33 Bridge to have a look. It was late summer; a perfect azure sky towered overhead. The marina that had existed on the north shoreline was now gone with nothing to mark its existence. Terry pointed out the great length the bloom had stretched that day in the 1970s, from Point Marker 27 west of the bridge to around the bend and completely out of sight to the east, perhaps covering as much as half the river's width. A bloom that covered that many square yards would have comprised millions of tiny jellies. It's overwhelming to think of so many in one place, especially when you remember that their first known foray into America in 1907 was confined to a twelve-foot tank.

"Seeing the jellyfish is a privilege," said Terry. "What gave the bloom the pinkish cast is a mystery. Perhaps it was just the way the light was reflecting off them that day."

By 1987, freshwater jellyfish had spread throughout the Tennessee Valley. Bruce Yeager reported on the drainage-wide occurrence of freshwater jellyfish. He stated that "the Tennessee River system represents one of the few examples in North America of watershed colonization, rather than isolated occurrence of this organism." Yeager cited historical records and forty-two collections made at thirteen sites along 673 miles of the river. Freshwater jellyfish had been found in seven mainstream lake reservoirs on the Tennessee River and in at least two tributaries: the Norris and Douglas Reservoirs.

By the time of Yeager's account, freshwater jellyfish had been documented at twenty-three locations in the Tennessee Valley and along the Tennessee River in Alabama and extreme northeast Mississippi. Twenty-three locations aren't a lot in forty-nine years, but most of the sightings came in the late '70s and early '80s, indicating that the jellies were becoming more common and widespread or, at least, more noticed. The year 1978 was a big one, with

C. sowerbii turning up at eight sites in Tennessee, but the little Cheshires were appearing and disappearing all around the globe.

This led to a host of common names. To list a few: in the United States and Great Britain, it is simply known as freshwater jellyfish; in Austria it's Süßwassermeduse; in the Czech Republic, medúzka sladkovodní; in Germany, Süßwasserqualle; in Finland, Lammikokmeduusa; in Lithuania, gėlavandenė medusa; in Sweden, Sötvattens manet; and in the Netherlands, Zoetwaterkwal. (Don't worry; there will be no pop quiz at the end of the chapter.) And the list of scientific binomials has been a jumble as well, but again the first published name has priority, the name supplied and misspelled by naturalist Lankester in 1880: *Craspedacusta sowerbii*.

"It's a strange fact about science that until an object or a phenomenon receives a name in some way it does not exist. Names really matter. They retrieve something from the endless chaos of anonymity into a world of lists, inventories, and classification. The next stage is to understand their meaning," wrote British paleontologist Richard Fortey.

AN ODD CREATURE WITH AN ODDER LIFE HISTORY

By the 1990s, more had been learned about the lifecycle of freshwater jellyfish. When a free-floating *C. sowerbii* egg hatches, the emerging tiny, flat, free-swimming larva is called a planula. Soon it settles onto an underwater surface. There it moves around for a short time before attaching one end of itself to the hard object. It soon develops into a polyp, a stalk-like hydra with no tentacles. The immobile polyp is a clear animal that looks like a miniscule, hollow bowling pin made of jelly. It's less than one-tenth of an inch long and is permanently attached to the underwater substrate: a rock, a plant, a tree stump, or perhaps even a floating object. As a polyp, *C. sowerbii* appears to be more plant than animal and can remain this way for years, feeding on whatever zooplankton (tiny animals) that haphazardly float by. The polyp's mouth is edged with special stinging cells called nematocysts. Inside each nematocyst is a tiny, barbed, whip-like structure. When a zooplankton floats by, the whip strikes out and pierces the animal's skin like a hollow harpoon. A chemical is injected, and the tiny morsel is paralyzed and consumed.

The polyp reproduces asexually, so there's no need for separate sexes. It merely grows a bud, an exact copy of itself, attached to its translucent body. In this way, if the conditions are right, a single polyp can become a colony of two, three, or more matching polyps, all attached to each other at the base.

The colonial polyps secrete a sticky mucous that in time becomes covered with all manner of particles, camouflaging the creature's location.

A polyp has another asexual trick up its metaphoric sleeve. Again, if conditions are favorable, it can grow a bud called a frustule that, unlike the polyp itself, can crawl away to another location. The frustule is a tiny cigar-shaped larva. There seems to be a correlation between polyp feeding and the distance the frustule can travel: the more energy stored, the longer the journey. The frustule eventually sets up camp for itself and develops into another polyp to produce a colony of its own—essentially clones. This is a remarkably creative way to expand an empire and live inconspicuously. In this manner, theoretically, the jellyfish polyps could spread to fill an entire lake. The only known predators of these polyps are crayfish and turtles.

In the winter, cold weather forces the polyps to contract into "resting bodies." In this dormant state, the polyps become flattened cellular disks known as podocysts, which surround themselves with a protective chitin-like membrane. It is believed that the podocysts can be transported from one body of water to another, carried by aquatic plants and animals, and perhaps are able to hitchhike on the feet of waterfowl such as herons. Dr Peard added that they can "even be blown about by the wind if they become exposed above the water line." Thus the podocysts are like space travelers held in suspended animation, waiting to be transported to new worlds. Miniscule aquatic animals being blown about like motes of dust. Some land in water. When warm weather returns, these dormant disks wake up and rehydrate becoming polyps once again, and new colonies are formed. I know, this sounds a little like Ridley Scott's 1979 movie *Alien,* but freshwater jellies are much more benign.

Still yet, a third type of bud may be produced asexually.

"In this case, a few cells form a small medusa bud attached upside down at the central region of the medusa umbrella near the top of the polyp," emailed Dr. Peard. "The small medusa bud grows to about one millimeter in diameter and develops eight small tentacles by the time it is released into the water from the polyp."

In the laboratory, it has been found that well-fed polyps cultured at 68°F will begin to produce medusa buds when the water temperature is raised to 77–80°F and will peak in medusa production in two to three weeks if the water is maintained at that temperature. Conversely, in the lab, when the water temperature is dropped to 42–50°F, the medusae "invert and lose much of their medusoid form." The jellyfish can't tolerate cold water.

Forgive me if I am going into too much detail describing their life stages—I have overwhelmed myself just creating this account—but the chance of you getting to see any of this is not great. It's okay to skip ahead, but this biography is a remarkable description of an astonishing life form that generally goes unnoticed.

The medusae themselves are round, between five to twenty-five millimeters (twenty-five millimeters equals 0.984 inches, the diameter of a U.S. quarter). When fully matured, a total of fifty to five hundred tentacles hang from various levels around the marginal ring; four of the tentacles are long and probably help the medusa stabilize itself while it floats up and down like gossamer goo. The outer umbrella-shaped bell is transparent, and the internal organs are a slightly opaque white. Like an umbrella, a central tube called a *manubrium* hangs down in the middle of the creature's mouth with four frilly lobes at the bottom. Four radial canals that originate at the edges of the stomach circulate nutrients. The medusae are either male or female, having four large, flat sex organs; attached to the same four radial canals, the gonads are usually opaque white.

But again, oddly—and I've already used the word "odd" six times in this account—as a general rule every bloom is either all boys or all girls—although, it has been observed (but only rarely in nature) that these segregated clusters do get together because sexual reproduction does happen, and occasionally eggs are created that give rise once again to free-swimming larvae. The cycle is reborn.

It is widely believed that *C. sowerbii* has found its way around the world through human activities. The importation and cultivation of exotic plants and the construction of dams that impound rivers have certainly benefited its spread. The colonial polyps have also been documented as underwater passengers riding on the hulls of ships or floating alga mats or pieces of wood.

It has also been suggested that the advent of plastics and the rise of floatable trash have given the hitchhiking polyps another means of quietly getting from place to place. If you've ever worked a shoreline trash cleanup such as the annual Ijams's River Rescue, you know that we humans carelessly use our rivers as garbage bins. Thousands of plastic bottles and disposable coffee cups float down the rivers of this country annually. They collect momentarily in quiet coves and behind dams until storm waters and high winds move them along. This could be one way the entire Tennessee River system has been colonized by the passive jellyfish.

Some believe the jellies originated in South America, probably somewhere in the Amazon regions of Brazil. Yet, most biologists now believe that *C.*

sowerbii originated in the Yangtze River system in China (the Chinese call them peach blossom fish) and was transported originally on ornamental aquatic plants. Since the late 1800s, the jellyfish have slowly spread to still-water locations around the world and to all continents except Antarctica. It is altogether possible that in their original home, the Yangtze River, social mixers, where the males and females could meet, were much less inhibited.

Predicting where the medusas will materialize next is difficult. From time to time, they make headlines in local newspapers because their appearance is such a *rara avis,* as if the Cheshire Cat suddenly appears in city hall only to disappear with a grin.

In September of 1997, they were found in Mead's Quarry Lake in south Knox County, very near my home. A sampling was taken to Ijams Nature Center before I worked there and TVA's Bob Terry was called in again to identify the mysterious creatures. A story about the jellies by Morgan Simmons made the front page of the *Knoxville News Sentinel.* "Delicate little beasts, but beautiful, and more fun to watch than a lava lamp," said Terry at the time. He took a small jarful home and was able to keep them alive for a short time, feeding them fresh spring water naturally filled of zooplankton. Three years later, in July 2000, the jellyfish appeared again in Mead's Quarry. Ben Nanny, Sean Blevins, and Maggie Michael, three CAC AmeriCorps members at the time, were near the water's surface and saw a small bloom. "At first we wondered what they were," said Blevins. "They were so small it wasn't readily apparent. But, when we looked closer, they appeared to be tiny jellyfish."

On September 9 of the same year, the *Kingsport Times-News* carried a story about their sudden appearance in the front-yard pond of Glenda Clemons in Scott County, Virginia, just north of the Tennessee state line. "Isn't this weird?" she is quoted to have said. The entire community was entertained for a time as if a traveling circus had come to town.

Freshwater jellyfish made national news in 2003. On September 22, National Public Radio's *All Things Considered* reported that an eleven-year-old schoolgirl named Alex Fegley had discovered the tiny jellies in a pond at Grand Island, Nebraska. She had become an overnight celebrity for being the first person to discover and verify the small jellies in her state. NPR's Robert Siegel interviewed Alex, who seemed quite blasé about her instant notoriety. Fame comes, then it goes, just like *C. sowerbii.* Siegel apologized, stating that NPR had picked up on the jellyfish invasion rather late since they had, after all, already been found in over forty states. They are now so widespread, Dr. Peard wrote, "they are no longer considered rare, just sporadic and unpredictable."

Since they first appeared in the United States in 1907, freshwater jellyfish have revealed themselves in every state except Alaska, Montana, Wyoming, North Dakota, and South Dakota and by the time you read this, they may have appeared in all of those. The spread of the weird jellyfish seems innocent enough; it has not proved as invasive as kudzu, at least not yet. Its Cheshire Cat act is more of a county fair sideshow curiosity. Yet, its hop-skip-and-jump journey around the globe—from Yangtze River, to botanical garden, to Benson Creek, to goldfish pond, to rock quarry, to the entire Tennessee Valley and beyond—does illustrate how, by simple means and random acts, an exotic species can find a way to get around.

As history shows, they're likely to appear just about anywhere on hot summer days, if conditions are right; and then they disappear from the spot, perhaps never to be seen again. Freshwater jellyfish are remarkable animals, simple, and efficient. Their very existence succinctly illustrates that life on our blue-green planet is exceptionally robust and diverse, even if some seem fragile and frail.

"Elegance incarnate, pulsing, contracting, almost flying through the water, apparently dancing to some music that our ears cannot sample," wrote Richard Fortey in his book about animals that time had left behind. "Yes, this is the nub of it: jellyfish are spookily beautiful, spun out of something that has little substance yet can engender complex form." Yes, fragile and frail but from a bloodline, if you can call it that, millions of years aged.

Bob Terry is now retired from TVA. When I visited him at his Black Oak Ridge home, where he lives with his wife, Jean, he was quickly able to find his sample bottle. It was tucked away in a plastic tub—his personal cabinet of curiosities—with an assortment of containers all filled with natural oddities floating in preservative: velvet ants, black widow spiders, giant water bugs.

Rummaging through the vials, he found what he was looking for and handed me a small bottle neatly labeled, "Freshwater Jellyfish. *Craspedacusta sowerbyi*. Mead's Quarry. September 18, 1997." Like the other containers in the collection, it was filled with alcohol but the tiny jellyfish inside had disintegrated; after all, it is a creature that's almost all water. "It's not easy to preserve them," said Terry. We both squinted, looking at the bottle's clear contents, swirling it around and looking again. Nothing really remained to mark its corporeal existence. It seemed, as is its whim, the Cheshire Cat had vanished once again.

"CURIOUSER AND CURIOUSER!" CRIED ALICE

After stalking *C. sowerbii,* a.k.a. *sowerbyi,* for years during proper season (the heat of a fading summer, August and September) and even finding a scattered few, I had not yet seen the elusive Mead's Quarry Cheshire Cat up-close. That ended with a phone call from Jim Matheny late in August 2015.

To say Jim is a reporter for WBIR Channel 10, the NBC affiliate in Knoxville, is a bit too simplistic. In a day when station owners require their reporters to do more, Jim does more. He's a news team of one—reporter, writer, videographer, editor, and producer—and he has won awards in many of those disciplines. He'll readily admit that TV journalism is his second career, but his résumé pre-newsman trained him in a lot of job skills that later coalesced into the toolbox he carries today.

Matheny's curiosity was sparked on his day off. But a good reporter really doesn't take a day off; there's always the hunger for the next story. He had rented a paddleboard to relax and explore Mead's Quarry Lake on a Sunday afternoon. It was there, under a robin's-egg-blue sky, just below the 180-foot cliff that once had been solid limestone, he encountered a significant bloom of jellies.

It was one of those "What the heck?" moments. Curiosity piqued, he called the nature center the next day and found me. And yes, I had the answers to his questions. I knew "What the heck."

After our half-hour conversation about their life histories—part asexual, part sexual; their transformation from planula to polyp to medusa; their fortuitous global journey from the Yangtze to Regents Park to Dead Horse to Mead's Quarry Lake—Jim felt he had enough to do a proper story. And in a world of three-minute reports, he felt sure he had enough for a longer feature about the evanescent jellies, quirky little Cheshires that they are. Then the writer/videographer in him took over and by the time we met on the lake a few days later, Matheny only needed a bit of on-camera me to flesh out their account.

Matheny's story aired on WBIR at 5:30 p.m. on Monday, August 31. It's perhaps one of the smallest living things the venerable NBC affiliate had ever showcased in such detail. Six months later, Matheny would win a regional Edward R. Morrow Award for this and two other nature features.

Watching the account, it looks like I'm the only one paddling around the lake chasing the Lilliputian invertebrates. That's a romantic Thoreauvian notion, but in this case it's untrue. Always nearby, just off camera, was a red canoe that contained the story's entire TV crew, all housed in newsman

Matheny. He had also figured out how to get his GoPro video camera to glide smoothly underwater behind his canoe using a length of twine, an empty water bottle for buoyancy, and wrenches for ballast. His cobbled-together creation should be forever known as the "Matheny Rig" because it worked perfectly. That *en plein air* video, plus what he clicked off at home in a make-shift miniature studio, made his jellyfish footage matchless. He even captured one of the jellies swimming just above a penny, proving that they were indeed coin-sized. Lincoln has never appeared in an odder juxtaposition.

Transparent, the little beasties are hard to notice and hard not to notice at the same time. Matheny's story generated a bit of buzz. Folks began to go to the quarry to rent paddleboards, kayaks, and canoes to look for them, a perfect curtain call to the summer of 2015.

Talk of the jellyfish bloom brought Brent LeTellier to the quarry lake. His daughter Nicole worked at the canoe rental site there. LeTellier and his brothers grew up on the coast and warm waters off Saudi Arabia. They routinely explored whatever flotsam and jetsam, living or dead, that washed up onto the beach, including the venom of various jellyfish. He was no stranger to abnormal aquatic life, and he was curious. LeTellier had heard that the fresh-water jellies at Mead's did not sting. Was this true? His experience with their ilk had taught him otherwise. Initially, he placed about ten on his forearm and got no obvious skin reaction, so he decided to up the ante and popped one in his mouth. His wife did the same.

"My wife, being the smarter one, immediately spit out the jelly after sensing a very slight tingling sensation" remembered LaTellier. "On the 9-volt battery to the tongue scale, she rated it around a two or three."

On the other hand, LaTellier did not feel any sensation for about thirty seconds.

"Then the tip and sides of my tongue became slightly numb. However, after about five minutes, my throat was scratchy sore like a very mild cold, and noticed a slight change in my voice, a drop in octave," he added.

After that, no further symptoms arose.

The adventurous LaTellier concluded, "The slight stomach discomfort experienced that night was probably better correlated to a spicy taco. Can't say our jellyfish tasting holds scientific validity, but they do have some venomous punch, just not as much as a good taco."

News travels fast. The jell-emonium garnered the interest of another TV station. News anchor and thirty-year veteran Alan Williams has worked for all three local TV news departments: WBIR, WATE, and WVLT. He's also from Knoxville, so he knew a good quirky local story when he heard one, perfect for kicking off the Labor Day weekend.

Alan and photojournalist Keith Smith met me at the same lake and we talked jelly. The gelatinous cnidarian with trailing stinging tentacles made the WVLT Local 8's six-o'clock news by the end of the week. That's the hard news hour, but who doesn't prefer a nice freakish feature to a convenience store robbery or home break-in?

ALONE AT LAST

Labor Day 2015, and it's quiet, without labor. I'm sitting at a desk in my darkened studio, sketching *C. sowerbii*, the results of which serve as the frontispiece for this sequence of events. A lone desk lamp lights my work. Before me is a gallon jar that once held Mt. Olive dill pickles; now it holds translucent jellies. Watching them undulate, move up and down in the water, is mesmerizing. Yes, indeed, Bob Terry, it's like watching a lava lamp. If I could keep them alive like goldfish or tetras, I would. But I know I cannot. Their medusa phase is short, so once I am finished sketching, I'll return them to Mead's Quarry Lake.

Can there be anything more fleeting? Even newsman Matheny noted, "You are fond of that phrase, 'Ephemeral by nature,' aren't you?"

"Well yeah," I replied. "It's the title of my next book, and I can't think of anything more metaphoric than these jellies. They come; they go. But don't we all?"

And even Lewis Carroll knew when to put away his Cheshire Cat.

Balea 2016JUN29

Monarch Butterfly
Danaus plexippus

I take this evanescence and lubricity of all objects,
which lets them slip through our fingers
when we clutch hardest,
to be the most unhandsome part of our condition.

—Ralph Waldo Emerson

IN THIS CASE, lubricity means "fleeting nature," or at least that's what the Sage of Concord had in mind. Perhaps he was even thinking about butterflies. Have you ever tried to catch one?

Working as a naturalist at a nature center can hardly be called work. It's a ten-year-old's fantasy job, and I have several very young naturalists—Chloe, Lucy, Josie, Judah, Asha, Aiden, Abby, Jacob, Annabel, Oliver, Jackson, Phia, Rachel, Riley—with résumé in hand, patiently waiting in the wings for me to retire. It's more like an everyday vacation. You really go on trips more for a change of scenery than anything else. In October 2003, I vacationed with Lindalee Fortney-Thomas on Cherry Grove Beach in South Carolina. The weather was ideal: sunny with warm breezes.

The great joy of being a naturalist is that you are never at a loss for amusement. All you have to do is go outside. Visiting an unfamiliar location heightens your senses; nature does not disappoint. Over the course of five days, we counted 607 passing monarch butterflies at Cherry Grove and at various other spots along the coast, south to Huntington Beach State Park. The monarchs kept winging by us one by one like animated glitter in a snow globe. I may have counted the same one twice, but considering the vast space we are talking about, I doubt it. Most of those I counted from the fourth floor balcony of a condo overlooking the ocean. At times, as many as four or five a minute fluttered by, seemingly in no real hurry. They have two forms of locomotion: either powered flight or gliding on favorable winds. This section of coastline serves as a monarch flyway because if you draw a line on a map from Cherry Grove to Huntington, the line points south to the gulf and beyond. Averaging roughly twenty-five to thirty miles per day, these monarchs were migrating south for the winter.

But this coastal flyway doesn't start at Cherry Grove. Six years later, Karen Webster and I spent a week at Avalon Beach, New Jersey, north of Cape May, the guests of Kimberly Dmytro. South of Avalon is Cape May Point State Park, a birding mecca, especially in the fall. From September to December, migratory birds pass over the narrow finger of land, the last piece of New Jersey shoreline before the Delaware Bay. If the conditions are not right, the birds linger in the area before crossing the open water. Wouldn't you?

First, warblers migrate through, then birds of prey, and finally, late in the season, the ducks. In early October, it's the raptors. There's a large, wooden bird-watching platform built between the lighthouse and pond where the Cape May Hawk Watch takes place. Most days it's crowded with people looking up or out or across, watching. The first day we were there was accipiter day: 358 sharp-shinned and 455 Cooper's hawks were counted. There were also 97 kestrels and 205 broad-winged hawks. Most were high overhead; you had to crane your neck skyward. But you can only do that for so long. In time, we noticed activity much closer to the ground. People with the Monarch Monitoring Project were netting the lithe lepidopterans and tagging them with tiny numbered stickers. This project also falls under the auspices of the Cape May Bird Observatory, a research wing of the New Jersey Audubon Society.

The butterfly count runs from September 1 until October 31, and since its inception in 1991, thousands of monarchs have been tagged on their way south. When we were there, artist and naturalist Louise Zemaitis and others with the monitoring program were tagging the orange and black butterflies and letting others release them.

Their next stopover would be Cape Henlopen and the Delaware shoreline, 140 miles across the bay. Karen and I had lunch on the porch at The Grille at Cape May Point, watching monarchs fly out over the water. After that it is on to Maryland, Virginia, North Carolina, and eventually Cherry Grove.

Of course, it doesn't stop there. Knoxville resident Debbie Cavanaugh remembers seeing monarchs one October several years ago at Seagrove Beach west of Panama City on the Florida panhandle. It was a perfect, calm day; the ocean was unusually flat. She and several other people were in shoulder-deep water, enjoying the gentle surf. They all were amazed as they watched dozens of the orange butterflies fly past them, headed straight out to sea over the Gulf of Mexico.

"It's just one of those kinds of memories that stay with you forever," said Cavanaugh.

STUDENTS OF NATURE

You do not have to be a ten-year-old to be fascinated by butterflies. One of the first life cycles we learn in school is that a caterpillar somehow goes through metamorphosis and changes into a butterfly: egg, larva, pupa, adult, all in a few weeks. Other insects do it, too, but it's those dainty, colorful, tissue paper-like creatures that garner our attention. How is it possible?

Some insects are like you and me. As infants, they are tiny replicas of what they will look like as adults. A one-minute-old silverfish looks like a tiny adult silverfish. Currently, the oldest known insect is named *Rhyniognatha hirsti*. It appeared during the Early Devonian Period, around 400 million years ago, when earth's first terrestrial ecosystems were being created. The first fossil turned up in a piece of chert in the village of Rhynie in Aberdeenshire, Scotland, in 1919. At first, no one knew what to make of the small thing, and it took a few years to figure out what it was and give it a name. The find makes the earliest insect older than flowering plants but younger than the ferns, horsetails, cycads, and conifers. It is believed that *R. hirsti* may have eaten fern spores and superficially resembled a modern-day silverfish.

Then something interesting happened, wrote Ferris Jabr for *Scientific American*: "Between 280 million and 300 million years ago . . . some insects began to mature a little differently—they hatched in forms that neither looked nor behaved like their adult versions. This shift proved remarkably beneficial: young and old insects were no longer competing for the same resources."

Like today's butterflies, the young ones ate one kind of food, and the mature ones ate another. They could coexist in the same place and not steal food from one another. Now this is the thing that will probably rock your understanding of life on Earth. The evolution of this survival strategy has been so successful that today, 65 percent of all animal species on our planet are metamorphosing insects. Let that sink in awhile and think about it. Sixty-five percent. That is according to one estimate on global biodiversity by the World Conservation Monitoring Centre.

So metamorphosis is not just a nature curiosity taught to fourth graders; it is a success story that is all around you—under your front porch, in your backyard, and on the empty lot down the street. The fact is made even more unbelievable when you look at the before and after of a monarch butterfly: a chunky yellow, black-and-white-striped caterpillar almost two inches long, looking like a festive Tootsie Roll, versus an orange and black-winged lepidopteran adult with a wingspan of up to four inches, an ephemeral insect with the delicacy of a paper Japanese lantern. The transformation from one to the other seems impossible, like an ancient alchemist's dream of turning lead to gold—so unimaginable that in the 1830s, a German naturalist named Renous was arrested for heresy in Chile for proposing that such was true. And you think we live in harsh times. To Chilean authorities of the time, morphing lead to gold was more believable.

Monarch caterpillars, like all other butterfly larvae, are eating machines born to consume leaves and grow large and plump quickly. For them, the world is one endless salad bar. Yet, nature has a lovely balance; each species has a host plant. Even accused heretic Renous knew that. For black swallow-tails it's fennel and Queen Anne's lace; for eastern commas it's elm trees; for gulf fritillaries it's passionflowers; for silvery checkerspots it's coneflowers; for painted ladies it's hollyhocks; and for cabbage whites, well, it's cabbage. No mystery there. The list goes on. It would not benefit butterflies as a whole if all their caterpillars ate the same leaves, so the lush green world has been divvied up. For monarchs it is the many plants in the milkweed family, which get their name from the milky thick latex they ooze. The most important food source is common milkweed *(Asclepias syriaca)*. Estimates are that 90 percent of monarchs that make it to winter have fed on this single species as a caterpillar.

Monarchs are aposematic, from the Greek *apo sema,* meaning, "away sign." It's a term coined by British evolutionary biologist Sir Edward Bagnall Poulton. His book *The Colours of Animals,* published in 1890, presented this anti-predator adaptation, as well as the importance of the exact opposite: dull-colored patterns that offer certain animals camouflage so they can hide in plain sight from predators.

The Scots have a word for it: "kenspeckled." It means "conspicuous; easily seen or recognized." Monarchs are certainly kenspeckled. Their bright, in-your-face orange and black markings warn would-be predators to stay away; they are foul tasting and toxic. It's a survival strategy that has served them well.

Monarchs are noxious because of the cardenolides or cardiac glycosides in their bodies that the caterpillars sequester from eating milkweed. These naturally occurring steroids act in heart-arresting—that is, heart-stopping—ways similar to digitalis. Once a brown thrasher attempts to eat a monarch, it upchucks, learns a valuable lesson and stays away from others. Monarchs are also healthier, with fewer parasites because of the cardenolides in their systems. It would be an absolute "Get out of jail free card" for monarchs, except that black-headed grosbeaks and black-backed orioles, two western and

Mexican species, have evolved into being cardenolide-tolerant. Nature surely doesn't abhor a vacuum, but it surely abhors an absolute. Giving monarchs absolute protection from all predators would alter the natural check and balance, and we might become hip-deep with monarchs after a few decades.

Most of us learned in elementary school about mimicry in nature. One animal looks like another because it gives it protection from predators. The example most often cited is that orange and black viceroy butterflies mimic monarchs. The same sickened brown thrasher that learns not to eat the latter will consequently avoid the former. It was taught as an example of Batesian mimicry, named for the English naturalist Henry Walter Bates, after his work on butterflies in the rainforests of Brazil. In this model, the palatable viceroy has evolved to look like the unpalatable monarch. Yet, guess what? The viceroy apparently tastes foul too. Studies conducted by David Ritland and Lincoln Brower with the Department of Zoology at the University of Florida suggest that the viceroy is just as unpalatable as the monarch. This makes their relationship an example of Müllerian mimicry, named after the German naturalist Fritz Müller, who first proposed the concept in 1878. In this model, both are toxic, and the duo have evolved as co-mimics, each imitating the appearance of the other to reinforce the warning to predators. Brown thrashers probably already knew this, so you do not have to worry about passing on the word.

The toxicity of a monarch is built up during its short life as a caterpillar, during which they go through five major developmental stages of growth. After each one, they shed their old restrictive skin much like a snake. Each distinct stage is called an instar, and after each, it is understandably larger than the previous instar as it eats and stores fats and nutrients to carry it through the nonfeeding pupal period.

Right out of the egg, the first instar is pale green and translucent, measuring as little as 0.08 inches. It would take three to equal the length of a short grain of uncooked rice. Over its larval life, it will go through four molts and develop the characteristic pattern of black, white, and yellow transverse bands and grow pairs of black tentacles on each end. Ultimately, it will reach a length of up to 1.77 inches (45 mm). That's an increase of 2,250 percent in roughly 14 days. In comparison, I grew from a twenty-four-inch newborn to a six-foot adult, an increase of only 300 percent, and it took eighteen years. And I certainly ate more than milkweed leaves.

There are really two forms of metamorphosis. Some insects go through incomplete or gradual metamorphosis with only three life stages: egg, nymph, and adult. The immature nymphs look like small adults but lack mature features such as wings and genitalia. This is true for grasshoppers, crickets, praying mantises, termites, cockroaches, and dragonflies. There is no pupal stage, no David Copperfield magic. It makes sense that gradual metamorphosis evolved before the complete. But it is the latter that produces one of the great wonders of nature, the pupa.

What goes on inside a monarch pupal chrysalis is nothing short of a miracle that took science a while to decipher, although it's not yet completely understood. (Metamorphosis for moths and beetles takes place inside cocoons, butterflies inside chrysalises.)

"First, the caterpillar digests itself, releasing enzymes to dissolve all of its tissues. If you were to cut open a cocoon or chrysalis at just the right time, caterpillar soup would ooze out. But the contents of the pupa are not entirely an amorphous mess," Ferris Jabr wrote.

"Some organs stay intact. Others, like muscles, break down into clumps of cells that can be re-used, like a Lego sculpture decomposing into bricks," noted Ed Yong for *National Geographic* online.

If you had a mind to and a good microscope, you could sift through the caterpillar ooze and find some rudimentary structures shared by both the larva and adult butterfly. Yong explained that 3-D scans of pupas "showed that the caterpillar's guts quickly change shape, becoming narrower, shorter and more convoluted." (I love it when science writers use earthy terms like "guts.")

Inside the caterpillar soup, you would also find small clumps of cells called imaginal discs. Each of these clusters is destined to be an adult body part: eye, wing, leg, genitalia. The caterpillar did not need such accouterments, but they will come in handy in its new life.

In some butterfly species, the imaginal cells remain dormant within the caterpillar throughout its short life. Yet, once a caterpillar gets tucked away inside its chrysalis and dissolves most of its tissue, these nascent organs use this protein-rich soup to fuel the growth of the adult body part. A fifty-cell imaginal disc can quickly grow to a fifty-thousand-cell monarch eye. Thus, a caterpillar reforms itself into a butterfly, a phoenix raised from the ashes of its own dissolved guts.

A monarch chrysalis is "like a rich jewel in an Ethiop's ear," to steal from Romeo, or, rather, the Bard of Avon himself. An "Ethiop" refers to someone from Ethiopia or other dark-skinned person. To the young Montague, Juliet's beauty shone as bright as a brilliant jewel on a black background. Such is the case with a monarch in its pupa stage, although it's a living jewel. Shaped something like a big toe on a size 8 foot, it's initially milky green and turns translucent as the butterfly inside begins to take its folded form.

Normally, a monarch caterpillar is instinctually adroit at finding a hidden place to molt into its chrysalis; after all, it is totally helpless during this portion of metamorphosis. But in late September 2013, one chose the armrest of a dark green bench in the plaza near a cluster of common milkweed at Ijams. It was discovered by retiree and volunteer Rex McDaniel and became a teachable location for students coming to the nature center. A monarch watch ensued.

As with all ectothermic creatures like insects, their lives are controlled by the ambient conditions. Depending on the temperature, the pupal stage can last from ten to fourteen days. For monarchs, metamorphosis from egg to adult can be as short as twenty-five days or as long as seven weeks during cooler springtime weather.

If all goes well inside the chrysalis and the butterfly successfully rearranges itself out of its own protein-rich goo and pull its guts into proper alignment, the adult emerges, expands, dries its wings, and flies away. It's nothing short of a miracle. And if the caterpillar's sole purpose was to eat and store away nutrients, then the winged adult's sole purpose is reproduction. The males and females have to find each other.

When it comes to the basic background biology on this butterfly's reproduction, a lot was unknown until the Monarch Lab at the Department of Fisheries, Wildlife and Conservation Biology at the University of Minnesota began its research. The program is under the leadership of Dr. Karen Oberhauser, who has been studying monarch butterflies since 1984.

Within adult monarchs, a pair of glands called the corpora allata, release a hormone. High levels of this so-called juvenile hormone cause eggs to mature in females and the male reproductive tract to develop. The Monarch Lab noted, "When monarchs mate, the male uses the claspers on the end of his abdomen to attach to the vaginal groove (ostium bursa) of the female. Once attached, the female cannot get away and the male transfers spermatophore components to the female."

Yet, only about 30 percent of mating attempts end in copulation, suggesting that females may be able to avoid mating with males they find unsatisfactory. Just what she is looking for in a mate could be the topic of a graduate-level thesis that would be most interesting to read. Both males and females mate more than one time, and we have already learned that red pandas want a mate with proper manners, while female hummingbirds look for tenacity.

In monarch males, sperm begin to mature during the third and fourth larval instars. Even in the caterpillar soup days inside the chrysalis, the bright red testes are easily visible in dissected male larvae.

The Monarch Lab continues, "Lepidopteran sperm are transferred within a protein-rich ejaculate called a spermatophore. This spermatophore can represent a significant investment by the male; some male monarchs transfer spermatophores that weigh up to 10 percent of their own mass!" (The exclamation point is theirs, but in this case I think it is justified.) "Mating monarchs can remain together for 16 hours or longer, and it is only at the very end of this period that sperm are transferred."

Should the mating monarchs be disturbed, the male is able to lift them both and fly the joined pair to safety. The union remains unbroken. Once copulation does occur, the sperm is stored within the female for later use. Lepidoptera have two ovaries; each consists of four ovarioles, which are essentially conduits for maturing eggs that move along it like an assembly line. Fertilization occurs just before the eggs are about to be laid, one at a time, as each passes down the common oviduct. According to Dr. Oberhauser, a female may mate several times and produce between 290 to 1,180 eggs. All butterfly mothers only lay their eggs on their host plants; it's the most maternal thing they can do to insure a healthy life for their offspring. And depending again on the temperature, the monarch eggs hatch in three to eight days to repeat the cycle.

Male monarchs are highly territorial. They will chase another butterfly, a bee, or even a bird out of their space. That is the first few generations of males. How did the late Muhammad Ali, the former world heavyweight champ, describe his boxing style? "Float like a butterfly, sting like a bee." But monarchs lack stingers, or claws, or teeth, or a jaw-dropping left hook. They are all bluff.

Okay, it's about to get really interesting again. Any given year, adult males and females that appear in mid August lack this urge to reproduce. They seem to have other things on their tiny little minds.

Most butterfly species in North America produce two or three generations a year. But it is the monarchs' last generation, the one that comes at the end of summer, that produces the most wonderment and, for decades, the most mystery. The monarchs we watched at Cherry Grove Beach in South Carolina in 2003 and the ones at Cape May Point, New Jersey, six years later flew with purpose.

WHERE DO THEY GO IN WINTER?

As a general rule, adult butterflies live only a few days or weeks, with each generation taking at least a month or so to go through metamorphosis depending on the temperatures. This means that the adult butterflies we see in the fall are the grandchildren or great-grandchildren of the first adults we saw in spring.

This holds true for all butterflies, with one exception. All adult tiger swallowtails die before the onset of winter. But somehow, each year, the last generation of monarch adults do not, as Dylan Thomas put it, "go gentle into that good night." For a long time it was believed they hibernated, but where? Strangely, this late summer generation cannot mate. They go into reproductive diapause, a period of hormonally controlled quiescence. Their sex organs do not mature until the following spring.

In late summer and early fall, all the adults seen in the east, in Point Pelee, Ontario, the skyscraper canyons of Manhattan, Eastern Point, Massachusetts, along the shore of Lake Superior, and thousands of other meadows, playgrounds, and backyards east of the Rockies seem to just be fluttering by. As a general rule, they're flying southward but are apt to turn up just about anywhere. On November 16, 2016, I was standing in downtown Knoxville on the corner of Locust Street and Clinch Avenue waiting for the crosswalk light to change when a lone monarch came jaunting past so close I could have reached out and touched it. But the shock of seeing it there at that moment froze me. Albeit a bit late, it was true to the season, following Clinch in the flow of traffic past the YMCA and the offices of University of Tennessee Press toward the old World's Fair site heading southwest. It was a sunny, mild afternoon, and if I could sing, I would have burst out with Beethoven's "Ode to Joy."

The French have a phrase, *joie de vivre,* that is generally translated as "a delight in being alive." I can think of nothing that illustrates this better than a butterfly, or as the French say *le papillon,* fluttering by. The monarchs don't seem to be in a hurry, they seem aimless and carefree, although they sometimes flutter by at twenty miles per hour, sometimes two feet above the ground, sometimes up to two miles overhead blown about by whatever breeze presents itself. They seem purposeless, yet nothing could be farther from the truth.

For years no one knew where the last generation of monarchs went; they just disappeared. Poof! Not a single egg, larva, pupa, or adult could be found in their summer time range. They just vanished. But where do they go?

My home, like thousands or perhaps millions of other homes, is at least partly shored up by the stacks of *National Geographic* neatly stored away in the basement. No matter what magazines you subscribe to, be it *Time, Good Housekeeping, Vogue, Rolling Stone,* or *TV Guide,* the yellow-bordered *National Geographic* is the one you simply cannot throw away. I have forty years' worth, roughly five hundred issues, and the one that I keep sequestered from the rest is dated August 1976. It arrived two years after I graduated college and disco music was on all the radios. Why so special? It's the issue that details the search for the missing monarch butterflies. On the cover is an attractive dark-haired woman named Cathy Aguado. She's covered with monarchs; the trees around her are covered with monarchs; and the ground is orange and black as well. The photo had been taken in January 1976. The cover story inside, "Found at Last: The Monarchs Winter Home," was written by sixty-five-year-old Frederick "Fred" Urquhart. He knew the topic well; it was his story. He was only twenty-six years old when he began his monarch research.

In 1937, Urquhart, a zoology professor at the University of Toronto, and his wife, Norah, decided they would find out where the monarchs go in winter. The Urquharts dedicated almost forty years of their lives to the project. Searches in Florida and along the Gulf Coast turned up no large numbers of wintering monarchs. How could this be? They determined early in their research that they had to tag the late-summer monarchs they encountered with a number so that maybe they could be tracked.

"But how do you mark a migrating butterfly, a delicate, featherweight insect that depends totally on freedom of flight?" asked Urquhart.

Early methods failed miserably. Gummed labels like postage stamps simply washed off in the rain. Finally, they tried small, printed, pressure-adhesive labels used for price tags on glass merchandise. It worked.

The Urquharts raised thousands of monarchs in their home in Scarborough, Ontario, tagged them, and then let them go. In 1952, the Urquharts began to recruit volunteers, citizen-scientists who were not academically trained scientists, to help them tag butterflies in numerous locations. Fred wrote a short plea for help that appeared in *Natural History* magazine. He got twelve responses, and the Insect Migration Association was launched. By 1971, he had over six hundred volunteer taggers. They were lawyers, shopkeepers, teachers, housewives, even kids.

Each tag had a distinctive number, and every so often a tagged butterfly would be found dead or netted alive somewhere farther south. On a large map, a line could be drawn from where the monarch was tagged and where it was found, a valuable piece of information. Over the course of time, the Urquharts had a map filled with lines all pointing to the southwest. They identified several distinct migration routes but were then flummoxed. Why did the trails seem to disappear in Texas in the late fall, only to reappear in the spring?

In 1968, the Urquharts spent the winter in Texas, driving along the border and eventually to the Pacific Coast, searching for large masses of overwintering monarchs. They found none.

If not Texas, were the lines on the map all pointing to Mexico? Could this be? That's a very long way to fly for something that weighs so little.

According to *National Geographic*, a monarch weighs between 0.27 and 0.75 grams, so on average, half a gram. But that's the metric system again. How can we nonmetric users relate to such a tiny amount? Here's a comparison. Take a one-dollar bill out of your pocket and tear it into two equal halves. Each piece should weigh half a gram. The same thing would work with a twenty-dollar bill, but that's a much bigger sacrifice just to make a point.

And that point is this: How could a life so frail, a butterfly that weighs the equivalent of half a dollar bill, fly from Canada to Mexico? Fred Urquhart must have asked himself the same question, but that's what years of research and dozens of lines drawn on a map seemed to suggest. Clearly there was a need to search south of the border. He needed to find volunteers that knew that country.

Finally, Norah wrote to Mexican newspapers, hoping to find volunteers. Early in 1973, Kenneth Brugger from Mexico City responded, "I might be of some help." He convinced Cathy Aguado, a Mexican-born naturalist and social worker, to join him. For months they roamed the country on weekends in his Winnebago, searching for monarchs. Aguado was a perfect partner. She was from the Mexican state of Michoacán, and the trail of recovered tagged monarchs seemed to be pointing there. And not only did she know the tiny villages and spoke the languages, both Spanish and the native Indian dialect, but she also knew her way through the thick mountain forests.

During the day, Kenneth and Cathy hiked the rugged, remote terrain; at nights they stayed in the Winnebago. (The couple married in 1974, which meant that one husband-wife team was completing the work of another.) They were dedicated, climbing ever higher, seven thousand feet, eight thousand feet, until finally on January 2, 1975, the couple found a high mountain summit called Cerro Pelón where the trees and even the ground were festooned with overwintering butterflies.

A week later, Kenneth and Cathy called the Urquharts to report the good news. One year later, Fred and Norah themselves came to visit the site they had sought for decades. The search that began in 1937 had come to a spectacular end.

"I gazed in amazement at the sight. Butterflies—millions upon millions of monarch butterflies! They clung in tightly packed masses to every branch and trunk of the tall gray-green *oyamel* trees," wrote Fred. "They swirled through the air like autumn leaves and carpeted the ground in their flaming myriads."

"Breathless from the altitude," he added, "my legs trembling from the climb, I muttered aloud, 'Unbelievable! What a glorious, incredible sight!'"

Indeed they were breathless from the altitude. The monarchs were spending their winters above nine thousand feet. It is mindboggling to think that some of the 607 monarchs I counted at sea level at Cherry Grove Beach in 2003 or the lone butterfly flying along Clinch Avenue in downtown Knoxville in 2016, might have ended up clinging to trees on a mountaintop in Mexico a few months later.

The locals in the area have long known that monarchs mystically fill the skies on or near the second day of November, the traditional "Day of the Dead." Two indigenous tribes, the Mazahua and the P'urépecha, have come to associate the return of the colorful butterflies with the returning souls of the their ancestors. Fred Urquhart died in 2002; his wife Norah in 2009. Kenneth Brugger died in 1998; his wife, now known as Catalina Trail, still lives. We like to believe that the souls of Fred, Norah, and Ken reappear there early every November.

In time, other monarch winter havens were found on the taller mountain peaks west of Mexico City. Today there are five official monarch sanctuaries there: Cerro Altamirano, Sierra Chincua, Sierra El Campanario, Cerros Chivatí-Huacal, and Cerro Pelón.

Many monarchs are killed along their arduous journey, but millions also make it. One estimate tallied three-hundred million. This yearly pilgrimage is miraculous since no monarch that makes the trip has ever been there before. It was their great-grandparents that spent the last winter there, clinging to the branches. Yet, somehow the insect's little bundle of nerve cells, loosely called a brain, simply knows where to go. How they make this, in some cases thirty-five hundred mile trip, to the same site each year is one of the planet's great mysteries.

Here's where it gets perplexing. You'd think the orange-and-black butterflies go to Mexico to spend a mild winter; but that's not so. They overwinter at elevations between ninety-eight hundred and eleven thousand feet, where the weather is cold, frosts are common, occasionally it snows, and there's little food to eat. The millions of monarchs huddle together, clinging to tree branches. It's not warm enough for them to be very active, but it usually does not get so cold that they freeze to death. Veteran entomologist Gilbert Waldbauer reported that they really go through a big chill that keeps them in a state of semi-dormancy. Their energy demands are low, which means that most of them will have enough fat reserves left to start the flight back north in the spring. The monarchs don't lose the precious little water their bodies contain because the mountaintops remain damp though the winter.

As science professor Loren Eisely wrote, "The world, I have come to believe, is a very queer place, but we have been a part of the queerness for so long that we tend to take it for granted. We rush to and fro like Mad Hatters on our peculiar errands, all the time imagining our surroundings to be dull and ourselves quite ordinary creatures." Well, our surroundings are not dull. All around us are miraculous things.

It's stunning to think that such delicate creatures fly so far to spend the winter in a refrigerator, but for them it works. So, if you see one fly past your yard on its way to Cerro Pelón, wave, "Adíos, amigo," and wish it well. And hope it packed its knickers.

Similar to the tops of the Great Smoky Mountains, the high peaks in Mexico that serve as the winter havens for the monarchs are mostly forested with conifers, primarily firs and pines with some cypresses. The dominant tree is a fir called the *"oyamel"* by the Mexicans. The international Monarch Butterfly Sanctuary Foundation has worked the past several years to collect funds to protect the mountaintops from being logged.

In 2000, Mexican President Ernesto Zedillo signed a decree to enlarge the protected monarch sanctuaries from 62 square miles to 216 square miles. In the core zone of each sanctuary, logging is forbidden.

THE REST OF THE STORY

We could leave this part of the narrative here and be happy that the mystery has been solved except for what radio broadcaster Paul Harvey used to call, "The Rest of the Story." For the overwintering monarchs clinging to the trees on the mountaintops of Mexico, their journey and life is only half over. Come spring, there's the return trip north. As I write this, it's March 27, 2016. And a check of the monarch tracking website "Journey North" reveals that adult butterflies from 2015 are beginning to show up in Texas, along the Gulf Coast, and Florida, heading north. For them the clock is now ticking. Their extra-long youth has ended. Their sex organs have matured; they must mate and fan out across the east in search of milkweed. The mated females may fly a thousand miles, laying hundreds of eggs along the way. The "Journey North" website notes that a female monarch was spotted today in Cypress, Texas. She was laying eggs. And she'll keep moving north. However, eventually she'll wear out her tattered wings and die, her winter on Cerro Pelón a distant memory. But her eggs hatch to become part of the first generation of the new cycle with each generation continuing its northerly track until roughly the summer solstice. That extra long day in June seems to trigger a halt. Then northward migration stops and monarchs stay put until mid August and their flow reverses, returning south. They also do not venture anywhere farther than the northern boundary of common milkweed plants: 50 degrees north latitude or roughly Winnipeg, Manitoba.

An additional advantage of locating the mysterious wintering sites of the butterflies was that it made it easier to estimate their numbers. Although there are other populations of monarchs elsewhere, the entire eastern migratory population overwinter huddled together. Instead of counting the number of individuals—a Herculean task—beginning in 1993 monarch census takers counted the number of acres covered with the butterflies and then estimated an overall population. Simple enough, but in early 2014, news sources around the world began to report an alarming change.

"After steep and steady declines in the previous three years, the black-and-orange butterflies now cover only 1.65 acres (0.67 hectares) in the pine and fir forests west of Mexico City, compared to 2.93 acres (1.19 hectares) last year. They covered more than 44.5 acres (18 hectares) at their recorded peak in 1995," reported Mark Stevenson for the Associated Press.

This translated to an estimated decline of one billion monarchs in the mid-1990s to only about 35 million in 2013, according to Marcus Kronforst, a professor of ecology and evolution at the University of Chicago who had studied monarchs. Many reports stated that their numbers had dropped 90 percent in just twenty years.

Why?

In some cases, it was bad weather. An intense storm on the mountaintops on January 12, 2002, killed an estimated 80 percent of the population. Another pair of storms in January and February 2004 killed 70 percent of that year's population. But those are freak occurrences, and the monarchs can recover from such. But what about the long term decline?

"The migration is definitely proving to be an endangered biological phenomenon," wrote Lincoln Brower, a leading entomologist at Sweet Briar College in Virginia. "The main culprit is GMO herbicide-resistant corn and soybean crops and herbicides in the USA [which] leads to the wholesale killing of the monarch's principal food plant, common milkweed."

"While Mexico has made headway in reducing logging in the officially protected winter reserve, that alone cannot save the migration," wrote monarch expert Dr. Karen Oberhauser. "A large part of their reproductive habitat in that region has been lost due to changes in agricultural practices, mainly the explosive growth in the use of herbicide-tolerant crops."

The herbicide in question was the weed killer glyphosate, also known as Roundup®. It was killing milkweed across millions of acres of the monarch's summer habitat in the Corn Belt.

Farmers cried foul. They were being blamed for the decline of monarchs. But there was some evidence to substantiate such a claim.

"Between 1995—the year before Monsanto introduced Roundup Ready soybeans and three years before it introduced Roundup Ready corn—and 2013, total glyphosate use on corn and soybeans rose from 10 million pounds per year to 204 million pounds per year. Roundup Ready varieties now comprise 94 percent of all soybeans and 89 percent of all corn grown in the United States," reported Seth Slabaugh for the Associated Press in October 2014.

"A 90-percent decline in the last two decades in what was once a common species in our backyards is pretty dramatic," said entomologist Sarina Jepsen, endangered species director at the Xerces Society. "There are a lot of threats, but the primary one is the twenty-fold increase in the use of glyphosate since the mid-1990s, coincident with the onset of genetically modified corn and soybeans to tolerate the use of Roundup."

This news report and others that followed in early 2015 sent shock waves around the country. True, we are talking about an insect, but it wasn't a weevil or cockroach or wasp. It was a beneficial pollinator and North America's most beloved butterfly to boot. The U.S. Fish and Wildlife Service deemed it a "charismatic insect" and sent out a call to action similar to the one that galvanized forces to save the bald eagle. To some, charismatic insect is an oxymoron, but to thousands of school kids and gardeners it's a given.

The good news: Roundup wasn't being used on 100 percent of the land and milkweed will grow practically anywhere. Millions of dollars were quickly allocated to grow milkweed wherever possible. Students began to plant milkweed around their playgrounds.

On May 19, 2015, President Barack Obama's Pollinator Health Task Force included in its larger strategy to help the beleaguered pollinating honeybee a plan to help the declining butterfly as well. The centerpiece of the plan is a monarch flyway along I-35 that runs north-south through America's heartland. It called for turning federally owned land along the interstate corridor into milkweed refuges for the butterflies. To make this happen, a billion "unruly" milkweed plants would be planted along a two-hundred-mile-wide corridor from Minnesota to Texas.

"We are going to get the most bang for our buck by concentrating on the prairie corridor," said Dr. Karen Oberhauser, one of two key scientists advising federal agencies on the monarch plan.

TAGGING ALONG

"If you want to catch a monarch," said Clare Dattilo. "Just follow Oliver."

I did not have to be told twice, I knew her ten-year-old son and knew his focus. I had worked with him at Ijams. I promptly fell in line with Team Oliver, which also included two other exuberant boys, Malachi and Carpenter. As we walked down a cobble-filled dry tributary of Abrams Creek—the name honors Old Abraham of Chilhowee, a prominent Overhill Cherokee chief in the 1780s—Oliver found a new buckeye with the dark sheen of Spanish mahogany.

"Put this in your pocket," he said as he pitched it to me. "It'll bring you luck."

I missed the toss and it fell to the ground. Had I just cursed my talisman? I'd soon put it to the test.

Friday, October 7, 2016, found me back in Cades Cove, this time on Sparks Lane not far from where Rachael Eliot and I searched for a short-eared owl nine months earlier. Clare Datillo and Aimee Davis are both volunteers for Tiffany Beachy in the Tremont citizen science program, and it was monarch-tagging season. Naturally, I tagged along. Datillo and Davis and their children were volunteers just like the ones Fred Urquhart first recruited in 1952. With us were several parents with children from the home school classes I lead at the nature center. When I do those outings, I only use first names. It's simpler. And it was good to see here: Marie with sons Carpenter and Auzlo; Amy with daughter Kylie; Christina with son Malachi; Aimee with son Will; Clare with Oliver, Annabel, and Fern; plus New Yorker Annie Novak, author of *The Rooftop Growing Guide,* who was in Tennessee chasing and tagging monarchs on her own researching a book on monarch migration.

After the botched buckeye toss, the first field we entered proved a problem. The drying, dying forbs: ironweed, goldenrod, thistle, tickseed, and frostweed were as parched and near lifeless as the streambed. Signs of the long hot summer were all around us. As tall as some of Team Oliver, the desiccated forbs made for poor visibility. Still we marched through the meadow mire. If there were monarchs in this morass they would be hard to find; plus, as I learned, it is not easy to run in a chest high dried flower arraignment.

We reversed direction, broke up, and fanned out. I lost Oliver but then relocated him and stuck by his side. He had that determined "will not be denied look" about him that you want in a partner. Plus, he had kid wisdom.

"Did you know," he asked as we walked along the gravel road, "You're more likely to cut yourself with a dull knife than a sharp one?"

"Really? Why is that?" I asked, confounded.

"I know. It doesn't make sense. But you're more careful with a really sharp knife than a dull one."

I like it when a ten-year-old drops his guard and talks about things that are important to know in his world. Insurance, mortgages, presidential politics, those concerns all come later.

In time, our fortunes changed after we entered a colony of low growing, white asters that were still soldiering forth. How could anything be brave enough to bloom in this arid autumn? Luckily for us they had because a migrating butterfly needs to eat. For a creature that flutters and stutters, moving along rather capriciously, they can be remarkably difficult to catch.

A bright orange gulf fritillary butterfly (*Agraulis vanillae*) gave me an adrenalin rush.

"It's only a gulf," observed Oliver. "You can tell by the way it flaps."

Okay. Lesson learned, more kid wisdom. He soon spotted the first monarch of our foray, and with a truly magnanimous gesture he stepped aside for me to net. He didn't need to show his prowess that would come later.

"It's yours," he said.

Nodding at his selfless act, I made it so. Swish! Later it was tagged with the number WJL735, just in case you see it.

The flowering colony of white asters proved to be a sweet spot, an oasis. That plus a favorable breeze that had kicked up from the northeast made the late morning and early afternoon bountiful. After my initial catch, Oliver caught three in one net, then four in a second, then five in a third, each time trying to outdo the catch of the one before. Others from our group began to join us. Multiple monarchs were caught and taken to Datillo and Davis to tag and record.

"Godspeed, you'll need it," said Oliver after each was released.

"Godspeed, John Glenn," said I, thinking of another sendoff. The NASA astronaut's journey in February 1962 seemed just as improbable.

As each one was released, it just fluttered away in a remarkably different manner than the hummingbirds. Yet, they each have incredible journeys that are far from being aimless. They have thousands of miles to go.

In all thirty-four monarchs were caught, tagged, and released by our group that October Friday. Oliver caught fourteen.

"This was the best trip I was ever on," said volunteer Davis. "Many times we come out and do not find a single one."

"Best day of the year!" Added Datillo.

Standing in the shade of a sycamore, I watched as tagged monarchs flew southwest after being released. They are not even halfway to Cerro Pelón.

Godspeed, John Glenn.

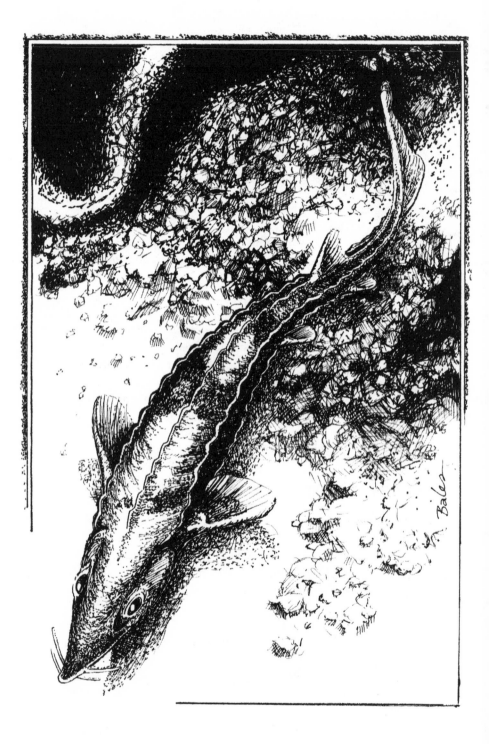

Lake Sturgeon
Acipenser fulvous

Nature loves to hide.
—Heraclitus of Ephesus

PART OF THE Persian Empire, Ephesus is an ancient city on the Aegean Sea at the mouth of the Cayster River. Now part of Turkey the region is noted for its beautiful surroundings. Even in 500 BC, people especially philosophers like Heraclitus liked to live in the midst of beauty. It inspires noble thoughts. This then is a story of noble thinking.

Located in downtown Chattanooga, the Tennessee Aquarium first opened its doors in 1992. The Scenic City's cornerstone attracts over seven hundred thousand visitors annually. They come to the facility to view more than twelve thousand live specimens representing almost eight hundred species of fish, birds, reptiles, and mammals, plus assorted plants. Originally it was billed as the largest freshwater aquarium in the world, but a 2005 expansion added a saltwater aquatic life building to the complex. It was a key component in the community-driven revitalization of downtown Chattanooga, the irony being not that such a homage to nature could help restore the fourth largest urban area in the state, but that it did. The not-for-profit educational institution is dedicated to the appreciation, conservation, and restoration of the nearby river, which the urbanization of the valley degraded in the first place.

Call it a paradox. A skeptic would ask, "How can a tourist attraction improve the environment?" Yet, it has done just that. Raising public awareness is the first step in any environmental movement. You can't improve a deteriorating situation if most people are unaware of the decline in the first place. If only a small percentage of the millions who come and go from the aquatic museum leave with an understanding of what's at risk, then it's a change for the good. Behind the very public attraction exists a large support organization—the Tennessee Aquarium Research Institute (TNARI)—which works to conserve and restore native aquatic species to the region. The Tennessee River is not alone in its plight. All of the major rivers in the world—Amazon, Orinoco, Fly, Volga, Yenisey, Zaire, Mississippi—and the countless numbers of plants and animals that live along them share the same dire fate. The people who built their villages along their banks have degraded them all. The bottom line is simple: humans and nature have to coexist, and people will always need clean, fresh water.

The Chattanooga facility's "River Journey" is a skillfully orchestrated descent from high to low that follows a drop of water from mountaintop to sea. My revisit in 2005 reminded me of its sublime design. Visitors move from the fifth floor's Appalachian cove forest—complete with free-flying birds and trees—down a mountain stream, through rivers, lakes, and delta swamp to the Gulf of Mexico. Along the way, they are introduced to appropriate inhabitants of each habitat: brook trout, spotfin chub, river otter, wood duck, yellowbelly slider, alligator. The "immersion" exhibits put you inside the habitats with the plants and animals. During my afternoon visit, I stood riveted by the scene before me, watching a male and female hooded merganser preen on a log in the pretend swamp. Perhaps they knew it was pretend, or perhaps they didn't; but they certainly didn't mind that this human, just four feet away, had invaded their private act of personal hygiene. The voyeurism was made even more sensational by the fact that absolutely nothing stood between us. If I had arms that were four feet long, I could have reached out and touched the grooming ducks, although warning signs posted near the exhibit strongly discourage that kind of viewer participation.

As you descend down the watershed, and your flow to the sea is slowed, there are side trips. One is Discovery Hall, a darkened gallery with carpet-covered walls and small individual tanks that contain spiny softshell turtles, hellbenders (large salamanders that never leave the water), painted river prawn, green tree frogs, and red-spotted newts. The object of the assorted collection is to give visitors better views of smaller species that would become lost in the larger exhibits. Beyond the hellbender was something even more alluring: a low-to-the-ground, eight-sided touch-tank.

The signs around the octagonal exhibit encourage onlookers to touch the tank's inhabitants: half-a-dozen large fish that have aged pedigrees. "They're really quite docile," said aquarium volunteer Bill Burch, "and don't seem to mind being touched." Curious, I complied, reaching into the swirling cool water to feel one of the passing lake sturgeons that swam along the bottom. They felt slightly rough, like wet leather or a rain-soaked football. Signs around the tank warn you to only use two fingers to resist the temptation to squeeze the passing fish.

"The Tennessee Aquarium is part of a group that's working to return these native fish to the river," added the friendly volunteer. Although the large bottom-feeding fish had once lived in the waters just outside the aquarium's five-story structure, they had disappeared from it for a variety of reasons. The six "touchable" sturgeons were of varying sizes: from about thirty inches on down, with the most senior being about five to seven years old, about the same age as the little girl standing beside me at the exhibit. She was dressed in a bright red outfit with the honorary title "Princess" printed in sequins across her blouse. Her brunette tresses were pulled back, held together with red, white, and blue ribbons. At first, she was timid; the large trolling fish seemed quite formidable, but urged on by her kindly grandfather, she soon became caught up in the experience. She laughed and grew ebullient as she reached her hands into the water repeatedly to feel the passing fish that were almost as long as she was tall. "I think they like you," Princess said, looking at me with a grin. "You think?" I replied wet to the elbow, knowing that we were touching animals both ancient and imperiled. As the three generations of humans stood in the darkened gallery marveling at the gentle creatures, I could not help but wonder: What would have Rafinesque have thought?

AN ODD FISH? HE WAS THAT INDEED

Constantine Samuel Rafinesque was an early American naturalist, a contemporary of John James Audubon. Simply put, he was Renaissance Man, described as a poet, botanist, geologist, economist, philosopher, philologist, historian, merchant, manufacturer, professor, surveyor, architect, inventor, banker, author, and editor. That's quite a résumé; yet first, and perhaps foremost, Rafinesque was himself a curiosity, an eccentric genius who was maybe even a bit crazy. An introductory letter, presented by Rafinesque to Audubon at their first meeting in Henderson, Kentucky, described him as being an "odd fish." He seemed perfectly comfortable with that description.

Born in 1783 in Turkey near Constantinople (in the same general area as Heraclitus our opening philosopher), Rafinesque's father was French and his mother was a citizen of Greece with German ancestry. He claimed that by the age of twelve he had read a thousand books on science and philosophy written in several languages. As an adult he invented an artillery piece for the Mexican army (they didn't buy it), a herbal elixir that purportedly would cure tuberculosis (he sold lots of it), and started a savings bank that paid 6 percent interest (it was very successful). He was also a winemaker and opened a distillery that made "very good brandy," which he himself did not drink because he hated strong liquors. But his one overriding passion was natural history. Rafinesque moved from Sicily to America in 1815 to study the plants and animals of the New World.

In the mid-1800s, Rafinesque roamed the vast wilderness of this country, weeks on end, collecting and cataloging new flora and fauna. During such forays, his beard grew long and his well-worn clothing became unkempt, soiled with the juices that oozed from the plants he pressed and carried on his back along with his leather-bound journal. I could not find a record of him collecting either jack-in-the-pulpit or Indian pipe, but if he encountered either, surely he did.

He slept where he could, ate what he found, and immersed himself in the vastness of virginal America. One can only imagine his utter sense of wonderment. The untidy naturalist is credited with discovering and naming more than one hundred new species, including the mule deer, alligator gar, Rafinesque big-eared bat, and numerous flowering plants. He pioneered the study of fishes in North America and was one of this country's first professors of natural history, the source of his lectures originating in what he had witnessed firsthand in the field.

He wrote profusely. If he thought it, he quickly churned out a pamphlet, book, or long monograph on the topic; and he also wrote dozens of articles for the *Saturday Evening Post*. One of his books, *The World, or Instability*, is essentially a fifty-four-hundred-line poem that contains his thoughts on angels and devils, stars and light, passion, peace, war, and women. Within the more lucid sections, he also lays down his thoughts on evolution a full twenty years before Charles Darwin published his own work on the topic. Rafinesque was tireless, his knowledge immense, and like any good scientist, he had an unquenchable thirst for the unknown.

On July 10, 1817, Rafinesque read one of his papers, "Addition to the Observations on the Sturgeons of North America," to the Literary and Philosophical Society of New York. The "odd fish" naturalist opined that the lake sturgeon was a "perfectly distinct species" and proposed to give the newly described fish the Latin name of *Acipenser fulvous,* meaning, "sturgeon of an overall fulvus (tawny, yellowish-brown) color." In addition to *Acipenser fulvous,* two other large fish Rafinesque discovered and named were the shovelnose sturgeon and the shortnose gar. Of the three, the lake sturgeon grows to be the biggest; it's the behemoth of the continent's freshwater interior. Reports vary; most accounts describe it as growing up to three hundred pounds, the equivalent of a beefy NFL lineman, and eight to nine feet long. That's incredible, considering it's a fish found primarily in lakes and deep rivers. (The largest freshwater fish in North America is the white sturgeon, which can reach a length of twenty feet and is found in estuaries along the Pacific Coast.) Watching a sturgeon patrol the water is to look back into a time when armored giants roamed the land and water.

Reports of large American fish had been around for years. Both the Abenaki and the Iroquois had legends of a large creature living in Lake Champlain. The Abenaki called it "Tatoskok." The lake runs north to south between New York and Vermont. In 1609, Samuel de Champlain was the first European to discover the large inland body of water.

The French explorer later wrote, "There is also a great abundance of many species of fish. Amongst others there is one called by the natives Chaousarou, which is of various lengths; but the largest of them, as these tribes have told me, are from eight to ten feet long. I have seen some five feet long, which were as big as my thigh, and had a head as large as my two fists, with a snout two feet and a half long, and a double row of very sharp, dangerous teeth. Its body has a good deal the shape of the pike; but it is protected by scales of a silvery gray colour and so strong that a dagger could not pierce them."

Champlain's account appeared in volume 2, chapter IX, of his journal. Although today it's believed that the French explorer saw his large creature in the St. Lawrence River and not in the lake that bears his name, his story has had a lasting effect in that part of the country. His account has been told, retold, and embellished for centuries. In a country full of "big fish" stories, it's the biggest. Today, the legendary Lake Champlain creature, otherwise known as "Champ" is North America's version of the Loch Ness Monster. Champ Day is celebrated every year in Port Henry, New York, with a parade and T-shirts and other Champ memorabilia sold by sidewalk vendors. As I write these words, June 21, 2016, the big fish festival is only twenty-six days away. Is it worth the 946-mile drive? I'm thinking.

Hundreds of eyewitness sightings have been reported since the late 1800s. Yet, like Scotland's Nessie, no hard evidence has ever been found, and all of the Champ reports can be attributed to being either driftwood, otters, gars, or sturgeons, either swimming alone or in groups.

REMARKABLE CREATURES BOTH ANCIENT AND LARGE

As a group, sturgeons are considered to be among the most primitive bony fish on earth. But unlike most bony fish, a sturgeon's skeleton is primarily cartilage like a shark's. Fossil remains of their extinct relatives can be dated back 350 million years, making them older than flowering plants but much younger than the freshwater jellyfish lineage. Sturgeons are also the largest freshwater fish on earth. The Caspian Sea's sturgeon, the Beluga, can reach twenty-six feet in length and is the source of the world's most prized caviar.

Of the five sturgeon species in the genus *Acipenser* in North America, two live in both salt and freshwater along the West Coast, and two do the same on the East Coast. Only one, Rafinesque's lake sturgeon, lives solely in freshwater in the continent's interior.

Huge lake sturgeon "were once common bycatch in the Great Lakes, where fishermen stacked them like cordwood on the shore," wrote Erika Engelhaupt for *National Geographic* in August 2016. "But populations have been drastically reduced by habitat loss, pollution and the popularity of the species' caviar."

Tennessee has somewhere between 302 and 319 freshwater fish species, making it the richest state in overall diversity. The Tennessee Valley has 160 native species. The bottom-feeding lake sturgeon is the biggest and can live up to 150 years on a diet of crayfish, mollusks, and insect larvae. Today, they can be found in the Great Lakes and Mississippi River Basin, but in the Tennessee Valley, they had all but disappeared over the past 150 years because of overharvesting, dam construction, and water pollution. At the southern edge of their range, the lake sturgeon of Tennessee do not grow as large or live as long as the northern populations, but they are still the biggest fish in the valley.

There were occasional reports of sturgeon being caught in the 1960s and '70s, but those encounters declined in numbers as the century wore on. Some children allegedly pulled one in near Island Home Airport in Knoxville in 1974, in the sluice between the island and the southern shoreline, but that was the last supposed appearance in the upper Tennessee River. That's also a waterway that borders Ijams. I have canoed it often in the past twenty years and heard of nothing sturgeon-like being caught there.

RETURN OF THE NATIVES

If you are an aquatic biologist or fisherman in Tennessee, July 19, 2000, was a big day. If your specialty is large game fish, it was monumental. On that date, approximately five hundred young lake sturgeon were released into the French Broad River just below Douglas Dam in Sevier County. In effect, it was a long-awaited homecoming, the beginning of an effort to reestablish a sustainable population. The reintroduction was a major undertaking that would take years to reach fruition. Needless to say, hopes were high. In a preliminary study the previous year, several had been released with radio tags. Their movements were tracked, and they dispersed evenly down the French Broad to the Tennessee River. One was even followed to West Knox County and Fort Loudoun Dam.

The return of lake sturgeon to the valley is a huge environmental effort with many partners. In addition to the Tennessee Aquarium, which hosted the event, the Southeast Aquatic Research Institute, the Tennessee Valley Authority, the Tennessee Wildlife Resources Agency, the U.S. Fish and Wildlife Service, the U.S. Geological Survey, and the World Wildlife Fund all had a hand in the project.

"The World Wildlife Fund recognizes the Tennessee River Basin as the most diverse aquatic place in the world," said Wendy Smith, director of WWF's Southeast Rivers and Streams Project, at the time of the initial releases. "Being able to reintroduce lake sturgeon is good news," she added. Because of the Clean Water Act of 1972 and continuing efforts by TVA, the water quality of the river system had improved enough to make such a reintroduction possible.

In the mid-1990s, now-retired TVA aquatic biologist Ed Scott noticed a remarkable comeback of fish communities and aquatic insects in the French Broad River. The return of the insects was important because they are one of the things that sturgeons eat. TVA's own "Shoreline Management Policy" has worked to stabilize eroding riverbanks, thus reducing the amount of sediment that enters the rivers. Sturgeons, like most aquatic life, do not fare well in muddy water. TVA has also worked to increase the oxygen level in local waterways.

I attended that first release with Peg Beute of Ijams Nature Center. Beute is the chair of the Water Quality Forum (WQF), a consortium made up of several organizations and agencies that consolidate their efforts to protect and improve local waterways. It's a group made up of dedicated people such as Tim Gangaware and Ruth Anne Hanahan with the Tennessee Water Resources Research Center at the University of Tennessee and Martin Pleasant with the Knox County Stormwater Department, who have worked for years in anonymity—often in hip waders removing trash from shorelines or stabilizing stream banks with riparian plantings—all in an effort to restore area rivers, creeks, and wetlands to some semblance of natural order. WQF members also work with hundreds of students in the classroom, on field trips, and outside doing community service projects.

The young sturgeon release site was just beneath the bridge downstream from Douglas Dam. I knew the location very well. Growing up in Sevier

County, I had often fished the same shoreline between the bridge and dam with my late father, Russell. He was eager to turn me into a fisherman, but I proved to be a poor angler. Lacking the patience of great blue heron, I spent more time exploring the rocky rip-rap that holds the riverbank in place than tending my line and lure. Watching the red and white float bob up and down in the water seemed hopelessly mind numbing. Being more Rafinesque than bass legend Bill Dance, I had yet to master the art of "mindfulness."

Many of the people at the release that July morning, especially the aquatic biologists, had already invested years in planning the initiative. Wearing T-shirts that boasted "Bring Back the Natives," they took turns carrying the young sturgeons to the water and patiently letting them go, one at a time. A defining moment in their careers, it was a selfless act they wanted to savor.

Having spent the first year of their young lives in much smaller artificial environs, the year-old sturgeon at first lay in the shallow water, seemingly bewildered by the newness of it all. They gulped, slowly gathering whatever awareness it takes for such creatures to move into the great unknown. Gradually, their senses alert, they swam away into the water's murky depths and their new life.

"For my eye perceives the world as fixed or fluid, as it wishes. The earth twitches, the mountains shimmer, as if all molecules had been set free," wrote Peter Matthiessen in *The Snow Leopard*. And the collective molecules we call lake sturgeon were being set free, and around us, the environmental world twitched. It was a new day.

As that July morning wore on, the onlookers watched Chris Coco, fisheries curator at the Tennessee Aquarium at the time, as he paternally carried fish after fish to the water and carefully let each one go, taking the time to inspect it as the young scion slowly moved away. As a curator at the aquarium, he had spent a great deal of time with the group of fishes already, and now he was setting them free. More than likely he would never see any one of them ever again. Poof, it just disappeared. After each year-old sturgeon swam away into the dark water, it would probably not be seen throughout its long life unless it happened to be caught somewhere downstream by a fisherman. It's hard to call a fish that can live a century ephemeral, but when they are gone from sight, they're gone. Yes, Heraclitus, "Nature loves to hide."

From an environmental standpoint, the next one hundred years are critical. To quote Charles Dickens, "It was the best of times, it was the worst of times." He was thinking about his own nineteenth-century England but writing about eighteenth-century France. Perhaps every generation thinks they live on the cusp, teetering between salvation and all-out ruination. But if we are going to undo the environmental wrongs of the past three hundred years, we need to start sooner rather than later.

Or is it already too late? The world's foremost biologist and biodiversity advocate, E. O. Wilson, knows we have to act fast. In his 2016 book, *Half Earth: Our Planet's Fight for Life,* Wilson, professor emeritus at Harvard University and recipient of two Pulitzer Prizes, proposed a wondrous solution. If we truly want to save 80 percent of the planet's species, we need to designate half the planet as a human-free nature preserve. Seems fair to me. We get half to argue over and sully, while the other 8.7 million species get the rest.

"I'm not suggesting we have one hemisphere for humans and the other for the rest of all life. I'm talking about allocating up to one half of the surface of the land and the sea as a preserve for remaining flora and fauna," said Wilson in a 2016 interview with the *New York Times.* "Large parts of nature are still intact—the Amazon region, the Congo Basin, New Guinea. There are also patches of the industrialized world where nature could be restored and strung together to create corridors for wildlife. In the oceans, we need to stop fishing in the open sea and let life there recover. If we halted those fisheries, marine life would increase rapidly. The oceans are part of that 50 percent."

Wilson is eighty-six years old. He knows his time is short. His proposal is for the long-term survival of the planet.

The reintroduction of lake sturgeon back into the Tennessee River is an act of "paying it forward." The fact that the river is clean enough once again to support these potentially nine-foot-long bottom-dwellers is a hopeful sign. The sturgeon reintroduction is also different because the progress is less observable; at the time indications of its ultimate success are years away. Earlier reintroductions of river otters and peregrine falcons into East Tennessee have gone well, but the population increase of both is easier to monitor. The visibly growing numbers prove the effort is working. The original peregrines that were returned to Alum Cave in the Great Smoky Mountains National Park have already reproduced multiple times. Today, an expanding number of these birds of prey can be seen throughout the region. River otters are also seen more and more frequently up and down the river, but what about the lake sturgeon? It takes the slow-developing fish almost two decades before they begin to reproduce and start to establish a sustainable population. That's a quarter of a human life that the "Return the Natives" partners will wonder how their project is progressing.

TIME PASSED

Since the initial release in 2000, everyone has patiently waited. The sturgeon reintroduction is complicated by their ability to vanish. Their progress is not easy to observe; indications of success can take years to ascertain.

Because of cost, reported Morgan Simmons for the *Knoxville News Sentinel* in 2011, "only a fraction of the released sturgeon were implanted with microchips designed for radio tracking. Most of the feedback has come from sport anglers and commercial fishermen who happen to catch [and release] a lake sturgeon and report it to the Tennessee Wildlife Resources Agency."

Scutes, large external scales, are removed in particular places to mark each fish and designate its release year. Some are also fitted with Passive Integrative Transponder (PIT) tags that are like the microchips commonly used in pets. Each tag, like a banded bird, has a unique number that can be used to identify an individual and its recorded history.

Researchers now know that the fish can move twenty-five miles a day. Since 2006, over 230 anglers have reported catching a sturgeon from locations as varied as Volunteer Landing in downtown Knoxville to Nickajack Lake west of Chattanooga. The reintroduction partners now use trotlines in the hope of catching maturing sturgeon to monitor their progress.

"We've had the best luck in November. We're not sure why," said Joyce Coombs, research associate at UT. "The commercial fisherman who set up trotlines for catfish were starting to also catch sturgeon. So they showed us the best places to set up our lines. The sturgeon seem to gather in the deepest holes."

In 2011, thirty-four were caught, weighed, measured, and returned to the water. "Lake sturgeon stocked in the Knoxville area have been found at least as far as Guntersville Reservoir in Alabama," said Ed Scott. "Although most seem to be staying in Fort Loudoun and Watts Bar Reservoir, according to our fall trotline surveys."

During the sampling week in November 2012, fifty-two were caught; the largest was nine years old. Released in 2003, it was now forty-nine inches long and weighed seventeen pounds.

"The success we're finding through the sampling shows that the reintroductions are working," said UT professor Larry Wilson of the Department of Forestry, Wildlife and Fisheries. "We're seeing that the sturgeon are dispersing from sites where they've been introduced and moving up and down the river system."

Ed Scott added, "We hope to observe spawning in the next five years."

Typically, lake sturgeon can migrate up rivers over one hundred miles to lay their eggs; however, some lake-bound populations do not migrate but instead spawn over rocky reefs. The construction of dams in the valley has limited migration but they will still find a way. Adult lake sturgeon do not spawn every year, but when they do, it's in the spring: April through June. As the water temperatures moderate to between 54 and 65°F, males assemble in shallow water—so shallow, in fact, that their upper bodies are often exposed. Receptive females are soon to follow and are flanked by one or two males. It can take an individual female from five to slightly over twenty-four hours to extrude her eggs, during which time the males fertilize them outside her body. Females spawn every four to nine years; males may spawn annually or every other year. Typically, females will produce between fifty thousand and seven hundred thousand eggs, but a large female may produce up to three million. The young sturgeons grow very slowly and don't begin producing young of their own until they're 14 to 25 years old. Males and females grow at the same rate, but the females live longer and grow bigger. In the Great Lakes, the typical lifespan of a male is 55 years. Females can live 80 to 150 years. Once reproduction is confirmed, TWRA hopes to legalize lake sturgeon as a sport fish, perhaps with an eighty-pound size minimum.

Since that initial release in 2000, every year young sturgeon have been stocked into the French Broad and Holston Rivers near Knoxville and the Cumberland River near Nashville. Angler reports are important because they provide information on movement and growth needed to monitor the success of the reintroduction program.

To alert the fishing public, TWRA posted a warning on the Internet: "If you have caught or sighted a lake sturgeon, please report it to either the TWRA office in Morristown or Crossville. We would like to know where it was caught or seen and the approximate length of the fish. Lake sturgeon is listed 'state endangered' in Tennessee; possession of the sturgeon is illegal and fish must be returned unharmed to the water as soon as possible."

FIFTEEN YEARS LATER

Some days are perfect. And some days are even more so. Thursday, October 8, 2015, was just one of those. The tulip trees were beginning to turn gold and even give up castoff foliage from their lower branches. Flowering dogwoods were adorned with burgundy leaves, their bright red berries delighting the mockingbirds. While in no real hurry, two turkey vultures launched themselves just before noon to soar lazily overhead, searching for any thermal with enough gumption to rise from the land. And for one thousand four-month-old lake sturgeon, it was a benchmark moment, a day to remember—that is, if such primitive fish have memories of their first taste of the natal waters they'll spend the rest of their lives exploring.

At Gap Creek School near Kimberlin Heights in southeast Knox County, there is a simple, small grave. Interred there is a fish, specifically a young lake sturgeon. The Gap Creek fifth graders are educational partners of the Tennessee Aquarium. It was not unusual that their fish died; most hatchlings do. That's why each adult female produces thousands of eggs.

At the school, Kelly Clemmer is their teacher. "We study endangered species. We use lake sturgeon as an example of what humans have done to the environment and what we are doing to make things good again," she said. The educational initiative began in 2006, and at one point the students had a lone lake sturgeon in a classroom aquarium. But when the solitary fish died, everyone in the school was devastated. They gave it a proper burial outside and hadn't quite recovered emotionally to care for another one.

Instead, every year the current fifth grade class meets with aquatic biologists from the Tennessee Aquarium, TVA, and TWRA to release juvenile sturgeon—Y.O.Y., or "young of the year"—into the French Broad River at Seven Islands State Birding Park, only a short distance from their school.

By 2015, the sturgeon partners have reintroduced more than 181,000 young of the year to the Tennessee and Cumberland Rivers since the project began below Douglas Dam that July day in 2000. The goal of the long-term program is to restore a self-sustaining population of the ancient fish in Tennessee. Since that first release, personnel have changed, lives have moved on, but the mission has stayed true to course. So far, the effort has proven very successful, with anglers reporting these fish downstream in Alabama and Kentucky. Biologists have also been encouraged by recent surveys to monitor the population between Knoxville and Chattanooga.

That perfect October day was the last sturgeon release of the year for the juvenile fish raised under the watchful eyes of Dr. Anna George and Dr. Bernie Kuhajda, aquatic conservation biologists, and their interns at the Tennessee Aquarium Conservation Institute in Chattanooga. The young fry had hatched from eggs collected in late spring from female sturgeons along the shallows of the Wolf River, a tributary of the Fox River that empties into Lake Butte des Morts in Wisconsin.

The male sturgeons swim upstream from the lake to the breeding grounds to be joined by the females a couple of days later. Wildlife agents simply walk out into the shallows to catch the large fish in nets.

A full fifteen years after their initial unveiling below Douglas Dam, I attended the early October release again with Ijams senior naturalist Peg Beute, plus the nature center's in-house veterinarian, Dr. Louise Conrad, and volunteer and former teacher Jane Rule. We were there to watch the fifth graders take turns carrying dip nets full of juvenile sturgeons to the shallows and let them swim away. Plus, as in years past, two of the young fish were going home to the nature center to be on display in the exhibit hall.

"They are quote, unquote, living fossils, but they are fish that have been around since before the dinosaurs," said Dr. Conrad. We weren't around to save the latter, but maybe we can revitalize the former.

Restoring a population of a long-lost species, be it furred, feathered, or finned, seems a Herculean task. Although beavers have managed to accomplish this on their own, there's little way a sturgeon could travel to the Tennessee River Valley without assistance. In the meantime, while we wait, we are back to our Dickensian question: Is it the best of times, or the worst? Is the glass half empty or half full? It's hard to watch trained aquatic biologists as they gently carry fish to the water's edge and let them slowly swim away and not think that the species' future is in good hands. If you only follow the news headlines, you get a lopsided view of our species, our humanity. Unless you are a fisherman or an ichthyologist, you rarely think of fish other than an occasional trip to a seafood restaurant. But they exist out there in our waters by the thousands. Ephemeral? They are virtually invisible. Very, very few of us will ever see a mature lake sturgeon. They're phantoms that patrol the depths of rivers and lakes. Even so, take comfort that this ancient behemoth has been returned to its rightful place in our biosphere. Again, from Dickens, "It's a far far better thing...."

Whooping Crane
Grus americana

"Hope" is the thing with feathers—
That perches in the soul—
And sings the tune without the words—
And never stops—at all.

—Emily Dickinson

WHOOPING CRANES barely exist. For over one hundred years, they have been close to the precipice, a downy feather away from disappearing altogether. For them, the ephemeral nature of life on earth is all too real.

In 1912, Edward H. Forbush wrote, "The Whooping Crane is doomed to extinction. It has disappeared from its former habitat in the East and is now found only in uninhabited places."

In many ways, the reclusive crane became the poster child for all endangered species in an era before that term even entered the popular vernacular. Never an abundant species, U.S. Fish and Wildlife reported that their total wild population had dwindled in 1941 to a low of only twenty-one total: fifteen western migrants and six left in the nonmigratory flock in Louisiana. To highlight the importance of wildlife conservation, in 1957 a three-cent postage stamp issued by the Post Office depicted a pair of parent cranes with two young ones.

Just a few years ago, it was impossible to imagine the leggy white bird would ever be seen again in the Tennessee Valley. That's why the morning of November 14, 2001, was historic. Seven wild whooping cranes had just spent the night at Hiwassee Wildlife Refuge in Meigs County just north of Chattanooga. How they got there is a remarkable story.

Whooping cranes are North America's tallest bird. Standing erect, they're just over five feet tall and appear solid white with long black legs; their red crown and cheek patches add a flash of brilliance to their faces. The ruby markings are bare, featherless skin that ends at the base of the spear-like bone-colored bill. Perhaps their most distinctive feature are their bustles. They look like billowy, white tails, but the handsome cabooses are created by the folded, long, secondary wing feathers that rest against their bodies and extend over the bird's hind quarters.

On the ground the majestic long-legged cranes strut rhythmically, reminiscent of palace guards—heads erect, ever watchful. Peter Matthiessen described the birds as the most statuesque on the continent. And who could argue with him? This air of nobility is not lost in flight. With a wingspan of eighty-seven inches—wider than I am tall—whooping cranes work the sky with strong, broad stokes, their necks fully extended. When they fly, it's also revealed that the tips of their wings, the long primary feathers, are jet black.

The name whooping crane comes from their loud trumpet-like calls: long rolling bugles described by some as *ker-loo, ker-lee-oooo.* It's a call both pure and primordial. The whoop can be heard up to a mile away and is produced from a five-foot-long trachea coiled like a French horn inside their breastbone. It's a resonance chamber few birds can match.

Whooping cranes are wary creatures fond of isolated marshes, wet prairies, and river shorelines. Unlike sandhill cranes, whoopers do not occur in large flocks but in small, isolated family groupings called cohorts. They are omnivores that eat a wide range of items—acorns, seeds, berries, roots, frogs, snakes, crayfish, insects, mussels, snails gleaned from the ground—but a researcher learned early that their favorite food is blue crab. Strutting through a marsh, they cautiously dip their long necks down to probe the soft mud for whatever tidbit presents itself.

Whoopers are monogamous, essentially mating for life and will not accept a new partner until a faithful one has died. Like sandhills, whooping cranes live long lives, perhaps as long as fifty years. In May 2016, it was announced that a sandhill crane wearing a leg band with the number 599-05468 had been recovered. The band was worn for thirty-six and a half years. From that, U.S. Fish and Wildlife estimated that the crane made round-trip migrations from Border, Wyoming, to Bosque del Apache, New Mexico, thirty-six and a half times. That's a total of 51,100 miles in a lifetime, or the equivalent of circling the earth more than twice.

At their breeding site, both the male and female whooping cranes work to build a nest of soft grasses on a raised mound of reeds, grass, or sod. The nest is generally in or near the water and the mated pair take turns incubating the clutch. Like most birds that nest on the ground, whooping crane hatchlings are precocial, which means that the chicks are well-developed at birth and quickly become mobile after emerging from the eggs; they more or less "hit the ground running." After hatching, both parents feed and guard the young that follow them through the marsh. Unlike hummingbirds or even red pandas, whooping cranes' fathers are active parents. The fledging cranes are able to fly after eighty to ninety days but remain with their protective parents for months. They have to be taught how to migrate and where to go. Their demeanor is almost antediluvian, suggesting an existence in a time before the time. Oh, and did I mention they are intense? They look you in the eye, poised to strike.

A KINSHIP WITH T-REX

In late spring of 2005, former Ijams executive director Paul James and I visited Patuxent Wildlife Research Center in Laurel, Maryland. Created in 1965 by an appropriations amendment sponsored by Senator Karl Mundt from South Dakota, the center is under the control of the U.S. Fish and Wildlife Service; its mandate is to work out captive breeding programs for whooping cranes and other endangered species.

After meeting with John French, the center's director, we were escorted inside one of the enclosures that housed captive whooping cranes. To be only a few feet away from one of these magnificent birds was exhilarating. I have worked with several intense raptors but none raised my level of caution as these look-you-in-the-eye birds. Like the red panda at the Knoxville Zoo, I was ready to scamper up a tree at the least sign of trouble.

The crane specialist with us held her outstretched hand in front of her to keep the closest whooper from pecking at either her or our eyes. They were old acquaintances; we were the strangers. It was a lot like the scene from the 2015 movie *Jurassic World,* with researcher Owen Grady holding a *Velociraptor* in check with his outstretched hand. In light of recent discoveries, a whooping crane and the now extinct theropod are not that far removed from one another.

"Dinosaurs have been getting slowly more birdlike for decades—perhaps not mainstream depictions, but at least in the minds of paleontologists," wrote Stephen Bodio for Cornell's *Living Bird.*

I remembered seeing *Jurassic Park* in the early 1990s with my very young nephew, Michael Brett, standing the entire movie between his father David and me watching the big screen dinosaurs. His older sister, Leighanna, seemed fine with the movie magic illusion, but Michael was transfixed. *Could this all be real,* he must have wondered. Well, not the amusement park part, but the giant reptile part, yes. But imagining all of those scary beasts covered with downy feathers seemed farfetched, at the time.

Since 1861 and the first discovery in Bavaria in southern Germany of the nearly complete fossilized remains of an odd reptile named *Archaeopteryx* that had feathers—yes, feathers—we have known something funny was going on around 150 million years ago, but connecting the dots has taken awhile. Reptiles have scales, not feathers; but just like our fingernails, they are all made of the same tough structural protein, keratin. So, there's a kinship.

If you think all dinosaurs were large like the brontosaurs in the old Sinclair Oil logo, you're off the mark. Many were small, odd-looking creatures. *Archaeopteryx* was raven-sized, and its discovery caused quite a ruckus in the scientific community. Major paradigm shifts generally do; apple carts do not like being upset. It is estimated that *Archaeopteryx* weighed about two pounds, had broad wings with rounded ends, and had an overall length of up to twenty inches. It also had claws, jaws with teeth, a long boney tail, and hyperextensible second toes known as "killing claws."

Of late, as new fossil remains have been unearthed, mostly from the Liaoning Province of China, paleontologists, and even dinosaur-obsessed kids like myself now know that many or most of the terrible lizards had feathers of some form and other birdlike qualities. Some even had toothless beaks. It's hard to imagine the very toothy *Tyrannosaurus rex* as being feathered, but world-renowned paleontologist Robert Bakker is now fond of describing the ferocious predator as a "20,000 pound roadrunner from Hell." Think about it; that's scary. As Bodio pointed out, the Age of Reptiles might also be called, "The Age of Big Weird Feathered Things."

A beautiful 2008 coffee table book written by paleontologist John Long and illustrated by acclaimed wildlife artist Peter Schouten titled *Feathered Dinosaurs* depicts over seventy now-named species of weird feathered things including *Appalachiosaurus montgomeriensis,* whose remains were unearthed in Montgomery County, Alabama, in 1982. Plus, the book published by Oxford University Press has six species of early birds. Truth be told, 100 million years ago, not only were there feathered dinosaurs, but also living with them were truly recognizable birds. Fossil finds of the past twenty years, around the world but principally at Jehol Biota in China, indicate that birdlife during the Age of Dinosaurs may have been just as diverse and colorful as it is today.

Amber is fossilized tree resin. Golden in color and transparent, it's long been considered a gemstone. But it's not a mineral like amethyst; it's plant based. Greek myth has it that when Phaethon, son of Helios, was killed, his grieving sisters were turned into poplar trees and their tears became solidified as amber. And if that weren't dramatic enough, sometimes these golden teardrops contain treasures inside—mosquitoes, ants, flies, leaves—perfectly frozen in time, like Victorian glass paperweights. These embedded treasures are called inclusions.

In June 2016, *National Geographic* announced that two intact, albeit small, feathered wings were found in 99-million-year-old Burmese amber. "Skin, muscle, claws, and feather shafts are visible in both samples, along with the remains of rows of primary asymmetrical flight feathers, secondary feathers, and covert feathers. All are similar in arrangement and microstructure to modern birds," wrote Kristin Romey.

Two entire wings preserved in toto. Perhaps invertebrate paleontologist Ryan McKellar summed it up the best: "It's mind-blowingly cool." That's not science speak; it's everyday speak, so I'll repeat it. It's mind-blowingly cool.

But all of the feathered dinos came to an end roughly 66 million years ago, when a small asteroid or large meteor hit the earth. POW! Its aftermath started a chain reaction that ultimately wiped out all the dinosaurs and an estimated 75 percent of all species on the planet. The Chicxulub event, so named because the impact crater is located off the Yucatán Peninsula near the town of Chicxulub, Mexico, produced Armageddon-like conditions.

"But, Uncle Lyn," queried my nephew Logan Brett, a geology student at the University of Tennessee, "what about the Deccan Traps?"

Oddly, it was his twenty-first birthday, and he was returning a congratulatory text with the mention of a concept I had never heard of. Scrambling, I looked up the work of paleontologist Greta Keller, who in a 2014 paper argued that massive volcano eruptions in the Deccan Plateau of west-central India 66.25 million years ago did in the dinos. The continuing eruptions created layer upon layer of hardened lava flows known by geologists as "traps," or steps. Ultimately these traps were 6,562 feet thick and covered half of what is now India. That's a major remodeling of planet Earth. Such a catastrophic molten outpouring filled the atmosphere with volcanic gases, particularly sulfur dioxide. Keller believes that this is what truly killed 75 percent of all life on Earth. There's a growing sense that the Chicxulub asteroid impact may have triggered the Deccan volcanism. It was a one-two punch that dramatically changed our planet.

"Strong ecologic recovery may have been impossible until the volcanism slowed down 500,000 years later," concluded Paul R. Renne, director of the

Berkeley Geochronology Center, in a paper published in the fall of 2015 in the journal *Science.*

Clearly, for a long period of time, Earth was not a hospitable place. How, then, did the early birds survive all this when the dinosaurs did not? The widespread fire storms and darkened skies created a planet-wide condition known as an impact winter. Adding to the centuries of volcanic eruptions and an atmosphere that was virtually unbreathable, it's something of a miracle that 25 percent of life did survive. In its wake, layers upon layers of dead or decaying plant material would have covered the ground. Just like all the leaves that fall in autumn, this build-up is called detritus. Millipedes, snails, worms, beetle grubs, and other insects are collectively known as detritivores; they eat this organic windfall.

Evolutionary biologist Stephen L. Brusatte, with the School of GeoSciences, University of Edinburgh, presented a new theory in the May 23, 2016, issue of the journal *Current Biology.* Brusatte posited that the birds (and, it would stand to reason, even the small mammals) that survived this mass extinction lived to another day because they ate the invertebrate detritivores and massive amounts of seeds lying dormant on the ground. The early birds did get the worms; they scratched through the debris very much like today's towhees.

Bottom line: all birds alive today owe their existence to their refuse-grubbing ancestors.

PERHAPS WHOOPERS WERE ALWAYS SCARCE

That's the basics of whooping crane biology and even a peek at their zoogenic roots, their long-ago, great-great-*ad-infinitum* grandparents scavenged for anything edible on the ground just like the extant cranes do today. But perhaps their most remarkable modern-day feature is their scarcity. Although listed as common in many early accounts, whooping cranes were probably never abundant. Modern estimates indicate that perhaps no more than two thousand—I've seen estimates as low as fourteen hundred—lived in North America at the time the first Europeans arrived. Passenger pigeons once existed in the millions, but the whoopers' paucity gives us a sense of perspective; even before Columbus made landfall in the New World or before that, the Vikings, some things were rare and elusive. There was a myth that circulated for decades even in the scientific community that although "they may not be common here, somewhere whooping cranes exist in a great flock." People searched for that great flock for years, but it never was found.

The graceful white cranes have always had a wariness of humans and kept an ever-watchful stance, leaving areas when settlers arrived. It's as if they had an innate sense that humans were trouble. The formal written history of this great bird has been told before; parts of it bear repeating for it's just as poignant today. It essentially begins with English naturalist Mark Catesby. While Catesby was in the Carolinas in 1722, on a trip along the coast, a Native American gave him the skin of a large white bird. He knew at once that it was a species unknown and undescribed. He recorded it as *Grus americana alba,* Latin for "crane American white." In 1748, another dried whooping crane skin made it to George Edwards in London. He included the bird's description in his book *A Natural History of Birds the Most of Which Have Not Hitherto Been Figured or Described.* (That's another long title; respectability was more important in those days than marketability.)

A few years later, in 1770, explorer Samuel Hearne recorded the following observation in Canada: "This bird visits Hudson's Bay in the Spring, though not in great numbers. They are generally seen only in pairs, and that not very often. . . . It is esteemed good eating. The wing bones of this bird are so long and large, that I have known them made into flutes."

In the early 1800s, the then-unknown wildlife artist and naturalist John James Audubon freely roamed the country drawing and painting the birds he found. Like the odd fish Rafinesque, he had a thirst to know what was out there, a vagabond searching to find himself. Unlike Rafinesque, Audubon was uneducated, but he had a trump card, an incredible artistic talent. In New Orleans, he found, killed, and drew a whooping crane. The artwork depicts a whooper, head bowed, about to eat two newly-hatched alligators. The watercolor of the crane was finished in 1821, and the two reptiles were added the following year.

Audubon had trouble finding supporters in this country. He was snubbed; both he and his work were deemed too flamboyant or, in the parlance of today, "over the top." To the stuffy world of 1800s academia, Audubon was indeed flamboyant. He was a Frenchman and spoke with a heavy French accent and with a certain *savoir faire.* He knew American birds and how to draw them. Not to be denied, he took his vision to England, a trip that ultimately changed the course of his life. The whooping crane painting is one of the pieces in his portfolio that he showed to the esteemed book engraver William Home Lizars. Again, in today's terms, Lizars was "blown away." He had never seen such a wonderful wildlife picture: an alligator-eating bird. Unbelievable. "Mr. Audubon," Lizars exclaimed, "the people here don't know who you are at all, but depend upon it, they *shall* know." Rebuffed and un-known in America, Audubon soon became the talk of the country across the Atlantic, bringing the English what they were most eager to see: glimpses of the natural history of the strange New World.

Audubon's fortunes may have taken off, but the 1800s did not bode well for the leggy white cranes. America was expanding. Settlers were rapidly sweeping into untamed places, shooting or spooking whatever got in the way. By the end of the Civil War, the late 1860s, it is believed that only about thirteen hundred cranes remained, but not for long.

Faith McNulty wrote, "It is probable that 90 percent of the whooping crane population disappeared in the thirty years between 1870 and 1900." Wetlands were drained or dredged and converted into more "useful" parcels. The vast prairies across the central states were tamed into farmland. In Louisiana, the habitats of the whoopers were remade into millions of acres of rice fields, and the newly arrived rice men shot the cranes that turned up among their crops. In 1918, at Sweet Lake east of Port Arthur, rice farmer Alcie Daigle shot twelve cranes in one day.

It wasn't just habitat loss that pushed the cranes to the edge. Irresponsible sportsmen killed them as well. On a slow day, when there was little to shoot at, a target that's solid white and five feet tall is very tempting. The fact that whooping cranes are vigilant made it feel more like sport. In 1888, the periodical *Sports Afield: A Journal for Gentlemen* posted the following report from a "gentleman" shooter in Grand County, Colorado: "Ducks and other water fowl are not as plentiful as they have been the seasons before. Cranes, though, are very numerous this season—some of them big white fellows. One was shot recently that measured 6 feet, 6 inches."

If this weren't enough, still other pressures worked against the cranes. There is a particular odd human obsession that haunts many; it's the longing to possess something rare and exquisite, whether it's a Fabergé egg or a vintage *Superman* comic book. The little blue Spix's macaw *(Cyanopsitta spixi)* of Brazil has been practically driven to extinction in the wild because wealthy collectors want to own one as a pet.

In the late 1800s, there was a genteel Victorian hobby that was quite popular: egg collecting. Each species of bird lays a unique egg. Collectors viewed their pastime as "scientific," and the study of eggs became known as oölogy. There was even a publication, *Oölogist,* that catered to egg fanciers. Once word began to circulate that whooping cranes were becoming scarce, every oölogist had to possess one of their eggs. The average whooping crane egg is four inches long, soft blue to khaki colored with brown and reddish-brown splotches.

Although collecting eggs seems innocent enough, this parlor hobby had its ruthless side, as an account written in 1876 by oölogist George B. Sennett attests. He was at Elbow Lake, Minnesota, shotgun in hand, when he found a pair of cranes, the female on the nest protecting the eggs that he desired. Sennett wrote, "The male stood on the ridge watching her closely for a few minutes, when, feeling all was safe he calmly commenced to plume himself in grand style and shortly walked off away from me, the proudest of birds. I slowly arose, turned, and gave her one barrel as she was rising from the nest and the next before she had gone six feet and dropped her in the water."

When you read something like this today, you cannot help but be incensed. This historic account documents a mated pair in the eastern migratory population, a flock soon to be driven out of existence. Yet, amateur collectors weren't the only problem. Men of science and museum curators were equally voracious. They too desired to possess something rare. They wanted mounted specimens, study skins, and eggs to file away in long, flat, wooden drawers. This same self-centered interest helped drive the nail in the coffin of other birds like the Carolina parakeet and, perhaps, the ivory-billed woodpecker.

When news of the whooping crane's plight became a topic of discussion, curators let it be known that they would pay a premium price: in 1887, top dollar was $2.50 a skin or a dozen for $24.00. By 1890, that cost had climbed, depending on the condition, to between $8.00 and $18.00 a skin. The coveted eggs at first sold for 50 cents apiece, but by 1890 the price had jumped to $2.00 each.

In today's world, this wanton destruction, even in the name of science, seems unconscionable. The sensibilities back then were different from our own. At this point, no one had ever dared to imagine that a species on the edge of oblivion could possibly be saved. Arthur Allen, founder of the Cornell Lab of Ornithology, wrote, "The whooping crane is so near the precipice of extinction that it is apt to topple over any moment. . . . Gradually we have come to our senses. Let us hope it is not too late."

An editorial in the *Christian Science Monitor* said it best: "Can a society, whether through sheer wantonness or callous neglect, permit the extinction of something beautiful or grand in nature without risking the extinction of something beautiful or grand in its own character?"

The question of the day became this: Can a rare species truly be saved?

Notions of preservation and conservation began to slowly percolate, but there were mountains of resistance to overcome; added to this was a lack of understanding of the species itself. To begin with, no one exactly knew the whooping crane's range. That couldn't happen today because thousands of ornithologists and amateur birders are outside every day, recording what they see and where they see it. It wasn't until an ornithologist with the U.S. Department of Agriculture named Wells B. Cooke began to pull together reports that an accurate picture of the declining crane population began to emerge. Wells used sightings from a wide range of people across the country and in 1888 published a bulletin on migratory birds. After this accounting, the plight of the whooping crane became clear. They weren't being found in very many places. Principally, there were only three known groups.

The eastern migratory flock was believed to have flown annually from Illinois across the Appalachians to winter along the Atlantic Coast and gulf. The last reported sighting of a member in this population probably occurred in the late 1920s, when a taxidermist killed a whooping crane near St. Augustine, Florida.

It was then realized that there were only two groups of whooping cranes left in the wild: a nonmigratory group that lived year-round in Louisiana and a western migratory flock that wintered on the Texas Coast on the Blackjack Peninsula. Where the Texas cranes spent their summers was a mystery, and why the Louisiana group did not migrate was also unknown. By 1937, only ten to fifteen cranes remained in Cajun country, and an unnamed hurricane that hit in August 1940 killed half of those. Soon only one was left. In 1950, Louisiana's sole whooping crane was caught and taken into captivity.

After that, all that remained was the one migratory group that wintered in Texas. By 1937, it was believed to be only twenty birds, but all probably weren't of breeding age. An early conservation law should have helped this population. The Migratory Bird Treaty of 1916 between the United States and Canada placed the management of migratory birds in the hands of the federal government. It declared a moratorium on the killing of all migratory birds. But like most early conservation laws, it was difficult to enforce. It's hard to change tradition, and hunters were used to shooting cranes as they flew over the Great Plains. Yet, ironically, it was the sportsmen who provided funds that finally turned the tide in halting the decline of whooping cranes.

First, the Duck Stamp Act of 1934 required hunters to purchase a stamp in order to hunt waterfowl, primarily ducks and geese. This user fee collected millions of dollars to purchase land for wildlife refuges. In 1937, as part of Franklin Roosevelt's New Deal, the Pittman-Robertson Federal Aid in Wildlife Restoration Act was also enacted. It placed an 11 percent excise tax on firearms, ammunition, and other hunting equipment. The millions raised were distributed back to states to aid in the recovery of game animals.

By now, biologists knew that protecting a portion of Blackjack Peninsula on the Texas coast was essential, and 46,712 acres were purchased for $463,500, establishing a refuge at Aransas Bay that was later called the Aransas National Wildlife Refuge. The timing of this purchase could not have been more critical. Without it, the wild whooping crane population would have probably disappeared in the 1940s. Nevertheless, the crane population remained precariously low for several years.

In time, Port Aransas became the center of focus for whooping crane recovery. In February 2007, Knoxville artist Vickie Henderson, who later became board of directors chair for Operation Migration, and I attended the Whooping Crane Festival held in the south Texas town annually in late February. We stayed as guests of Tom Stein, refuge biologist and whooping crane coordinator for U.S. Fish and Wildlife.

Now that the Texas wintering grounds of the whoopers were saved, it was determined that the summer breeding grounds needed protection as well. But where did the cranes spend their summers?

In the late 1940s, the National Audubon Society entered the picture. This early environmental organization was named in honor of John James Audubon, the artist who benefited from his painting of a whooping crane a century earlier. It was payback time. In 1946, biologist Robert Allen was named director of the new Cooperative Whooping Crane Project and spent the remainder of his life devoted to the cranes. He was described as being "fiercely dedicated"; his iron will was coupled with sensitivity and gentleness. In addition to studying the basic biology and life history of the birds to learn their critical needs, he set out to discover their mysterious summer nesting grounds. His fieldwork for Audubon was very similar to research carried out in the late 1930s on ivory-billed woodpeckers by James T. Tanner. (See my book *Ghost Birds*.)

Each spring, whooping cranes flew north and disappeared into the vast expanse of uppermost Canada. With the help of the U.S. Fish and Wildlife Service and the Canadian Wildlife Service, Allen combed the region for eleven summers, from Hudson Bay to the Pacific Ocean and from the U.S. border to the Arctic Circle. He traveled more than six thousand miles by jeep and twenty thousand miles by plane, spending many frigid nights huddled inside a tent. It's not easy finding twenty birds if they don't want to be found. At one point, he drove an unheated government truck. When the windshield froze over, he used the heat from his bare hands to melt the ice. The hunt became one of the greatest wildlife searches in North American history.

During the winter of 1951–52, the wild western population only numbered twenty-one; a few others lived in captivity in zoos. The whooping crane ancestors may have survived the mass extinction of 66 million years before, but the modern descendants were in real trouble. That year, while the summer search for the flock was in full swing, a widespread media blitz was carried out to educate hunters and the general population about the crane's predicament. Reports began to appear in local newspapers across the country. In the fall of 1952, all twenty-one cranes plus three juveniles returned to Texas—a hopeful sign.

In 1955, Allen recorded the following after thirty-one days of travel: "Let it be known that at 2 p.m. on the 23rd day of June, we are on the nesting ground with the Whooping Cranes! We have finally made it!"

The cranes were hiding in an area already protected: Canada's Wood Buffalo National Park, a refuge set aside for the conservation of woodland bison. It straddles the border between Canada's Alberta province and the Northwest Territory. True to their nature, the whooping cranes had chosen an isolated location, far from civilization near the Arctic Circle. It's much farther north than anyone expected and meant that the cranes' annual migration covered a round trip of roughly fifty-two hundred miles.

That year, the wild population had climbed to twenty-eight, and by 1969, J. B. Owen reported in the *Knoxville News Sentinel* that the population had climbed to fifty-five. Clearly the population was increasing, albeit incredibly slowly. Could more be done?

Earlier, in 1950, the first whooping crane hatched in captivity was born at Patuxent; the mother was a captive female on loan from the New Orleans Zoo. Audubon's Robert Allen was in charge of that project as well. He had been studying crane interaction for years. This birthing proved that captive breeding could speed up their return, but that recovery suffered a setback when Allen, their devoted champion, unexpectedly died of natural causes on June 28, 1963.

The study of whooping crane biology revealed that the mated female normally lays two eggs, but the parents usually raise only one. Many birds produce more eggs than they need. In essence, the extra ones are insurance in case the older siblings die. It was decided that some "extra eggs" could be removed from nests and raised artificially. To some degree this improves the chances that the remaining sibling survives since its parents turn their full attention to feeding and protecting it.

Starting in 1967, scientists from Canada and America began to remove "second eggs" from the nests of wild cranes summering at Wood Buffalo.

These eggs were flown to the Patuxent Wildlife Research Center and incubated; they became the nascent captive breeding flock.

In 1975, yet another program was attempted. Fourteen eggs were removed from whooper nests in Wood Buffalo and placed into sandhill crane nests in Idaho. Sandhill cranes are a similar but smaller species. They're closely related to whoopers, and it was hoped that the wild sandhills would become protective foster parents. Once the adopted cranes were grown, it was believed that they would follow their foster parents when they migrated to a wildlife refuge in New Mexico, thus slowly establishing a second migratory flock of whoopers that intermingled with the sandhills.

Most of these adopted whoopers did not survive. They routinely flew into power lines that the smaller, more agile sandhill cranes were able to maneuver around. The whooping cranes that did survive grew up "species confused." Wouldn't you? Perhaps believing they were sandhill cranes, they hadn't learned the elaborate mating rituals necessary to encourage mating and didn't view their fellow whoopers as possible partners. Thus, no pair bonds were formed. This program was soon abandoned and replaced by other efforts. But at least another attempt to save the species had been made.

In 1973, two Cornell University graduate students, Ron Sauey and George Archibald, established the International Crane Foundation (ICF) on the Sauey family horse farm in Baraboo, Wisconsin. Horse stalls became crane pens, an incubator was installed, and enclosures were built. The name "International" was not just a throwaway moniker; it was an ambition. Initially, ICF worked with brolga and eastern sarus cranes from Australia. Techniques learned in the captive breeding of these two species were soon used to raise endangered whoopers. The first chick hatched in Baraboo was named "Gee Whiz."

So where does that leave us? In the late summer of 2005, Ijams wildlife biologist Pam Petko-Seus, Paul James, and I visited with George Archibald at ICF in Wisconsin. Archibald knows more about cranes and the perils they face than anyone in the world. It was hard to contain our admiration. He was then maybe, kind of, sort of, starting to feel good about the whoopers' chances of survival. He reflected back on all that had happened in his lifetime.

As early as the late 1970s, the establishment of a new, wild, nonmigratory flock was being discussed. This would replace the group that had lived in southern Louisiana until the 1940s. A site of expansive savanna and marshland around Kissimmee, Florida, was chosen because it was very similar to the bayous of Louisiana. By 1989, both Patuxent and the ICF were having great success raising young whooping cranes called colts. Soon after hatching, the young birds imprint on the first large moving object; if it's a person, they will grow up "people friendly." Losing their wariness of humans isn't a desirable trait for any wild animal. To get around this, caregivers dressed in white crane suits tended the impressionable young cranes. The costume, complete with a realistic adult-crane head puppet, was designed to hide the human form. Handlers in the white garb taught the young hatchlings how to eat and drink, even what kind of food to look for. The costumed humans did their best to imitate natural rhythmic crane movements. They were earnest surrogate parents—albeit rather large, bulky ones.

In 1993, eight new whooping cranes that were raised in Wisconsin and two from Patuxent were released at Three Lakes Wildlife Management Area near Kissimmee in Central Florida. They were on their own—wild and free. As the years passed, researchers learned and techniques improved. The initial survival rate was disappointing. Predators, mostly bobcats, killed many, but the project continued. In time, the older whoopers began to form pair bonds and build practice nests. A few eggs were even laid, although raccoons often stole them, but the young future parents were learning as they matured.

Real progress finally came in 2000. A mated pair of whooping cranes that had been hand-raised by humans and released in Florida successfully hatched two chicks on their own. They were the first wild whoopers born in the United States in six decades. (Remember, the wild western flock cranes are born in Canada.) The two did not last long. The first disappeared from the nest in ten days, perhaps the victim of a great horned owl. The shredded body of the second, probably killed by a bobcat, was found a few weeks later. This second youngster was only a few days from fledging. The deaths of the two young cranes were disappointing but understandable. Even at Wood Buffalo in Canada, it's believed that predators kill up to 50 percent of all wild crane nestlings. Raising a young crane until it's old enough to fly to safety is not easy. The effort to establish a population of nonmigratory cranes in Florida continued for fifteen years and was finally terminated in 2008. Problems with survival, reproduction, drought, habitat loss due to development, and the overall costs plagued the program. In all, between 1993 and 2005, 289 captive-raised, nonmigratory young cranes had been released into Osceola, Lake, and Polk Counties in central Florida, but as of 2015, only 8 survived.

With the continued growth of the wild Wood Buffalo/Aransas flock and the successful rearing programs at Patuxent and ICF in Wisconsin, a new dream was being bandied about. Could the eastern migratory flock be re-established? It was feared that an ill-timed hurricane or even disease could decimate the natural Texas migratory population. Historically, there had once been an eastern migratory flock as evidenced by the crane skin given to Mark Catesby in the 1700s.

CAN YOU TEACH A CRANE TO MIGRATE?

Standing in a room full of people that included Bill Lishman, you first noticed his tall, lanky stature. The bearded Canadian is an artist and creative thinker. His forty-foot stainless steel Iceberg sculpture was officially unveiled outside at the Canadian Museum of Nature in Ottawa, Ontario, on June 17, 2016. Known by many as "Father Goose," Lishman first reached international fame in the fall of 1993 when he and pilot Joe Duff taught eighteen Canada geese how to migrate from Ontario to a wintering site at Airlie Center in Warrenton, Virginia. The young geese followed the two men in ultralight aircraft as though they were their parents. The project was so captivating that it was reported on ABC's *20/20* and generated such widespread public interest that it spawned a major feel-good motion picture, *Fly Away Home*. In the movie, actor Jeff Daniels portrays Lishman.

With the success of the goose flights, Lishman and Duff founded Operation Migration (OM), a nonprofit organization registered in both Canada and the United States in 1994. Their new dream: teaching whooping cranes how to migrate. In time, Lishman retired, and Joe Duff became OM's director.

The next year, OM began studies of cranes' flying habits. For the next few years, they worked with the smaller sandhill cranes that had been raised by costume-wearing humans at Patuxent. Procedures were tested and refined. In 1997, seven sandhills were ultralight-led from Ontario to Virginia, and the next spring six of them flew back on their own to Ontario. Returning home on their own was an important part of their foster parenting. They had to understand where home was.

In 1999, the joint Canada/United States Whooping Crane Recovery Team sanctioned OM—in essence, giving their go-ahead to the ultralight-led migration program. To accomplish such an ambitious undertaking, the Whooping Crane Eastern Partnership (WCEP) was formed. The consortium was made up of several nonprofit organizations and governmental agencies from both Canada and the United States.

By 2000, the stage was set for a complete dress rehearsal. In early fall, the OM team led eleven costume-reared sandhill cranes from Necedah National Wildlife Refuge in Wisconsin to St. Matins Marsh Aquatic Preserve on Florida's Gulf Coast. Necedah is a 43,656-acre refuge established in 1939.

The dress rehearsal to Florida took forty days and covered 1,250 miles. The following spring, the sandhills returned to the north unaided. But sandhill cranes are the world's most numerous cranes. It was time to start working with the world's most endangered: whooping cranes.

Early in 2001, eggs hatched at Patuxent were raised by costumed humans under the tutelage of wildlife biologist Dan Sprague. The young, leggy colts were taught to walk behind a taxiing ultralight. It was a surreal sight, but a lot that was about to transpire over the next fifteen years was extraordinary. In July, Secretary of the Interior Gale Norton announced that the experimental program had been authorized. It was the official U.S. governmental blessing. On July 12, ten crane colts were moved to Necedah to imprint on the area and begin flight school. At the refuge that summer, they continued to follow ultralights driven by pilots, surrogate parents wearing white crane suits.

By October, the recovery team was ready to attempt the journey that only a few years before seemed impossible. They hoped to avoid bad weather and make the one-thousand-plus-mile trip from Wisconsin by way of Tennessee to Florida in less than two months. To have a successful day's flight, conditions had to be ideal; if they weren't, both cranes and humans stayed on the ground. Duff reported that they needed cold air to keep the cranes from overheating. They also needed calm conditions or southerly winds.

At 7:15 a.m., October 17, 2001, the small cohort of eight young whooping cranes left Necedah, dutifully flying in formation behind three ultralights. At Ijams Nature Center in Knoxville, educator Peg Beute followed their progress on the Internet. When she called with the news that the troupe was on the ground in the Tennessee Valley, I jumped at the chance to see them take off, and we left Knoxville at 4:00 a.m. Whooping cranes roosting in East Tennessee was historic. And if ever you have to get up early to see history in the making, Peg is the person you want to go with because usually she brings fresh-baked biscuits. The human/crane troupe had covered a total of 658 miles since leaving Wisconsin. They were bivouacked at Hiwassee Wildlife Refuge in Meigs County. The protected area is a six-thousand-acre parcel—twenty-five hundred acres of land and thirty-five hundred acres of water at the confluence of the Hiwassee and Tennessee Rivers. The lake waters of Chickamauga Dam back up into the location, creating quiet, protective coves. The new cranes had spent the night in a protective pen near Hiwassee Island, the site of the Native American village where some historians believe De Soto's men had camped 461 years earlier. The former farmland is now managed by the Tennessee Wildlife Resources Agency and has become a gathering place for thousands of wintering sandhill cranes. It was important for the migrating whoopers to learn the location as well.

If conditions were right, the experimental crane caravan was scheduled to depart at 6:30 a.m. the next morning, November 14. After the two-hour drive from Knoxville, Peg and I stood bundled and chilly with wildlife photographer Dick Dickenson, watching the site from the edge of a field near a gazebo built for the public. We were a good distance from the traveling crane troupe and would remain so. People are not allowed anywhere near the endangered cranes unless they are one of the OM costumed trained handlers.

As daylight began to seep into the valley, a small flock of noisy sandhill cranes flew in and a northern harrier hovered briefly over the field in front of us. The people who had gathered to see the cranes hopped back and forth from left foot to right, partly to keep warm and partly because it was hard to contain the nervous energy that percolated through their systems. A cool predawn fog hanging over the water kept the whoopers on the ground until 8:51 a.m., but as the fog slowly lifted, we watched the three ultralight aircraft circle "cranelike" above the holding pen half in the water. In time, the young cranes followed, spiraling up to fall into formation behind one of the motorized foster parents heading south. The surreal moment got even more so, as is often the case when history is being made.

After leaving Hiwassee, the group flew 67 miles to Gordon County, Georgia. The flying caravan eventually reached the Chassahowitzka National Wildlife Refuge in Florida on December 1. The trip had taken forty-eight days (twenty-four flight days and twenty-four grounded-by-weather days) and had covered 1,164.2 miles. For the next several weeks the young cranes spend their nights inside a protective pen, watched by costumed humans. After a time, they slowly become independent cranes left to migrate north on their own in the spring.

After that initial migration, with adjustments made in the methods, routes, and stopovers, more than two hundred young cranes imprinted on the parental ultralights and their costumed pilots to fly south for the winter every fall for fifteen years. Beginning in 2005, a new technique was added to supplement the OM ultralight-led group. Called Direct Autumn Release (DAR), young cranes were released in small groups with older, now-experienced whooping cranes that could teach the migration route to their young charges. It was hoped that in time the captive-bred, but now wild, adult cranes would pair-bond and raise young cranes of their own, thus creating a self-sustaining population. It worked. In 2006, a young crane designated W1-06 was the eastern flock's very *first* wild-hatched chick to survive. Yet, over the following decade the crane partnership noticed that the artificially created flock was somewhat lacking in their parenting skills. A lot of chicks simply did not survive. Cranes being raised by humans in crane suits and taught to follow ultralight aircraft were somehow missing some important life lessons.

"We have two separate problems," said Sarah Converse, a research ecologist with the USGS. "One, the eggs don't make it. Two, even if the eggs make it, the chicks don't make it." The cranes form pair bonds and mate, but fewer than one in ten of the reproducing pairs raises a chick that lives more than four months. The cranes were simply not learning how to be good parents; an important, intangible lesson wasn't being taught. Humans can only do so much.

In January 2016, with great disappointment, U.S. Fish and Wildlife announced that it was ending the project with the hope that there were enough whooping cranes in the wild to carry on with human protection but without human interference. The self-sacrifice, hard work, long hours, and dedication of all involved with Operation Migration have to be applauded. Never in human history had such a project been conceived and maintained for fifteen years.

The good news: in February 2016, it was announced that the western Wood Buffalo/Aransas flock was up to 308 whooping cranes, including 39 juveniles. From a low of only 21 whooping cranes in 1941, today there are over 600 captive and wild cranes, including two separate migratory populations. It has taken seventy-five years, one man's lifetime, to grow the population, to right a wrong one tiny step at a time, one agonizing setback at a time. But as the Roman poet Ovid once said, "Dripping water hollows out stone, not through force but through persistence."

SATISFACTION

With the recovery of the bald eagle (see my book *Natural Histories*), as it now stands, the National Audubon Society lists the whooping crane as number three on its list of most endangered birds. The ivory-billed woodpecker and California condor are numbers one and two.

In March 2016, after a day of writing part of this book, I went for a walk on the new Cherokee Farm Greenway near where I live. It was late; the sun had essentially set, since heavy clouds were moving in. Rain was on the way, light fading. As I returned to the car at Marine Park by the Marine Corps Reserve Center, a large white bird flew in over the river to the upstream shoreline of

Looney Island. "Wow!" I thought. "A great egret." But just as it dropped its landing gear and tilted its wings to slow for touchdown, I saw the unmistakable black primary feathers. It was a whooping crane returning north, finding a place for a sleepover. In years past, other whoopers have been spotted on the island downstream from the Buck Karnes Bridge in Knoxville, but this was a first for me, and only a mile from my house as the crane flies.

We end as we began: "'Hope' is the thing with feathers— / That perches in the soul— / And sings the tune without the words— / and never stops—at all."

Bala

11 JULY 2016

Coy-Wolf-Dog?

Canid species

Observe always that everything is the result of change,
and get used to thinking that there is nothing Nature
loves so well as to change existing forms
and make new ones like them.

—Roman Emperor Marcus Aurelius

COYOTES, WOLVES, AND DOGS are, as the late baseball player and idiom artisan Yogi Berra might have said, "three sides of the same coin." And in this case, the former Yankee catcher and turn-of-phrase-ologist would have been correct. In 1972, on his way to the Baseball Hall of Fame with his family, Yogi also said (or is credited with saying), "We're lost, but we're making good time."

It is generally believed that gray wolves are lost to the East. We killed them all; yet, it's also safe to say that there's a DNA near match lying somewhere near you in the form of a border collie or Yorkie or one of those hyper Jack Russell terriers, not to even mention the coyote-looking canid creeping through your neighborhood at night scavenging your garbage. Yes, Yogi, wolves are lost, but their genetic material is making good time.

For me, driving to Ijams is a quick trip. And you never know what you'll see or hear along the way. The first week of December 2013, I saw something I had never seen. It happened just after I'd crossed Chapman Highway on East Moody. At the time, this was the major in-and-out route for the business district from the south side, because repairs were being made to the Henley Street Bridge. With cars zipping by, there it stood, bold as Bratwurst.

At first glance, I thought I'd spotted a skittish, scrawny dog watching traffic from a hillside; yet, in a flash, I realized it was *no dog*. There was a coyote *(Canis latrans),* or at least a coyote-like creature a scant two miles from downtown Knoxville, south of the river, during the noon hour, a brazen assault on my worldview. Wow. (I think we all need flexible worldviews, don't you?)

Lindbergh Forest is even closer to the city. It was created as one of the early "automobile suburbs" of Knoxville. We smile at the notion of this today since it is only one mile—as the crow flies—from downtown. Developed in the 1920s, the wooded neighborhood is named in honor of Charles Lindbergh, the American aviator who became world famous after his nonstop flight from the U.S. to Paris in 1927. He was the talk of the town, as was soon the development. Located in south Knoxville, just across the Tennessee River from the heart of downtown, today it's on the National Register of Historic Places. Lindbergh Forest is noted for its heavily wooded home sites with numerous mature trees. Many of its homes are also detailed with Tennessee marble quarried in the area.

Former Ijams Board Chair Karyn Adams and her husband, Bruce Cole, and sons Auden and Crispin live in the picturesque location. Adams is energetic with a quick smile that radiates the room. She loves being outside, that's what lured her to the nature center located nearby. She even jogs and bikes to downtown. In 2013, her neighbors reported seeing this beautiful animal several times. Finally, she saw it in their yard early one morning.

"It didn't move like a dog; didn't sniff the ground. It was self-assured, elegant in motion, paying attention, not shy. It owned the place," said Adams. "Bruce was able to slip outside to get the best photos he could, a testament to how unruffled the animal was by a human in sight and range."

It was in no real hurry; wasn't skittish, or lurking. Bruce's photos portray a confident canine at home in its surroundings. That's the point: only a river separated it from the courthouse and busy business district. It was living closer to downtown than 90 percent of the city's residents and it was comfortable being there. The animal I saw off Moody and what Karyn and Bruce saw in their nearby yard were different; mine was scrawny, theirs was full-bodied. And they weren't dogs, but what were they?

A LOOK BACK

Prehistoric North America was the great spawning ground for all horse species; the same can be said about canids. If we could climb into Mr. Peabody's WABAC (pronounced Way-Back) Machine with Sherman—those of you who remember television's *The Adventures of Rocky and Bullwinkle* know what I'm talking about—and set the dial for 37 million years ago, long before the Gray Fossil Site was created, we'd find in the Great Plains and Texas the progenitor to all modern-day wolves, coyotes, and dogs. Mr. Peabody himself would have a vested interest in this journey since he is an uber-smart beagle wearing glasses.

The earliest fossilized remains in this storied group were unearthed at an airstrip in Presidio County in southwestern Texas. The species was designated *Prohesperocyon wilsoni* by Dr. Xiaoming Wang, the same noted vertebrate paleontologist who helped assign the name *Pristinailurus bristoli* to the prehistoric panda we met earlier.

Many canid species came into being and died out over the next 30 million years. From the fossil record, paleontologists currently know of 177 species that evolved, lived thousands of years, and went extinct, further illustrating Macbeth's "brief candle, life's but a walking shadow" soliloquy. Three subfamilies once existed in North America. Caninae survives today, but two of the other linages are gone. In case you're a fan of TV's *Jeopardy!* and like to fill your brain with mind-numbing trivia, the two extinct subfamilies are Hesperocyoninae (dawn dogs) and Borophaginae (bone-crushing dogs). In May 2016, it was announced that a new dog-like fossil of one of these lost branches had been found in Maryland. Given the name *Cynarctus wangi* to honor Dr. Wang, it was a heavy-set, bone-crushing bruiser.

"Someone tell *Game of Thrones'* Jon Snow he picked the wrong canine companion. An animal even more badass than dire wolves existed in North America 12 million years ago, and its jaws were so strong it could crush an elephant's bones," declared science writer Max Plenke. The elephant bones the badass was crunching were mammoths. In time, other species will undoubtedly be unearthed. All of these early carnivores look dog-like, but they were not true dogs. That would come later.

A now extinct lineage commonly known as bear-dogs roamed the planet for roughly forty-four million years. As the name suggests some were as big as bears and somewhat distantly related to dogs. On October 11, 2016, it was announced by the Associated Press that a jawbone from an early ancestral bear-dog had been found, of all places, in a drawer at the Chicago's Field Museum. Originally discovered in Texas in 1946, the fossil had gone into hiding yet again another six decades, unidentified, before being rediscovered by post-doctoral researcher Susumu Tomiya, who works at the museum.

"It's almost like they feel that once a specimen's been described, they've learned everything they can from it," said Dr. Steven Wallace, curator at the

East Tennessee Natural History Museum we visited in the panda chapter. "Sometimes the coolest discoveries come right out of a museum."

Roughly nine million years ago, a modest group that could eat both meat and plants evolved. Named *Eucyon* (Greek for true dog), it came into existence in North America. Being an omnivore has its advantages; there is almost always something to eat.

This genus thrived and spread, eventually making its way to Eurasia roughly seven million years ago during an ice age. There it spilt rapidly into several species, filling empty niches and leading to the first true *Canis* (Latin for dog). One lineage produced today's gray wolf *(Canis lupus)*, which was eventually able to return, roughly eight hundred thousand years ago, to its ancestral homeland, moving from Arctic Eurasia to Arctic North America. The formidable predator was just moving into new territory, following large mammal prey: elk, mountain sheep, goats, caribou, and bison. It had no real memory of its genealogical roots. In a sense, it's like the line from the John Denver song, "Coming home to a place he'd never been before."

As a group, gray wolves are highly successful; currently there are forty recognized subspecies around the world. The ancestors of the coyote splintered off from the ancestors of the gray wolf between one and two million years ago. As a species, the western coyote *(Canis latrans)* has been around roughly one million years.

Wolves are bigger, hunt in familial packs for large prey, and occupy the forests, hence an alternate name: timber wolf. Coyotes are loners or hunt in mated pairs for small game: raccoons, frogs, fish, rodents, snakes, birds, and even vegetable matter or fruit. They scavenge and live in the open spaces. Wolves kill coyotes, and coyotes fear wolves. To a degree, wolves are the coyotes' sworn enemies.

Historian Joseph Mussulman reported that the Lewis and Clark Corps of Discovery first encountered a coyote on August 12, 1804, northwest of today's Onawa, Iowa. They attempted to collect a specimen to return to their benefactor, President Jefferson, but failed. The following spring, Captain Meriwether Lewis recorded a description of what he called the "prarie woolf" [*sic*] on May 5, 1805, in northeastern Montana. (Keep in mind this is one year before Noah Webster published his first dictionary, *A Compendious Dictionary of the English Language*. In it, he popularized features that would become a hallmark of American English spelling—*center* rather than *centre, color* rather than *colour,* and so on. Before Webster, spelling was more freestyle.)

Meriwether Lewis recorded:

The small woolf or burrowing dog of the praries are the inhabitants almost invariably of the open plains . . . they frequently watch and seize their prey near their burrows; in these burrows they raise their young and to them they also resort when pursued; when a person approaches them they frequently bark, their note being precisely that of the small dog; they are of an intermediate size between that of the fox and dog; very active, fleet and delicately formed; the ears large erect and pointed the head long and pointed more like that of the fox; tale long; . . . the hair and fur also resembles the fox tho' is much coarser and inferior; they are of a pale redish brown colour; the eye of a deep sea green colour small and piercing; their tallons [claws] are reather longer than those of the ordinary wolf or that common to the atlantic states, none of which are to be found in this quarter, nor I believe above the river Plat.

Lewis and Clark's Expedition lived off the land the 860 days they traveled from St. Louis to the Pacific Ocean and back. In late September 1805, the Corps of Discovery—plus Sacagawea, Old Toby, and his son—killed and ate a coyote for supper. Historian Mussulman noted that it "wouldn't have done much to fill 35 empty stomachs by itself, since a full-grown coyote in its best days tips the scale at somewhere between 25 and 35 pounds—head, tail, bones, innards and all."

In the early 1800s, the terms "barking dog" or "burrowing dog" were most often used for Lewis's "prarie woolf." The word "coyote" would not enter the lexicon until the native Mexican Aztec word *coyotl* appeared in print in 1824. Over the next sixty years, the moniker morphed from "coyjotte" to "collates" to "cayeute," before it was finally standardized as "coyote," now pronounced either ki-YOH-tee or KI-yote, depending on personal preference. American naturalist Thomas Say first assigned the binomial for scientific purposes for the coyote as *Canis* (Latin for "dog"), and *latrans* ("barking").

Before our European ancestors came to North America, gray wolves, a.k.a. timber wolves, lived in the forested areas, while coyotes lived in the open spaces. The smaller coyotes knew to stay out of the wolves' domain. But as the woods were cut and farmland grew, the wolves were either forced out or simply killed—shot, poisoned, or trapped, then killed.

Here we have a historic clash of cultures: one human, one canine. The European immigrants to North America brought with them bad blood, an intense fear and hatred of wolves. It was deeply engrained in their folk tales. In ancient Greece, *Aesop's Fables* included a cautionary tale of the Big Bad Wolf, while the basic story of Little Red Riding Hood exists in different forms in most Old World countries. French peasants told the tale as early as the tenth century, which first appeared in print in 1697 as *Le Petit*

Chaperon Rouge, while the Italians had an oral version, *La finta nonna* ("The False Grandmother"), that can be traced back to the 1300s. Generation after generation of children learned that wolves ate grannies or, even worse, little girls in red caps. Even more sinister, if there could be such a thing, was belief in the werewolf, or Greek *lycanthrope,* a man who periodically becomes a bloodthirsty wolf; this goes back to Roman courtier Petronius (27–66 AD).

The fabled "monster within" foreshadows Swiss psychiatrist Carl Jung's work on the subconscious "shadow aspect" of our own personalities, which erupt periodically. Jung felt that we all have a shadow, the dark repository of the aspects of our own personalities we consciously refuse to acknowledge. Our shadow is hidden in our subconscious. One's personal interiorities can be either positive or negative, but most of us readily accept our positive qualities. Psychological projection is a theory in psychology in which humans suppress their own unpleasant impulses, even denying their existence by pushing them into their shadows while loudly loathing the same traits in others.

Could the same be true with our hatred of wolves? Do we perceive them as vicious because of our own shadowy predilection for violence?

Humans and wolves are both apex predators at the top of their food chains; both are efficient killers—intelligent, highly adaptable, hunting either alone or in groups. In their two respective worlds, they have no rivals. But what happens when the two worlds collide? Is our enormous rancor toward wolves the projection of our own Jungian shadows? Do we perceive them as being more loathsome than they really are?

As a rule, our two worlds do not intersect. They fear us as much as we fear them, sort of a mutual distrust. And *Canis lupus* really do not eat grannies. There has never been a single human death reported from a wolf attack in the lower forty-eight states, although there has been one death in Alaska and one in Canada. And in both cases, the victims may have provoked the wolves by not keeping a proper distance from them.

Worldwide, mosquitoes are the biggest killers, hands down. But let's compare apples to apples. In this country, on average annually, 130 people are killed by deer, almost exclusively because of collisions in cars; 100 people die as a result of horse-related activities; 58 are killed by bees, wasps, and hornets, mostly due to anaphylactic shock after a sting; 28 are killed by dogs; 20 are killed by cows; 7 by spiders; 5.5 die from rattlesnake bites; 1 is killed by a bear; 1 by a shark; and zero by wolves.

But as far as the animosity between humans and wolves is concerned, the stage was set early for tension when we imported our easy-to-kill livestock—cows, sheep and goats—and eliminated the wolves' naturally wary prey—deer, caribou, and bison. It has been estimated that once there were 250,000 to 500,000 gray wolves in North America. The settlers began to reduce those numbers as soon as they moved into a new area. Still, there were wolves until the U.S. government implemented a nationwide policy of wolf destruction, a decree to drive the predator to extinction.

"In 1902, Theodore Roosevelt called the wolf 'the beast of waste and destruction,' and in 1907 the United States Biological Survey declared the extermination of the wolf to be 'the paramount objective of the government,'" wrote conservation scientist John A. Wiens.

Bounties were set for this government-sanctioned persecution. In the 1908 *Yearbook of Agriculture,* D. E. Lantz, assistant biologist with the Biological Survey wrote, "The following are the provisions of law in force in the several States and Territories authorizing the payment of rewards for the destruction of noxious animals."

The edict went on to list what the government would pay in every state in the bounty program for each dead wolf. Here are some examples: Arizona, $25; Colorado, $2; Indiana, $20; Kansas, $5, Minnesota, $7.50 or $3 for wolf cubs; Missouri, $3; Montana, $10; Nevada, 50¢; Wisconsin, $10 for a mature wolf, and $2 for a cub under six months old; and my home state, Tennessee, $2.

Consequently, the wolf population plummeted. By the 1950s, they had been essentially eradicated from the United States—canid genocide—and the human-leery, sneak-around-alone-in-the-night coyote population naturally grew. They were a better fit to live near people—more doglike, scavenging for scraps and eating the rats and other rodents that followed civilization.

Here is the irony. We fear wolves but adore the third member of our canid trio, a wolf subspecies: *Canis lupus familiaris,* or simply *Canis familiaris,* the family dog. And dogs kill far more people in this country than wolves do, although wolves do have a taste for livestock.

Many animals have been more than just tamed, but domesticated. All horses, cows, sheep, goats, yaks, ducks, cats, the list goes on, come from wild ancestors. But the very first to be brought into the society of humans were dogs. Since prehistoric times, dogs and humans have been companions. All scientists seem to agree on that, but here is where the debate begins. For years, the accepted theory was that the domestication had apparently happened in several locations around the globe. And there was hard evidence to back it up.

Perhaps the most poignant find was made by two Israeli zoo-archeologists named Davis and Villa who announced a remarkable discovery in 1978: a double burial in Mallaha, near the old Huleh Lake in the upper Jordan Valley of Israel. The Mallaha site belonged to one of the last hunter-gatherer groups, the Natufian people. The human in the grave was old—some accounts say it was a woman—lying with a puppy; her left hand had been placed over its body, suggesting an affectionate relationship.

"This hand is wrapped around the chest of the puppy, and the person's head is resting on top of the puppy. The intimacy of these two individuals is truly remarkable and argues strongly for a relationship that is more than a mere casual association," wrote vertebrate paleontologist Xiaoming Wang. The grave dates back 13,500 years. Clearly, humans and dogs have been heartfelt companions for at least that long.

Other sites as far apart as Seamer Carr in North Yorkshire, England, and Bonn-Oberkassel in Germany have also been found with canid remains. The latter dates to about fourteen thousand years ago, and the buried dog was part of a human double grave. All were similar burials suggesting a human bond with a dog. It has been speculated that in several locations wolves began to follow roaming bands of hunter-gathers to steal from the bone-scrap piles and slowly developed a relationship with the humans and their throwaways, a boon for the canid. The humans in return got a partner to help with hunting and later herding, plus an alarm system to guard the campsite, and even a food source, should the need arise. So it was win-win, except for the "let's eat Fido" part.

Then in 1997, this tidy little story started to unravel. Science loves to turn itself on its ear every so often as we saw with the feathered dinosaurs in the last chapter. Long accepted theories can crumble in a hurry when new evidence surfaces.

The genetic studies of the last thirty years have rewritten a lot of textbooks. Animals, including humans, have two types of DNA, nuclear (nDNA) and mitochondrial (mtDNA). The genes coded for by nDNA are responsible for external characteristics and for behavior. I have blue eyes because my father did. My love of the outdoors is behavioral and probably came from my farm-girl mother. On the other hand, mitochondrial DNA is separate from nDNA and is found in the mitochondria of the cell. The gene coding here is strictly regulatory and has little effect on external appearances or behavior in comparison to nDNA. But mitochondrial DNA comes solely from the female parent, so in a sense, it's purer, making it a good generational yardstick. By comparing mtDNA from two closely related species, geneticists can get a reasonable sense of how long ago the separation between the two occurred.

"The domestic dog is an extremely close relative of the gray wolf," wrote Dr. Robert K. Wayne, "differing from it by at most 0.2 percent of mtDNA sequence. In comparison, the gray wolf differs from its closest *wild* relative, the coyote, by about 4 percent of mitochondrial DNA sequence." So wolves and dogs have been separate entities for a much briefer period than wolves and coyotes. But how brief?

In a study published in 1997, Dr. Wayne and colleagues at the University of California at Los Angeles analyzed mtDNA from 162 wolves at twenty-seven localities worldwide and from 140 domestic dogs representing sixty-seven breeds and set a date of separation of up to 135,000 years ago. Many to most scientists had real trouble accepting this long-ago date because there was no physical—that is, bone evidence—to back it up.

Three studies were published in the November 22, 2002, issue of the journal *Science* to help clear the muddy waters that were mucking up the origin of dogs. One suggested that all dogs could be traced back to only a few wolves, perhaps from the same population somewhere in East Asia, and that these are the mothers of almost all dogs alive today. And that domestication may have happened only once, probably around 15,000 years ago. The new, highly prized human-friendly proto-dogs proved to be so popular that their off-spring spread quickly around the continent.

Additionally, "Dr. Peter Savolainen, a former colleague of Dr. Wayne now at the Royal Institute of Technology in Stockholm, has proposed a date that is more palatable to archaeologists," wrote Nicholas Wade for the *New York Times*. "On the basis of DNA from several wolf populations and from the hairs collected off 654 dogs around the world, Dr. Savolainen calculates a date for domestication either 40,000 years ago, if all dogs come from a single wolf, or around 15,000 years ago, the date he prefers, if three animals drawn from the same population were the wolf Eves of the dog lineage."

New research published in the journal *Science* in June 2016 suggests that dogs were domesticated from two separate wolf populations on either side of the Old World, one in Europe and one in Asia, with the two groups eventually meeting in the middle, although European ancestry has all but disappeared from today's dogs. But when you think of a two-thousand-year-old dog, don't imagine a collie or beagle or pug. Modern breeds have only been around a few hundred years. For most of evolutionary history, *Canis familiaris* looked like the semi-wild "village dogs" that hang around small gatherings of indigenous peoples around the globe.

Today, there are close to 340 breeds recognized by the Fédération Cynologique Internationale (FCI), the world governing body of dog breeds. Owners have manipulated each to have desirable traits, although selective breeding can go too far. The English bulldog is good example of a breed in trouble. It's a breed that dates back to the 1630s and today it's much too in-bred; the breed's gene diversity is sadly lacking.

"Their skeletons have also been modified through selective breeding over time, to the point that many English bulldogs are now essentially deformed. . . . Many suffer from joint disease, including hip and elbow dysplasia, and ruptures in the spine," wrote Mary Brophy Marcus for *CBS News*. "The lifespan of a purebred English bulldog, the fourth most popular dog, is not long." They have breathing, dental, and skin problems, immune system issues, and difficulty giving birth naturally (most puppies are delivered by Caesarean sections) or, for that matter, even conceiving naturally. Left to their own devices, the breed would go extinct in short order. It's hard to look at the University of Georgia's stocky mascot Uga and think ephemeral, but short-lived he truly is. Since 1956—that's sixty years—there have been ten Ugas. The physical differences between Uga I and Uga X are striking, as the modern-day version has been pushed towards a greater degree of deformity.

"Dog breeds were created by human beings," wrote Evan Ratliff for *National Geographic*. "The village dog created itself." What might be called the forever dog, you and I would simply call a mutt, but these motley canines have more ancient wolf royalty in their bones than any shih tzu.

In North America, the archeological evidence suggests that these same village dogs came with their human companions across the Bering Land Bridge early. Also known as Beringia, the land bridge was up to 620 miles wide. It wasn't an icy glacier, as you might imagine, but rather a grassland steppe that stretched for hundreds of miles into the continents on either side. So much of the planet's water was frozen and tied up in ice that sea levels dropped and the land bridge was exposed. Simply put, Asians, the ancestors to Native Americans, walked to the New World with their companion dogs.

The first evidence of this human-dog bond in North America was found in the 1950s in the Bonneville Basin around the Great Salt Lakes region. "It's from Danger Cave, in Utah, between 9,000 and 10,000 years old. They came early, but it's not clear if it was with the absolutely first people," noted Darcy Morey, a zoo-archaeologist from the University of Tennessee at Martin, who focuses on the archaeological evidence of canine-human companionship, shown most clearly by dog burials.

"There's plenty of evidence in the Southeast that dogs were companions of Native Americans, as far back as seven thousand years ago, certainly by the Middle to Late Archaic Period," said retired UT anthropologist and professor emeritus Dr. Charles Faulkner in a conversation we had in June 2016. "There's some evidence they were eaten, perhaps only ceremonially; with the Great Plains Indians, yes, and the Iroquois to the north, yes, but here, not so much. The Eva site in West Tennessee had plenty of evidence of dogs with humans."

The prehistoric Eva site is in Benton County. The UT Archaeology Department and the Work Progress Administration (WPA) conducted excavations at the location in late 1940 before it was submerged under Kentucky Lake, an impoundment created by the completion of the Kentucky Dam on the Tennessee River. In a very short time, numerous artifacts were unearthed at Eva: points; blades; butchering tools; bone artifacts like awls, needles, fish-hooks, and a necklace composed of snake vertebrae; and the graves of 180 humans and eighteen dogs.

COY-WOLF-DOG?

With this, the stage was then set for the next act in our canid drama. We had three ingredients in our stewpot; they just had to be stirred. Gray wolves, coyotes, and dogs were all in North America, the same place their ancestral progenitor named *Eucyon* first appeared seven millions of years earlier. With these three gene pools in place only recently, something very interesting began to unfold.

Charles Darwin said it first and said it best: "Thus, from the war of nature, from famine and death, the most exalted object which we are capable of conceiving, namely, the production of the higher animals, directly follows. There is grandeur in this view of life, with its several powers, having been originally breathed into a few forms or into one; and that, whilst this planet has gone cycling on according to the fixed law of gravity, from so simple a beginning endless forms most beautiful and most wonderful have been, and are being, evolved."

Karen Webster once lived with her daughter, Rachael, in an apartment that borders Sharp's Ridge Memorial Park in the heart of Knoxville. The park is bordered on the south by the city's main north-south thoroughfare, Broadway Avenue. On the north flank, Webster could hear the traffic on busy I-640, and there's an often-used railroad track nearby. It is, in a word, urban. Over 104 square miles of civilization surrounds Sharp's Ridge, a 111-acre forested island in the middle of the largest city in East Tennessee. The sandstone ridgeline, home to several radio and television towers, rises two hundred to three hundred feet above the surrounding limestone valley floor. An abandoned fire tower marks its highest point.

One evening in late spring 2015, Webster looked out of her bedroom window and saw a mother raccoon followed by four or five young pups. So many young mouths, Webster had empathy for the mom's responsibilities. The parade of masked raccoons emerged from the wooded ridge behind the apartment on an obvious animal trail through an understory of privet. The scene was well lit from an overhead streetlight, and she watched as the cuddlesome parade high-stepped through the mowed lawn to forage, presumably the neighborhood's trashcans.

"Within thirty seconds, I saw another animal standing at the edge of the woods on the same animal trail," said Webster, remembering the ominous scene. "It was also watching the raccoons."

We met Webster in the red panda chapter. She once worked at the Knoxville Zoo as the small mammal keeper. She knows small mammals and knew she was seeing something she had never seen before.

"It was big, well-fed with a beautiful coat, bushy tailed and its head was surrounded with fur like a husky, but it was not a dog. It was furry, 'wolfy' like," she said. Webster had seen coyotes before; this was fuller bodied. She also once worked for a local veterinarian and knows dog breeds and is used to picking them up. She estimated that this mystery mammal weighed up to forty-five pounds. It did not notice her watching from the second-floor window since it was too focused on its own agenda: dinner.

"Quickly, it dashed out of the woods and grabbed one of the raccoon pups," she remembered. It squealed in a pitiful alarm as it was carried away from its mother back into the forest to disappear forever.

Webster was used to seeing such shocking scenes on PBS but not in her own backyard. Truth is, the raccoon population in the East is exploding, and a wily midsized predator was needed to help keep a natural balance. And, true to form, nature rushed to fill that niche. Empty niches do not last long. Webster's eye for size was accurate as well, and what she saw might not have been a by-the-book coyote but a new modernized version.

That story began long before Webster saw the raccoon pup snatched from its mom. And what she observed outside her very urban apartment window did merit the attention of PBS in the form of a nature documentary titled, "Meet the Coywolf," although that story was not quite complete.

For years it was the general belief that coyotes would never make it across the Mississippi. It was a western species confined to the openness of the Great Plains. The east was too crowded and civilized.

Then there was an odd urban legend making the rounds. It proposed that insurance companies and various wildlife agencies had conspired to release coyotes throughout the East. The insurance companies supposedly hoped that the wily predators would be able to reduce the deer population and, in turn, lower the number of claims filed as a result of deer and automobile collisions. Roughly 130 people die annually in such accidents, and vehicle damage amounts to more that $1.1 billion.

Both the insurance and wildlife people strongly denied the story. Besides, western coyotes are predators that *can* kill animals as big as white-tailed deer, but they prefer much smaller prey like mice, moles, snakes, frogs, raccoons, squirrels, groundhogs, and lizards, plus their diet includes fruit, berries, seeds, carrion, and garbage. The more roads we build, the greater the supply of available roadkill. In this way, the scavenger coyote benefits humankind by helping clean up the bloody highways while we sleep. Why then should a coyote mess with deer? They are not as picky as wolves, another key to their success.

In fact, the opposite was true; wildlife officials had spent millions of dollars, with little success, trying to control coyote populations already in the East. In 2003, U.S. Fish and Wildlife killed a reported 75,724 coyotes to try and slow their spread, but it seemed to have had little effect. Coyotes have no federal or state protection like other wildlife. Hunting season is year round; there's no bag limit. Thousands can be shot; yet still they multiply and thrive.

Dr. Stan Gehrt, associate professor with the School of Environment and Natural Resources at Ohio State University, studies the coyotes in the Chicago area. "They need no protection," said Gehrt. "As we continue to remove these animals off the landscape, they continue to replace themselves, to the point where not only have we not lowered their numbers they have increased their range. And are now found in more parts of North America than they have ever been before." Coyotes have a phantom-like ability to blend into the most unlikely places. Gehrt estimated that there are two thousand urban coyotes in the greater Chicago area.

So, when did the coyotes first cross the uncrossable Mississippi River? It appears they didn't move west to east as you might think but rather west to northeast into the Great Lakes region and Canada, first appearing in western Ontario in the early 1900s, then heading south into New York State by the early 1920s. Unlike wolves, coyotes are solitary animals, and young ones may disperse one hundred miles from where they are born. They find voids to fill. Traditionally a western species, in recent years coyotes have expanded their range into the East all the way to the Atlantic Coast. They are replacing the natural red wolf population that our ancestors eliminated. Coyotes first appeared in Cades Cove in the Great Smoky Mountains in the 1980s. Vermont naturalist Warner Shedd reported that there are probably more coyotes in this country today than there have ever been. They are now found in every state, from the Pacific to the Atlantic Ocean, from Canada to the Gulf of Mexico. They have even been found in New York City's Central Park, and how much more urban can you get?

BUT ARE THEY TRULY COYOTES?

Something interesting happened when coyotes moved into three-thousand-square-mile Algonquin Park in Ontario. They encountered an isolated, remnant population of eastern wolves *(Canis lupus lycaon),* a wolf subspecies. And whereas western wolves will kill the smaller coyote, the last of the eastern band, perhaps out of necessity, began to mate with their closely related cousins, producing hybrids sometime around 1919. The eastern wolves became a genetic bridge.

There's an "amazing contemporary evolution story that's happening right underneath our noses," said Dr. Roland Kays with the Department of Forestry and Environmental Resources at North Carolina State University. Some call the bigger coyote a "coywolf," but Kays himself prefers the term "eastern coyote." Kays earned his PhD in zoology at the University of Tennessee in 1999 and points out that the term coywolf doesn't quite fit.

If an organism reproduces asexually, it makes an exact copy of itself like the freshwater jellyfish polyps. Very efficient, but static. Who would want to go to a dinner party with seven exact copies of themselves? Yes, everyone would be good looking, but there would be no give-and-take in the conversation. Is there anyone that narcissistic?

Sexual reproduction stirs the mix, creates variety, and spawns speciation—the creation of a new species. The textbooks say that two distinct species cannot successfully reproduce. If they do, they create weak or sterile offspring. But what if the textbooks are wrong? Botanists know that plants routinely hybridize. Welcome to the difficult world of plant identification.

The esemplastic (from the Greek *eis en plattein:* "to shape into one") nature of DNA that comes from two living organisms and combines into a single unified entity is what drives this story. Heck, it's what drives life on Earth. But in this case, the DNA comes from separate species and produces a mix, a hybrid. And the hybrid can have the combined weaknesses of the parents, or the combined strengths. Nature rewards the latter. And nature has rewarded the coywolf coyote, mostly because there's a huge niche in the deforested and de-wolfed east and a lot of raccoon prey.

"They have long legs. They have thick fur. They look very wolf like," said John Pisapio, wildlife biologist at the Ontario Ministry of Natural Resources. "We have a medium-sized carnivore living in our midst. A formable creature, which is going to do very well."

The so-called coywolf is bigger than its coyote parent but smaller than its wolf parent. The new coywolves have shorter snouts and ears, and have a bigger, more muscular jaw and stronger bite for bringing down large prey, like deer. In that aspect, they are wolfish. The coywolf or, if you prefer, eastern coyote has rapidly expanded throughout the East in the past thirty years or so. And as a group, coywolves demonstrate an escalating boldness at living near people. They are intelligent, confident animals, and they are watching us, figuring us out, learning our habits. They are primarily nocturnal, active while we sleep or active at sunset or dawn. But don't be alarmed; they are also cautious of people, even paranoid. Like city pigeons, house sparrows, and Norway rats, they have worked their way into the biota of our cities, moving along pathways we've created: railroad tracks and interstate buffers where few people ever go.

But why move into a noisy urban environment? Why even go near people? By moving along railroad tracks, the new eastern coyote can access city parks, golf courses, vacant lots, and even neighborhoods in the middle of the night because these urban larders generate more prey—mice, rats, raccoons, Canada geese—than rural areas. In an urban setting, a coywolf only needs a three-square-mile territory as opposed to twice as much in rural areas. And in many ways, this new candid is the most intelligent urban animal we have. They slip in and out of our backyards unseen. And many people who do catch a glimpse mistake them for stray German shepherds.

What Webster witnessed in her backyard is a growing phenomenon. Should we keep our cats and small dogs in at night? Yes, most definitely. Should we fear for our own safety? No. They are 99.99 percent skittish around people. But for every rule there's an exception. There has only been one death of a human reported. In 2009, a nineteen-year-old woman, an aspiring musician named Taylor Mitchell, was attacked and killed as she walked alone on a hiking trail in Cape Breton Highlands National Park in Nova Scotia, Canada. The popular Skyline Trail is easily accessible and experiences twenty to twenty-five thousand visitors annually. So, why poor Mitchell? No one knows.

Coywolves hunt alone or in pairs, forming lifelong pair bonds. And there's enough easy small prey in any city to meet their needs. They are the number-one predator of raccoons and Canada geese, two urban animals whose populations are growing unchecked. They are observational learners like dogs and move through our world undetected, perhaps becoming the most adaptable, malleable animal on earth.

"It's entirely possible that after so many decades of intense efforts to remove them we've created an animal that's more and more adaptable, even more intelligent than they were to start with," said Dr. Gehrt. The ever-increasing urban environment is driving their evolution; they're adapting to better exploit the bountiful habitat and largely go unseen by the bipedal mammals that built the cities.

Yet like the famous Ginsu knives sold on television: but wait, there's more. One reason the term coywolf is not completely accepted or accurate is that it is not quite that simple. Coyotes will also mate with dogs, although it's not as common. The two usually aren't in the mood to reproduce at the same time, so it's almost a non sequitur. But it does happen.

In the early 1980s, the state of Illinois killed ten thousand coyotes annually for their fur. According to Donald Hoffmeister, author of *Mammals of Illinois,* it's estimated that up to 15 percent of those were coydogs. A little closer to home, twelve miles from where I live, coydogs were reported as being troublesome for small pets in 2014.

"The fact that they stuck around even after the humans came out and harassed them a little bit is very strange. So, it leads me to believe that maybe it's a cross between a dog and coyote. That happens in nature. If a coyote can't find a mate it will breed with a domestic dog," said Tennessee wildlife officer Matt Cameron. It was reported in October, the time of year when cubs separate from their mothers, and that maybe was why they were wandering into more urban areas, looking for new homes.

So what are we talking about here: coyotes, coywolves or coydogs?

This is one reason why Dr. Roland Kays is uncomfortable with the media's use of the term coywolf and prefers eastern coyote. Something big *is* happening, namely the evolution of a whole new species, but it is far too early to label it.

"There is no doubt that there is a hybrid canid living in the eastern US, and that it is the result of an amazing evolution story unfolding right underneath our noses," wrote Dr. Kays. "However, this is not a new species—at least not yet—and I don't think we should start calling it a 'coywolf.'"

The term leads one to believe that this new predator is half coyote and half wolf, which it is not. There are three separate species involved in this genetic stew—western coyotes, eastern wolves, and dogs, good old *Canis familiaris,* all so closely related they can interbreed when push comes to shove. And when the western coyotes started moving east of the Mississippi River, push came to shove because there was no other option.

Just what *is* and *is not* a separate species is not always easy to define. Different biologists have different parameters. One says "to-MAY-toe"; the other says "to-MAH-toe."

"The concept of species is a difficult issue fraught with intricate philosophical and practical problems," wrote Wang. The textbook definition goes: A species is a group of individuals that (or potentially) interbreed in nature and produce viable offspring.

"An alternative view of species loosely called the *evolutionary species concept* allows the fact that when populations begin to diverge from each other, regardless of their reproductive potentials, they embark on different evolutionary trajectories," Wang noted.

So if the closely-related-but-separate coyote and wolf interbreed, are their young coyotes or wolves? Or are they on a separate evolutionary trajectory? Maybe.

"Hybridization across species is a natural evolutionary phenomenon. The old notion that an inability to breed should define what a species is has been abandoned by zoologists (with a resounding 'I told you so' from botanists). Even modern humans are hybrids, with traces of Neanderthal and Denisovan genes mixed into our genome," wrote Dr. Kays.

What?

Yes. You are a hybrid mix of perhaps as many as four different, early, human-like species. Most of this comingling took place thousands of years ago, so it's only a small piece of your genetic makeup. But evolution loves a variable gene pool to work with. When you think about the wide range of modern-day humans—from Australian aborigines, to Pacific Islanders, to Native Americans, to Han Chinese (19 percent of humans are Han), to the African Maasai people, to a Japanese Sumo wrestler, to the petite four foot nine inch American gymnast Simone Biles or lanky six foot four inch swimmer Michael Phelps—you realize there's a lot of pliability in our own genetic code.

DNA profiles of all of those *Homo sapiens* would look identical, except for a gene here and a gene there; and mixed into all those genetic bits and pieces could be a snippet of Neanderthal DNA. Scientists looking at full human genomes have concluded that most Europeans and Asians have between 1 to 4 percent Neanderthal DNA. My ancestors immigrated to America from

Europe. So if I have a trace of Neanderthal in me, how might it affect me? Geneticists have found that a specific bit of Neanderthal DNA significantly increases the risk for nicotine addiction. Luckily for me, I do not smoke; but my father did, and that's what wrecked his health, eventually killing him.

According to Dr. Kays, with eastern coyotes the exact genetic mix of coy-wolf-dog depends on location. The coyotes in the Northeast are mostly 60 to 84 percent coyote, with 8 to 25 percent wolf and 8 to 11 percent dog. Kays pointed out that when you move south or east, this mixture slowly changes. In Virginia, animals average 85 percent coyote, 13 percent dog, and 2 percent wolf, while coyotes from the Deep South generally have just a dash of wolf and dog genes mixed in: 91 percent coyote, 4 percent wolf, and 5 percent dog.

"Tests show that there are no animals that are just coyote and wolf (that is, a coywolf), and some eastern coyotes that have almost no wolf at all," Kays added. "All eastern coyotes show some evidence of past hybridization, but there is no sign that they are still actively mating with dogs or wolves. The coyote, wolf, and dog are three separate species that would very much prefer *not* to breed with each other. However, biologically speaking, they are similar enough that interbreeding is possible."

So where does that leave us?

It leaves us in a front row seat to see evolution in action, a new species in the making on a separate evolutionary trajectory than its ancestors. The only problem is that we are not talking about something as observable as gray squirrels or chickadees. It's a sensational story with but a fugacious hold on our attention because its narrative swirls around a sizable mammal we rarely see, even though there are probably millions in the East living all around our cities and towns. They have mastered the art of blending into the background; they're transitory, only giving us a fleeting glimpse every so often. And poof, they are gone. It was once believed that natural selection worked slowly, taking thousands of years to create a new species. We now know it can happen much faster than that if there's a niche that needs filling.

A couple of years ago, I took a shortcut to Cherokee Trail and UT Hospital past the old Candora Marble Factory off Maryville Pike in south Knoxville. Candora Road passes the former industrial site and climbs a short incline to a railroad embankment. As I slowed, to the right stood a coy-wolf-dog (your guess). It watched me, and we made brief but meaningful eye contact before the beautiful creature turned and trotted away along the embankment. It was an almost perfect moment that remains crystal clear in my mind. Somewhere in my brain is a synapse labeled *Candora canid*. I have no idea what was going through its mind, but it showed no fear. It seemed to be, more or less, studying me, as I was it.

Perhaps it was confidently thinking, "I know far more about you than you know about me."

And if so, it was right.

Southern Pine Beetle

Dendroctonus frontalis

> Everything goes, everything comes back;
> eternally rolls the wheel of being.
> Everything dies, everything blossoms again;
> eternally runs the year of being.
>
> —Friedrich Nietzsche

QUIDDITY. It means the essential nature of a thing. It's a word not used often enough; that's why I offer it here.

That being said, the essential nature, the quiddity, of beetles is to go forth and adapt, to fill every nook and cranny, occupy every niche, succeed in a staggering array of forms.

By overwhelming numbers, beetles rule. Since 1758, over four hundred thousand different species of beetle have been discovered, described, and named by the world's scientists. That's over ninety-four thousand days, which translates into an average of close to four species a day. Many beetles that have been collected wait in drawers, yet to be identified. By the time I finish writing this paragraph, a new beetle species has probably been discovered somewhere on the planet.

If you were to sit down and make a list of all the different kinds of plants and animals known to science—about 1.75 million species—20 percent of that list would be beetles. They can be found in practically all environs, both urban and wild, and range in size from too-small-to-see to more-than-a-handful. The feather-winged beetle, *Nanosella fungi,* found in the eastern United States measures a miniscule 0.035 millimeters in length. (It would take 714 of them lined up end to end to make an inch.) The longest beetle on record is *Titanus gigantias,* found in the rainforests of French Guinea and

Brazil. One specimen in captivity measuring 6.3 inches in length died the first week of March 2005. It had been on display at the Museum of Natural History in Oxford, England.

In the Tennessee Valley, the eastern Hercules is the beefiest beetle. About the size of a Cadbury Easter egg, pale lichen green in color, they're the robust right tackles of the insect world in my locale. In the summer of 2001, I kept one alive for several weeks feeding it chunks of banana. We did programs together for groups of children and adults. It even made an appearance with me on WBIR's *Live at Five,* hosted that day by Russell Biven and Nicole Henrich. Measuring almost 2.5 inches in length, it was for three minutes the most famous beetle in town.

CAN WE IDENTIFY EVERY LIVING THING BEFORE IT'S TOO LATE?

Biodiversity is the sum total of all the plants and animals that live in a given area. The greater the biodiversity, the healthier the location, be it vacant lot, city park, forest, country, continent, or entire planet, what astrobiologist and author Carl Sagan called the "Pale Blue Dot." You define the perimeters and there's biodiversity within it. But until this millennium, no one had ever cordoned off a truly significant parcel to do a complete inventory of all life living inside its boundaries.

Such a census would discover crucial information. More than just a check-list of species names, it would be a complex living database of species locations, habitats, population densities, symbiotic relationships, and predator-prey interactions—in other words, what ecologists call a community within a defined space, showing all possible connections, like the ghost plant connected to the underground fungi, connected to the roots of an American beech—the web of life.

A brainchild of renowned ecologist Dan Janzen, the first such inventory was supposed to take place in the rainforests of northwest Costa Rica. Because of bureaucratic difficulties, however, the location was changed to the Great Smoky Mountains National Park. The All Taxa Biodiversity Inventory (ATBI) underway in the Smokies is the first major thorough search of its kind. The ATBI being conducted by the nonprofit organization Discover Life in America began in the year 2000; it's goal is to inventory all the animals, plants, fungi, and algae that live within the park's half-million acres, a lofty ambition since no such inventory had ever been undertaken. Counting all the species found in eight hundred square miles is a daunting task, and it's still underway. As of May 2016, a total of 19,250 species had been identified.

"We've discovered over 970 species new to science and added more than 9,000 new records of species for the Great Smoky Mountains National Park which has almost doubled the number of species known in the park," said Discover Life executive director and friend Todd Witcher. The so-called daunting task has garnered national and international acclaim. Witcher proudly added that author, biologist, and world's most famous entomologist E. O. Wilson "has written about us in his new book *Half-Earth: Our Planet's Fight for Life* and we've partnered with the E. O. Wilson Biodiversity Foundation to do more research around the region and even around the globe!"

To date, 2,562 species of beetle have been found living in the Great Smokies alone. Metaphorically, if cockroaches occupy the bowels of the ship, beetles are in a stateroom all their own. No comprehensive field guide of the world's beetles will ever be written because such a book would be too heavy to lift and virtually outdated as soon as it rolled off the presses. The last time such a project was attempted was more than seventy-five years ago. It took Wilhelm Junk and Sigmund Schenkling thirty years to produce their *Coleopterorum Catalogus*. Published in parts from 1910 to 1940, it was later bound into thirty-one volumes. There's a copy of the opus at UT's Ag-Vet Library; it takes up sixty-two inches of shelf space and reportedly lists almost 221,500 species of beetle. As staggering as that work is, by today's count it's roughly 179,000 beetles short. Terry Erwin, a beetle expert with the Smithsonian Institution, has estimated that there may be as many as eight million species of beetle in the tropics alone, most of which are waiting to be discovered. Yet, despite their remarkable success, most adult beetles are ephemeral, their time is measured in days not months.

Beetles belong to the insect order Coleoptera, which means "sheath wings," a moniker that describes the hard covers—modified front wings known as elytra—that protect the insect's folded, membranous true wings. People who specialize in the study of beetles are therefore called coleopterists and true beetle experts are few and far between, simply because of the sheer voluminous nature of the topic. If you would like to become an expert on a particular natural subject, I'd recommend North American ferns. Once you can identify about one hundred species, you'd have a pretty good grasp of your subject matter. Beetles, on the other hand, would take a lifetime to master—two lifetimes, probably.

YOU NAME IT, AND BEETLES
EITHER LIVE ON IT OR EAT IT

"And you, be ye fruitful, and multiply; bring forth abundantly in the earth, and multiply therein," reads Genesis 9:7. Every time I think of this passage from the King James Bible, I think of beetles.

Why are there so many kinds of beetles? The first part of the answer is time. Beetles have been around 240 million years, giving them eons to disperse, adapt, and entrench. As other life forms evolved, particularly the flowering plants, beetle forms were modified to follow their lead. The rich biodiversity of our planet was a boon to the highly adaptable insects. Beetles are specialists. Some species live on just one kind of tree and no other place. Finding all these host-specific beetles is a challenge. In 1982, the Smithsonian's Terry Erwin isolated just one species of rainforest tree, *Luehea seemanii,* in Panama. He collected 163 kinds of beetles indigenous to that species of tree alone.

Second, beetles are well designed. The hard coverings that protect their delicate true wings are masterpieces of bioengineering. They allow beetles to go into places that other delicate insects like butterflies could never go without ripping their wings to shreds. These hard coverings also allow beetles to retain moisture so that they don't dry out in arid locations or drown in wet ones.

In 2002, nine-year-old David Royce was swimming in his neighborhood pool in west Knox County. Something floating in the water caught his eye. It had worked its way into the trap that's designed to catch the flotsam and jetsam that routinely fall into swimming pools. The young naturalist recognized it to be the lifeless body of a reddish-brown male stag beetle. David carried the waterlogged corpse home. His mother, Jennifer, planned to help him pin the splendid specimen for his insect collection. The cadaver was laid out with all due respect on its back with the kitchen counter serving as a funeral bier. It needed to dry a bit, or so that was the plan. After about four hours though, they noticed that the legs on the critter's left side were "twitching." Shortly, the legs on the right side twitched as well, followed by an exploratory back and forth motion from the antennae. Like Dr. Frankenstein's monster, it was alive. Pretty soon the beetle was moving about—back from the dead.

According to the National Wildlife Federation's insect expert David Herlocker, beetles have the ability to survive long periods of time in watery conditions that would drown you and me. "The openings to the breathing system of a beetle are located on the abdomen, underneath the wings. When they are immersed in water they can pull these wings in tightly and seal off the openings to the outside, while slowly using the air trapped between their body and wings." The colder the water the better, because their metabolism slows and they use less oxygen. Herlocker injected, "There's no such thing as a sick insect; they are either well, or dead."

Beetles also have evolved a varied palate. Some eat leaves or suck plant juices, or chew on wood; each species has a specialty. They also eat other types of insects, carrion, and dung. In fact, no matter what you can think of—other than solid rock—there's a beetle specially adapted to consume it. The modest little ladybug beetles found in your garden eat the aphids attacking your plants, while on the other end of the acceptability scale, the Colorado potato beetle feeds on your potatoes, while the red flour beetle feeds on stored grains. There are also asparagus beetles, bean beetles, and spotted cucumber beetles; all of them are ready to help you harvest your crop, so some beetles can be pests in the garden.

But, as if to underscore the meaningful versatility of the order, one group of beneficial predator beetles is now being raised in a lab at the University of Tennessee. In May 2005, the Lindsay Young Beneficial Insects Laboratory (LYBIL) was dedicated at the UT Agricultural Experiment Station only a short distance from my Chapman Ridge home. Named after the late Lindsay Young, a Knoxville philanthropist, the first mission of the new facility was to raise mass quantities of *Sasajiscymnus tsugae.* That's a mouthful, but suffice it to say that these tiny—adults are two millimeters long—solid-black ladybug beetles are from Japan. There they specialize in eating hemlock woolly adelgids—small, aphidlike insects that can kill a hemlock tree. The predator ladybugs keep them in check in Asia, but in this country the woolly adelgids are decimating the hemlock forests, which have no natural defenses.

In the case of *S. tsugae,* both the adult and the larva attack the conifer-killing woolly adelgids that secrete fluffy white wax about themselves and appear as tiny puffs of cotton. From late 2003 to 2011, LYBIL produced more than 915,000 adults of the predator black ladybugs, releasing approximately 745,000 on federal and state lands in the southern Appalachians. Seen as a natural biological control, they will, it's hoped, reproduce and thrive, bringing the adelgid infestation under control, or at least reducing it to a non-damaging level. Private property owners with hemlocks are now able to go online and buy their own supply of the predator beetles using the search term "Sasajiscymnus tsugae for sale."

Tiny *S. tsugae* can save a tree and ultimately a forest, but another petite beetle can do the opposite.

DEATH BY A THOUSAND BITES

The hard coverings that protect beetles make them little tanks. It also allows them to exploit all sorts of places: under rocks and logs, and even into and under the bark of living trees. If you've ever chopped down a tree with an axe, you know they're formidable structures to bring down. If we all still had to chop our own firewood to keep warm in the winter, we'd still live in small houses. Keeping a big enough woodpile to heat modern-day houses would exhaust most homeowners.

On the other hand, the southern pine beetle (SPB), *Dendroctonus frontalis*, is a champion wood excavator. Its genus name, *Dendroctonus,* means "tree-killer." It's one of the group of insects collectively called the "southern pine bark-beetle guild," and it infests all species of pines but favors Virginia, short-leaf, and loblollies. There are about six thousand species of bark beetles on the planet, including five hundred that live in the United States and Canada. Most eat only the bark of a tree, and most have little impact.

When populations are low, SPB are very hard to find, and infestations seem to be limited to weak, sick, downed, or damaged trees. Periodically, however, populations explode, causing outbreaks that spread over many acres and states, advancing during the heat of summer at rates up to fifty feet per day. At the time of such outbreaks, swarms of beetles overwhelm even healthy trees and once a tree is colonized, it cannot survive; thousands of acres of once-healthy pines may be lost. It's been estimated that between 1960 and 1990, SPB caused $900 million in damage to southern forests. An infestation in Honduras in the early 1960s spread over 4.9 million acres; about seventy-seven thousand pines were killed every day.

Historically, outbreaks have occurred every six to twelve years and generally lasted two to three years, but of late, the interval between outbreaks has been decreasing while their severity has intensified. Part of this change is weather related. Long summer droughts and forest fires weaken trees, and mild winters do not kill as many of the dormant beetle larvae.

The outbreak of 1999–2002 was the severest on record in Tennessee. Morgan Simmons, a staff writer for the *Knoxville News Sentinel*, reported in 2001 that the infestation had already killed one hundred thousand acres of pines in Tennessee, and that tally excluded trees in the Cherokee National Forest and Great Smoky Mountains National Park. It reached epidemic levels in fifty-seven counties, including all those located in the Tennessee Valley.

The outbreak was so tenacious it moved into locations, particularly mid-state, that had normally never been affected. "For as long as we've kept beetle records, we've never had as many counties infested at one time," reported Bruce Kauffman, forest health specialist for the Tennessee Division of Forestry.

The Catoosa Wildlife Management Area, located twenty miles north of Crossville, is considered one of the crown jewels of the more than ninety wildlife areas across the state managed by TWRA. Funded by hunters and fishermen, the eighty-two-thousand-acre tract is mostly forested, far removed from the large natural meadow that early settlers found there. But that changed in the late 1990s. Pine beetles moved in, and ultimately over fifteen hundred acres of dying pines had to be cut. A massive amount of shortleaf pine, aged seventy to ninety years, was lost, destroyed by the aggressive beetles.

The story took an unexpected turn, however. Planners were discussing the reintroduction of native warm-season grasses when a walk though the cleared site revealed that bluestem and other North American tall meadow grasses were returning on their own. The land was beginning to convert itself back to the original savanna that existed when bison and elk roamed the high plateau of Tennessee. Even a pine forest can come and go. So ephemerality is relative. Again, somewhat surprisingly, we are reminded of Macbeth's "brief candle, life's but a walking shadow" soliloquy.

Unlike the gypsy moth and balsam wooly aldelgid, the southern pine beetle is native. Their outbreaks have been occurring for perhaps thousands of years. When French botanist François André Michaux traveled through the valley in September 1802, he passed miles of pines along the way that had only recently died. He was mystified and was told that the die-off happened every fifteen or twenty years. It's now believed that he was observing an early outbreak of pine beetles.

A MONOGAMOUS BEETLE?

From a naturalist's point of view, the southern pine beetle has an intriguing biology. To begin with, they're monogamous, which is very unusual for something so small, only two to four millimeters in length (about the size of a grain of rice). Using the same device I've used before, it would take ten of them lined up end to end to measure an inch.

Prairie voles, elephant shrews, and human beings, generally, form long-term mutually exclusive pair bonds (only about 3 percent of all mammal species are monogamous). In the avian realm, whooping cranes, bald eagles, and many other birds of prey mate for life, but most of the animal kingdom do not. Monogamy allows a mated pair to work together to produce offspring with a greater likelihood of success. Most insects ensure the survival of their species by producing overwhelming numbers—females lay lots of eggs. The SPB employs both strategies. The female produces many eggs, and when she works with a male, more of the offspring are successfully reared. In the South, a mated pair of SPB may produce several broods together before they die.

Mating season begins in the spring. Each new female overwinters inside an infected tree, first as an active larva and then as a metamorphosing pupa (like a moth inside a cocoon). After she emerges from her pupal cell, the SPB female must bore her way out of the dying tree and fly to a new one, so it's the female that chooses a new host. There she begins to excavate a tunnel and secretes the pheromone frontalin. The pine reacts to the initial attack by exuding sticky resin. Drawn by the smell of frontalin and resin, males and even additional females find the newly infected tree.

Once on the tree, the males begin to search for the females' entrance tunnels bored into the bark. When the portal is located, the male clears away the accumulated frass (debris or excrement produced by the female) built up inside the tunnel. Occasionally, two males will find the same entrance hole, and a fight may occur, with the larger of the two generally winning the contest. The victor then enters the tunnel; he secretes a second pheromone called verbenone, which is designed to counter the female's and discourage other males and even females from landing on the host tree. This "switching" mechanism forces subsequent waves of beetles to find new trees.

Meanwhile, the female hollows out a nuptial chamber. After the pair-bond forms and they have mated inside this shoe-shaped chamber, the monogamous couple go to work on the tree. The female constructs gallery tunnels into the soft inner phloem of the tree. The phloem lies just beneath the bark; it's the conductive tissue by which sugars made in the leaves are moved to the roots. The excavated galleries are winding serpentine tunnels that, at times, even crisscross each other; essentially it's a maze with curved walkways. The female also cuts egg niches into the walls of the galleries. Inside each, an egg is laid and covered by a thin wall of fine debris. Each gallery ultimately has up to thirty egg niches. As she finishes each section, the male works to clear frass and fine sawdust created by the excavating. Every so often, ventilation holes have to be bored to the outside, weakening the tree even more. When the pair finish their work, they may reemerge from the tree and move to another location on the same pine or another tree altogether. Under ideal conditions in the southern-most portions of their range, the parent beetles may construct up to five systems of egg galleries, raising an equal number of broods. Thus, their teamwork approach pays off.

Southern pine bark beetle eggs hatch in three to nine days, and as larvae, the young beetles feed on the tree's phloem, creating yet more tunnels that are perpendicular to their parents' egg tunnels. As the larvae develop, they work their way to the tree's outer bark, where they form their pupal cells. Pupation lasts five to seven days, and when the young adults emerge, they'll tunnel to the surface and fly away to begin the entire process over again. In this way, several generations may be created before the onset of winter, when the entire process has to shut down until spring.

During the warm months of summer, metamorphosis speeds up, beetle development is faster, and infestations expand more rapidly. The entire life-cycle can be completed in thirty to forty days. The pine's only line of defense is the oozing of sticky resin, but if enough beetles attack a tree simultaneously, resin pressure drops and production ceases. A pine riddled with entrance, exit, and ventilation holes loses moisture. The tree is also opened up to sec-ondary infections of fungi, bacteria, and yeast; all hasten the tree's ultimate death.

Before we label pine bark beetles as an abominable pest, absolute savages four millimeters long, we should look at them from their point of view. Their goal is not to ravage the trees but simply to raise a family and ensure their genes are passed on to the next generation, like ticks and botflies. Most of the time they colonize dead or dying trees to begin the process of decom-position, returning the woody plant's accumulated nutrients to the soil.

Their specialized, monogamous teamwork is remarkably rare, another creative beetle adaptation. Before our arrival in this part of the world, out-breaks were probably quite small and localized, like wild fires caused by lightning strikes—just one of nature's ways of rejuvenating a forest. Their recent outbreaks have been more severe, and quite possibly, we are to blame. Two principle reasons are generally cited: monocultural pine plantations and climate change.

When forests are managed as cash crops, one species of pine is generally planted. An infestation of pine beetles can spread quickly through the entire tree farm. As tree specialist Jim Cortese pointed out to me, "Dutch elm disease was more severe in the North than the South because northern urban plan-ners planted elm after elm along city cities. In the South, elms were generally more randomly planted, making it harder for an epidemic to spread." On the Cumberland Plateau, many pine plantations grew loblolly pines exclusively for the pulp industry. Loblollies are native to damper southern bottomland and may have already been stressed living on the higher, dryer plateau. These large stands of loblollies proved to be particularly vulnerable during the SPB outbreak of the early 2000s.

Many foresters are now questioning the practice. Was managing mono-cultural forests in crop-like fashion for short-term monetary profit the right thing to do? "Or do we respect forests for what they are and treat them ac-cordingly—as diverse, natural-capital ecosystems that collectively affect the health of the whole world?" asked Chris Maser in *Distant Thunder: The Jour-nal of the Forest Stewards Guild*. A diverse natural forest produces oxygen, collects and stores fresh water, holds soils in place, and serves as home to countless organisms, including pollinators and insect-eating birds and bats. Again, it's the web of life.

The second factor, which may lead to more severe and widespread SPB epidemics, has to do with climate. Many would cite global warming. Win-ter temperatures in a region that are cold enough to be lethal determine the northern limit to the pine beetle's range. One scenario predicts that with a temperature increase of just a few degrees, SPB outbreaks will become com-mon in Ohio and southern Pennsylvania, locations where they rarely occur. Occasional epidemics will begin in Wisconsin, Michigan, New York, and Massachusetts, northern states that historically have been off limits.

I recall having lunch many years ago with a friend when the subject of global warming came up. "I don't know what the fuss is all about," she in-jected. "Personally, I wouldn't mind if it were a fewer degrees warmer all the time." I grimaced, not knowing where to begin my lengthy rebuttal.

"PINE BEETLES DEVASTATE THE ONCE UN-DEVASTATABLE [*SIC*] WEST"

Historically, in western North America, the winters were too cold and the summers too short for a bark beetle to have much of an effect. But things have changed and apparently the mountain pine beetle (MPB, *Dendroctonus ponderosae*), has adapted to the change. As a rule, the bark beetle tribe lay eggs under the bark of dead or dying trees. A few species burrow into verdant trees, but they do it in small, isolated numbers. Good old MPB are like the Borg on *Star Trek: Next Generation*: they attack in mass and "resistance is futile."

Even in a bad year, MPB would confine their assault to a given region, but in the past two decades they have targeted half the continent. Sixty million acres of forests, especially lodgepole and ponderosa pines, have been laid waste from northern New Mexico through Canada. It is unprecedented. British Columbia is the Canadian province between Washington State and the Yukon; historically, it has long, pine beetle–killing winters and short, beetle-reproducing summers but not of late. An estimated 60 percent of its mature pine forests may be dead by the time this outbreak ends.

"Nature is always changing. But the mountain pine beetle is a troubling omen. It shows that global warming can push even native species to go rogue. At some point the epidemic will run its course, leaving a wake of ghost forests and altered ecosystems," wrote Hillary Rosner for *National Geographic.*

Warmer weather and the resultant drought have stressed the trees; their resistance is low. Longer summers have given the beetles time to expand their population, as well as their range, both horizontally and vertically up to higher elevations in the mountains. And again, like the southern cousin, this is not an imported immigrant like chestnut blight or Asian emerald ash borer. It is a native species taking advantage of our warmer, drier planet and the trees that have been put in peril by our use of fossil fuels.

It brings to mind the cartoon panel that Walt Kelly did for Earth Day 1971. Showing Pogo surveying his trashed swamp, the winsome possum laments, "Yep, son, we have met the enemy and he is us."

Is there any way to see a silver lining in one beetle species that is almost too small to see causing such widespread destruction?

"People always say things like, 'A thousand acres were lost,'" said U.S. Geological Survey forest ecologist Craig Allen. "But they weren't actually lost. The land is still there, full of new life again. I personally lost friends in the fires—individual ancient trees I knew and loved. But these systems are in the process of adjusting. Nature goes on."

Nature goes on, it's tenacious. Is that the lesson here? To a degree, it's the lesson of this entire collection. Species are ephemeral. Forests are ephemeral. Continents? Well, on a planet that's over four billion years old, even our landmasses are ephemeral too. They come and they go, but nature goes on. If, someday, when the only thing left is a barren, desolate planet, somewhere a seed will sprout, and the whole crazy, diverse world will start anew—although, I do think that there are beetles that specialize in living among devastation and that they will survive, just as the feathered dinosaurs we now call birds survived 66 million years ago.

This brings us back to Nietzsche's Eternal Recurrence and even parallel universes or a multiverse, something physics students are bantering about at this very moment. If our world exists, then logic dictates that a world like our own can recur. It happened once, so the probability it can happen again is greater than zero. And if space and time are infinite, then logic dictates that our existence must recur an infinite number of times.

So where does that leave us? Pay your overdue library book fines. You don't want that hanging around. It'll only come up again in a slightly different form.

The renowned British biologist and philosopher J. B. S. Haldane was once asked what his years of studying nature had taught him about the Creator. It is said that Haldane replied that he must have "an inordinate fondness for beetles." As we saw in our last chapter, Haldane's response seems comfortably apropos. But even over four hundred thousand species of beetles pale by comparison when you consider that an estimated five billion species have lived on our planet and more than ninety-nine percent of those are now extinct. Freshwater jellyfish have survived but the four-tusked elephant that Dr. Wallace and the good folks at Gray are currently reassembling did not. So it's just as easy to think that our planet—and probably thousands of hospitable planets like it—has an inordinate fondness for *life*. Species come and go, ephemeral all, and should we ultimately devastate our planet rendering it uninhabitable for humans, nature will simply hit reboot, and Nietzsche's eternal recurrence will come into play.

Whether or not Haldane said such a thing about beetles has often been debated, but it has been repeated so many times it has become part of the coleopteran mythos. I first heard it from the late Dr. Bob Harris while roaming the trails at Ijams almost twenty years ago. Harris was a retired anesthesiologist and a lifelong naturalist who volunteered at the nature center leading groups of students around the park's many trails. Today, I carry on his tradition as will someone after me when my ephemeral days are over. Dr. Harris would often encounter beetles scurrying about and earnestly pause to watch them; he was fascinated by their remarkableness, as they were, to a degree, a metaphor for all of nature itself, tenacious and adaptable.

Dr. Harris (known by most who knew him as Dr. Bob) was well traveled with a discerning eye—and heart—for natural beauty. In November 1999, I accompanied him on a canoe trip to his favorite place on Earth, the Okefenokee Swamp, the same wetland that was home to cartoonist Walt Kelly's Pogo, Howland Owl, and Churchy LaFemme, a mud turtle by trade.

On that trip, our human swampy trio was rounded out by a marine educator now retired from NOAA, Cathy Sakas, the writer and host of two Emmy-award-winning nature series: *The Coastal Naturalist* for Georgia Public Television and a documentary series called *Secret Seashores*. After one particularly memorable afternoon's paddle down Minnie's Run on Billy's Lake, Cathy and I turned to see Dr. Bob sitting in his canoe, crying. Yes, crusty old Dr. Bob was in tears. When we asked him why, he simply responded, "It's just all so beautiful."

It was just six years later when Ijams's wildlife biologist Pam Petko-Seus and I visited Dr. Bob at St. Mary's Hospice in Knoxville. It was bittersweet; all three of us knew he was dying. Yet, there was a profound peacefulness about him, interspersed with moments of tears as he spoke of his early days at the nature center, the camaraderie, and the groups of students.

What do you say to a man when you know his end is near? How to convey his importance? Or is it inevitable that such things go unsaid and we're cursed to live with your silence?

After a time, our rambling conversation drifted toward the spiritual. Dr. Bob, a true pantheist, saw divinity everywhere he looked in nature. Just six days before he died, he told us that after a lifetime immersed in the natural world, the three things he cherished most were hearing a wood thrush sing, watching fireflies twinkle at night, and seeing the aurora borealis on trips to the North; all had an undeniably sacred quality to him. He spoke of these events with tearful tenderness.

"I know of no pleasure deeper," said nature filmmaker Sir David Attenborough, "than that which comes from contemplating the natural world and trying to understand it."

Dr. Bob knew this pleasure because for him, "It was all so beautiful."

As I write these words to close out this book, it has only been a few hours since a wildfire in the Chimney Tops region of the Great Smoky Mountains National Park was whipped to a fury by hurricane force winds that topped out at ninety-miles an hour. A fierce swirl of glowing-embers-turned-firestorm swept down out of the mountains after dark and flowed through Gatlinburg, Tennessee, like Old Testament wrath.

The small resort community is my hometown, Baskins Creek my natal waters. I lost nothing material but everything memorable. Hundreds of people lost all that was tangible, everything they owned, only barely escaping down the mountain roads with fires blazing all around them. Online videos posted by some of the fourteen thousand evacuees are horrific. The town is now cordoned off. The ruins smolder. Residents are not allowed back in until all the fires are out and officials assess the carnage, searching for victims. Currently the death toll stands at thirteen but that will probably rise.

I went to Pi Beta Phi Elementary School located beside Arrowmont School of Arts and Crafts. My boyhood home was a short walk from both of these, and I walked it often. I graduated from Gatlinburg-Pittman High School, lived and worked in the festive, resort town for decades, walked up and down the Parkway, Reagan Drive, Airport and River Roads more times than I could possibly put a number to. I knew people who lived in Greystone Heights and wrote my first published words for the *Mountain Press*, the local newspaper. I've hiked the trails in the foothills, around and below Mt. Le Conte and the creek that bears its name many, many times. My family's roots go back to the 1880s and the watersheds of Roaring Fork and Baskins Creek. Our ancestral homes of Alfred Reagan and Jim and Ephraim Bales are maintained by the park service. Monday's fury of fires was reported in many of these places. At this point, no one quite knows what is left.

Tennessee Governor Bill Haslam said it was the worst fire in Tennessee in the past one hundred years. A three-acre brushfire quickly became a seventeen-thousand-acre blaze in a matter of hours. The current estimate is that over three hundred homes and businesses were damaged or destroyed within the town's city limits. Before I could finish this book's closing I received word that one of those was our family home, a two-story house with high gables on the hillside built in 1949. It was where my mother and father spent their entire sixty-plus year marriage. It is, or was, the fountainhead of all my childhood memories. The house had only recently been sold and was being remodeled for a new family. In a scant few hours, perhaps much less, every single home on Baskins Creek Road burned to the ground. There is nothing to go back to; nothing left but cinder blocks, ashes, and cobblestones carried up from the creek.

What do you say when a piece of you is burned away? One man's life can last decades but parts of it are astonishingly ephemeral.

"Whereas ye know not what shall be on the morrow. For what is your life? It is even a vapour, that appeareth for a little time, and then vanisheth away," James 4:14.

SOURCES

Short-eared Owl

Davis, Donald E. Personal correspondence. August 2016.

Davis, Marcia. "Birdlife: Spooky Myths about Owls." *Knoxville News Sentinel,* October 25, 2009.

Heinrich, Bernd. *One Man's Owl.* Princeton, NJ: Princeton University Press. 1987. See p. 5.

Knudsen, EI. "The Hearing of the Barn Owl." *Scientific American* 245, no. 6 (1981): 113–25.

Soniak, Matt. "Why Is Bird Poop White?" *Mental Floss* magazine blog, July 22, 2012. http://mentalfloss.com/article/31262/why-bird-poop-white.

Stroud, Emily. "Every Day Is Bird Day for ET Couple." WBIR *Live at Five at Four,* January 6, 2016. http://www.wbir.com/news/local/five-at-four/every-day -is-bird-day-for-et-couple-1/11308328.

Townsend, Charles Wendell. "Short-eared Owl." In *Life Histories of North American Birds of Prey,* edited by Arthur Cleveland Bent. 1938. Reprint, New York: Dover Books, 1961. See pp. 169, 179.

Van Norman, Alan. "Owls See World Distinctly with Unusually Large Eyes." *Bismarck (ND) Tribune,* February 25, 2010.

Zickefoose, Julie. "Midnight Rambler: Eastern Screech-Owl." *Bird Watchers Digest,* September/October 2013, 2.

Jack-in-the-Pulpit

Atlas, James. "Is This the End?" Sunday Review Opinion. *The New York Times.* November 24, 2012. http://www.nytimes.com/2012/11/25/opinion/sunday /is-this-the-end.html.

Banks, William H., Jr. "Ethnobotany of the Cherokee Indians." Master's thesis, University of Tennessee, 1953. Available online at http://trace.tennessee.edu /utk_gradthes/1052/.

Barras, Colin. "The Abominable Mystery: How Flowers Conquered the Earth." BBC online, October 16, 2014. http://www.bbc.com/earth/story/20141017 -how-flowers-conquered-the-world.

Fortey, Richard. *Horseshoe Crabs and Velvet Worms: The Story of the Animals and Plants That Time Has Left Behind.* New York: Alfred A. Knopf, 2012. See p. 252.

Loewer, Peter. *Thoreau's Garden: Native Plants for the American Landscape.* Mechanicsburg, PA: Stackpole Books, 1996. See p. 50.

Moisset, Beatriz. "Jack-in-the-Pulpit and Its Cruel Deception." *Pollinators* blog, September 19, 2010. http://pollinators.blogspot.com/2010/09/jack-in-pulpit -and-its-cruel-deception.html.

Rice, Tim, and Elton John. "Circle of Life." *The Lion King.* Disney, 1994.

Spivack, Charlotte. *Ursula K. Le Guin.* Boston: Twayne, 1984. See p. 48.

Thoreau, Henry David. *The Journal of Henry David Thoreau.* 1837–1851. Reprint, New York: Dover, 1962. See p. 1478.

Appalachian Pandas

Aurelius, Marcus. *Meditations.* iv. 36. Bartlett's Quotations online. http://www .bartleby.com/100/718.html.

Bristol, Larry. Personal conversation, May 6, 2006; e-mails, June 2006.

DeSantis, Larisa R.G. and Steven Wallace. "Ancient Ecology and Climate of the Gray Fossil Site," *Gray Fossil Site: 10 Years of Research.* Symposium Report, 2011. See p. 19.

Fortey, Richard. *Horseshoe Crabs and Velvet Worms: The Story of the Animals and Plants That Time Has Left Behind.* New York: Alfred A. Knopf, 2012. See p. 276.

Fulwood, Ethan L., and Steven C. Wallace. "Evidence For Unusual Size Dimorphism in a Fossil Ailurid." *Palaeontologia Electronica* (Society for Vertebrate Paleontology), article no. 18.3.45, Sept. 2015. http://palaeo-electronica .org/content/2015/1313-dimorphism-in-pristinailurus?fb_actionids =1022065497825770&fb_action_types=og.likes.

Johnson, Mary Gay. "Panda Preserve could Save Species." *Knoxville Journal.* August 26, 1987. See p. A2, A4.

Lundquist, Judy and Steven Wallace. "Gray Fossil Site: A Unique Fossil Site and Museum Opens to Visitors in the Mountains of East Tennessee." *Smoky Mountain Living.* Spring 2007. See pps. 38-39, 71.

MacClintock, Dorcas. *Red Pandas: A Natural History.* New York: Charles Scribner's Sons, 1988. See pp. 3–4.

McRary, Amy. "Red Panda Getting a Playmate." *Knoxville News Sentinel,* October 23, 1987. See p. B1.

Moore, Harry. *The Bone Hunters: The Discovery of Miocene Fossils in Gray, Tennessee.* Knoxville: University of Tennessee Press, 2005. See p. 11.

Schaller, George B. *The Last Panda.* Chicago: University of Chicago Press, 1993. See pp. 261–67.

Wallace, Steven C., and Xiaoming Wang. "Two New Carnivores from an Unusual Late Tertiary Forest Biota in Eastern North America." *Nature* 431 (September 30, 2004): 556–58.

Wallace, Steven C. Personal phone call November 3 and interview November 21, 2016.

Woodruff, Aaron. "Bristol's Panda (*Pristinailurus bristoli*)." *Life in the Cenozoic Era* blog, January 23, 2015. http://cenozoiclife.blogspot.com/2015/01/bristols-panda-pristinailurus-bristoli.html.

Cerulean Warbler

Beachy, Tiffany-Ahren. "Cerulean Warbler *(Dedroica cerulean)* Breeding Ecology and Habitat Selection, Initial Response to Forest Management, and Association with Anthropogenic Disturbances in the Cumberland Mountains of Tennessee." Master's thesis, University of Tennessee, August 2008. See p. 151.

Bent, Arthur Cleveland. *Life Histories of North American Wood Warblers.* Part 1. 1953. Reprint, New York: Dover Publications, 1963. See pp. 329–37.

Boves, Than James. "Multiple Responses by Cerulean Warblers to Experimental Forest Disturbance in the Appalachian Mountains." PhD diss., University of Tennessee, 2011. See pp. 207–8. Available online at http://trace.tennessee.edu/utk_graddiss/1169.

Chu, Miyoko. *Songbird Journeys: Four Seasons in the Lives of Migratory Birds.* New York: Walker, 2006. See p. 194.

Darwin, Charles R. *Journal of Researches into the Natural History and Geology of the Countries Visited during the Voyage of H.M.S. Beagle round the World, under the Command of Capt. Fitz Roy, R.N.* 2nd edition. London: John Murray, 1845. See p. 49.

Franzen, Jonathan. *Freedom.* New York: Farrar, Straus and Giroux, 2010. See pp. 300, 485.

Frost, Robert. "Fragmentary Blue." *The Poetry of Robert Frost.* New York: Holt, Rinehart and Winston, 1979. See p. 220.

Hamel, Paul B. *Cerulean Warbler: Status Assessment, April 2000.* U.S. Fish and Wildlife Service, April 2000. Available online at https://www.fws.gov/midwest/es/soc/birds/cerw/pdf/cerw-sa.pdf.

Johnson, Trisha. *Cerulean Warbler, Dendroica cerulea, Species Account and Cumberland Habitat Conservation Plan Survey Results.* Cumberland HCP Science Advisory Committee. Available online at http://www.cumberlandhcp.org/files/Cerulean_Warbler_species_acct.pdf.

Juniper, Tony. *Spix's Macaw: The Race to Save the World's Rarest Bird.* New York: Atria Books, 2002. See p. 113.

Moreno, Maria Isabel, Paul Salaman, and David Pashley. *The Current Status of the Cerulean Warbler on its Winter Range.* Fundación ProAves Colombia and American Bird Conservancy, August 2006. Available online at http://www.fws.gov/midwest/es/soc/birds/cerw/morenaetalo806.html.

Pearson, T. Gilbert. *Birds of America*. Reprint: Garden City, NY: Doubleday, 1936. See part 3, pp. 132–33.

Pendergrast, Mark. *Uncommon Grounds: The History of Coffee and How it Transformed the World*. New York: Basic Books, 2010. See pp. 259, 369.

Rainbolt, George W. and Sandra L. Dwyer. *Critical Thinking: The Art of Argument*. Cengage Learning, 2014. See p. 30.

Rosenthal, Elisabeth. "Heat Damages Colombia Coffee, Raising Prices." *New York Times,* March 9, 2011. http://www.nytimes.com/2011/03/10 /science/earth/10coffee.html?_r=1.

Shepard, Odell, editor. *The Heart of Thoreau's Journals*. Dover, 1961. See p. 106.

Stoeffel, Kat. "Cerulean Warbler: New York's Latest Literary Darling." *Observer* online, January 12, 2011. http://observer.com/2011/01/cerulean-warbler -new-yorks-latest-literary-darling/.

Weidensaul, Scott. *Living on the Wind: Across the Hemisphere with Migratory Birds*. New York: North Point Press, 1999. See pp. 258, 261, 262.

Wilson, Alexander. *Wilson's American Ornithology*. New York: Arno and The New York Times, 1970. See pp. 185–86.

Zickefoose, Julie. *The Bluebird Effect: Uncommon Bonds with Common Birds*. Boston: Houghton Mifflin Harcourt, 2012. See p. 21.

Ghost Plant

Banks, Iain. *Excession*. Bantam Spectra. New York. 1998. http://www.obooksbooks .com/books/3447_2.html.

Banks, William H., Jr. "Ethnobotany of the Cherokee Indians." Master's thesis, University of Tennessee, 1953. See p. 97. Available online at http://trace .tennessee.edu/utk_gradthes/1052/.

Coffey, Timothy. *The History and Folklore of North American Wildflowers*. Boston: Houghton Mifflin, 1993.

Dickinson, Emily. "Part Four: Time and Eternity." *The Complete Poems of Emily Dickinson*. Boston: Little, Brown, 1924.

Erichsen-Brown, Charlotte. *Medicinal and Other Uses of North American Plants: A Historcal Survey with Special Reference to the Eastern Indian Tribes*. New York: Dover Publications, 1979. See p. 317.

Finger, John R. *The Eastern Band of Cherokees*. Knoxville: University of Tennessee Press, 1984.

Freeman, E. M. "In Praise of Parasitism." *Scientific American* 44, no. 1 (1937): 67–76. JSTOR Scholarly Journal Archive. http://www.jstor.org.

Gortner, R. A. "What Is a Plant?" *Science* 57, no. 1482 (1923): 614. JSTOR Scholarly Journal Archive. http://www.jstor.org.

Hoig, Stanley W. *The Cherokees and Their Chiefs*. Fayetteville: University of Arkansas Press, 1998.

Kunze, Richard E. "Monotropa uniflora, L." *Botanical Gazette* 3, no. 6 (1878): 54. JSTOR Scholarly Journal Archive. http://www.jstor.org.

Lounsberry, Alice. *A Guide to the Wild Flowers*. New York: Frederick A. Stokes, 1899. See p. 170.

McMahan, Carroll. "Upland Chronicles: Decoration Day Is an Honored Sevier County Custom." *Mountain Press* (Sevierville, TN), May 9, 2015.

Milius, Susan. "Mistletoe, of All Things, Helps Juniper Trees." *Science News* online. January 2, 2002. https://www.sciencenews.org/article/mistletoe-all -things-helps-juniper-trees

Millspaugh, Charles F. *American Medicinal Plants*. Philadelphia: John C. Yorston, 1892. See pp. 411–12.

Perdue, Theda. *The Cherokee*. New York: Chelsea House, 1989.

Sanders, Jack. *Hedgemaids and Fairy Candles: The Lives and Lore of North American Wildflowers*. Camden, ME: Ragged Mountain Press, 1993.

Simmons, Morgan. "UT Herbarium Collection Numbers 550,000 Species." *Knoxville News Sentinel*, October 13, 2003.

Stokes, Donald, and Lillian. *A Guide to Enjoying Wildflowers*. Stokes Nature Guides. Boston: Little, Brown, 1985. See pp. 179–83.

Volk, Tom. "Tom Volk's Fungus of the Month for October 2002." University of Wisconsin-Madison website. http://botit.botany.wisc.edu/toms_fungi /oct2002.html.

Ruby-throated Hummingbird

Garrison, Greg. "Life Stories: Founder of Hummingbird Study Group Expanded Banding and Love of Birds in Alabama," *AL.com,* September 23, 2014. http:// www.al.com/living/index.ssf/2014/09/founder_of_hummingbird_study_g .html#incart_river.

Oliver, Mary. *New and Selected Poems: Volume Two*. Boston: Beacon Press, 2006. See p. 90.

Sargent, Robert. "Migration Basics." *Hummingbirds.net*. http://www.hummingbirds .net/migration.html.

———. *Ruby-throated Hummingbird*. Mechanicsburg, PA: Stackpole, 1999. See pp. 9, 43, 45.

Freshwater Jellyfish

Allman, George J. "On '*Limnocodium victoria,*' a Hydroid Medusa of Fresh Water." *Nature* 22, no. 24 (1880): 178–79.

Carmody, Deirdre. "A Park Census: From Trees to Reptiles." *New York Times,* April 25, 1983.

Carroll, Lewis. *Alice's Adventures in Wonderland*. 1865. Reprint, San Rafael, CA: Classic Press, 1969. See p. 43.

Castle, Kevin. "Rare Freshwater Jellyfish Found in Scott County Pond." *Kingsport (TN) Times-News*, September 9, 2000.

Erwin, Autumn. *"Craspedacusta sowerbyi." Animal Diversity Web*. University of Michigan, Museum of Zoology. animaldiversity.org/accounts/Craspedacusta _sowerbyi/.

Fortey, Richard. *Horseshoe Crabs and Velvet Worms: The Story of the Animals and Plants That Time Has Left Behind*. New York: Alfred A. Knopf, 2012. See pp. 52–53, 148–49,

Garman, Harrison. "The Sudden Appearance of Great Numbers of Fresh-Water Medusas in a Kentucky Creek." *Science* 44, no. 1146 (1916): 858–60.

Hargitt, Charles W. "Occurrence of the Fresh-Water Medusa Limnocodium, in the United States." *Science* 26, no. 671 (1907): 638–39.

———. "Occurrence of the Fresh-Water Medusa, Limnocodium, in the United States." *Biological Bulletin* 14, no. 4 (1908): 304–18.

———. "Distribution of the Fresh-Water Medusa, Craspedacusta, in the United States." *Science* 50, no. 1296 (1919): 413–14.

Kennedy, Steve. "Freshwater Jellyfish." *Skin Diver* 33 (October 1984): 26.

Lankester, E. Ray. "On a New Jelly-Fish of the Order Trachomedusae, Living in Fresh Water." *Nature* 22 (June 17, 1880): 147–48.

———. "The New Freshwater Jelly Fish." *Nature* 22 (June 24, 1880): 177–78.

LeTellier, Brent. Personal email September 2, 2015

"London Zoo." *Tour UK* website. http://www.touruk.co.uk/london_sights/london zoo1.htm.

Lytle, Charles F. "Development of the Freshwater Medusa Craspedacusta sower-bii." In *Developmental Biology of Freshwater Invertebrates*, ed. Frederick W. Harrison and Ronald R. Cowden. New York: Alan R. Liss, 1982. See pp. 129–47.

Mayer, Alfred Goldsborough. *Medusae of the World*. Washington, DC: Carnegie Institution of Washington, 1910.

Muscatine, Leonard, and Howard Lenoff. *Coelenterate Biology: Reviews and New Perspectives*. New York: Academic Press, 1974. See p. 344.

"Nonindigenous Aquatic Species: *Craspedacusta sowerbyi* Lankester 1880." United States Geological Survey website. http://nas.er.usgs.gov/queries/FactSheet .asp?speciesID=1068.

Peard, Terry. *Freshwater Jellyfish* website. freshwaterjellyfish.org.

———. Personal e-mail, August 27, 2003.

———. Personal e-mails, August 2016.

Pennak, Robert W. *Fresh-Water Invertebrates of the United States*. New York: Ronald Press, 1953. See pp. 104–5.

———. *Fresh-Water Invertebrates of the United States: Protozoa to Mollusca*. New York: John Wiley, 1989. See pp. 114–16.

Pennington, Wendell, and John W. Fletcher. "Two Additional Records of *Craspedacusta sowerbyi* Lankester in the Tennessee River System." *Journal of the Tennessee Academy of Science* 55, no. 1 (1980): 31–34.

Powers, Edwin B. "Fresh-water Medusae in Tennessee." *Science* 88, no. 2291 (November 25, 1938): 498–99.

Sasaki, Gen-yu. "Freshwater Jellyfish *(Craspedacusta sowerbyi)*." *Microscopy UK* website. http://www.microscopy-uk.org.uk/mag/artnov99/fwjelly.html.

Schmitt, Waldo. L. "Freshwater Jellyfish Records since 1932." *American Naturalist* 73, no. 744 (1939): 83–89. JSTOR Scholarly Journal Archive. http://www.jstor.org.

Siegel, Robert. "Jellyfish Turns Up in Nebraska." *All Things Considered*. National Public Radio, September 22, 2003.

Simmons, Morgan. "Freshwater Jellyfish Found in ET Quarry." *Knoxville News Sentinel*, September 23, 1997.

Taylor, Steve. "Freshwater Jellyfish: No, You're Not Seeing Things." *Sports Afield* 255, no. 6 (2002): 57.

Theroux , Mary. "Freshwater Jellyfish." *Tennessee Conservationist*, July/August 2007, 24–26.

Yeager, Bruce L. "Drainage Occurrence of the Freshwater Jellyfish, *Craspedacusta sowerbyi* Lankester 1880, in the Tennessee River System." *Brimleyana: The Journal of the North Carolina State Museum of Natural Sciences* 13 (July 1987): 91–96.

Monarch Butterfly

Eiseley, Loren. *The Star Thrower*. Times Books, 1978. See p. 3.

Emerson, Ralph Waldo. *The Works of Ralph Waldo Emerson. Four Volumes in One*. New York: Tudor Publishing, 1961. See p. 270.

Jabr, Ferris. "How Did Insect Metamorphosis Evolve?" *Scientific American* on-line, August 10, 2012. http://www.scientificamerican.com/article/insect-metamorphosis-evolution/.

———. "How Does a Caterpillar Turn into a Butterfly?" *Scientific American* online, August 10, 2012. http://www.scientificamerican.com/article/caterpillar-butterfly-metamorphosis-explainer/.

Marcotty, Josephine. "Calling All Milkweed: Federal Pollinator Plan Needs a Billion Plants for Monarch Butterflies." *Duluth (MN) Star Tribune*, June 6, 2015. http://www.startribune.com/calling-all-milkweed-federal-pollinator-plan-needs-a-billion-plants-for-monarchs/306383591/.

Oberhauser, Karen. "Reproduction." Monarch Lab, University of Minnesota website. http://monarchlab.org/biology-and-research/biology-and-natural-history/breeding-life-cycle/reproduction/.

Slabaugh, Seth. "Activists: Herbicides Threaten Monarch Butterflies." Associated Press article published in *Washington Times*, October 18, 2014. http://www.washingtontimes.com/news/2014/oct/18/activists-herbicides-threaten-monarch-butterflies/?page=all.

Stevenson, Mark. "Monarch Butterflies Decline; Migration May Disappear." Associated Press article published in *USA Today*, January 29, 2014. http://

www.usatoday.com/story/news/world/2014/01/29/monarch-butterflies
-decline/5028977/.

Urquhart, Fred A. "Found at Last: The Monarch's Winter Home." *National Geographic,* August 1976, 161.

Yong, Ed. "3-D Scans Reveal Caterpillars Turning into Butterflies." *Not Exactly Rocket Science* blog, *National Geographic,* May 14, 2013. http://phenomena .nationalgeographic.com/2013/05/14/3-d-scans-caterpillars-transforming -butterflies-metamorphosis/.

Lake Sturgeon

Benson, Thom. "Tennessee Aquarium & Partners to Release 1,000 Lake Sturgeon Near Knoxville." Tennessee Aquarium Media advisory. Personal email. October 5, 2015.

Bibb, Kelly Ann. "Saving Southeastern Aquatic Species." *Endangered Species Bulletin,* September/October 1999. www.thefreelibrary.com/Saving +Southeastern+Aquatic+Species-a059644038.

Coombs, Joyce. Research Associate University of Tennessee. Personal email. July 10, 2013.

Dreifus, Claudia. "In 'Half Earth,' E. O. Wilson Calls for a Grand Retreat." *New York Times,* February 29, 2016. http://www.nytimes.com/2016/03/01/science /e-o-wilson-half-earth-biodiversity.html?r_=1&_r=0.

Engelhaupt, Erika. "The Ones That Got Away Get Huge." *National Geographic,* August 2016. See p. 10.

Etnier, David, and Wayne C. Starnes. *The Fishes of Tennessee.* Knoxville: The University of Tennessee Press, 1993.

"Fishes First Described by Rafinesque." University of Evansville website. http:// faculty.evansville.edu/ck6/bstud/raffish.html.

Fulgham, Kathie. "Lake Sturgeon Make Historic Return to French Broad River." Tennessee Aquarium. Press Release (2000).

Gilbert, Bil. "An 'Odd Fish' Who Swam Against the Tide." *Smithsonian,* January 1999, 112–25.

"Lake Sturgeon Fact Sheet." Tennessee Aquarium website. www.tnaqua.org /Newsroom/sturgeonfacts.asp.

Matthiessen, Peter. *The Snow Leopard.* New York: Viking Press, 1978. See p. 105.

Meurger, Michel. *Lake Monster Traditions: A Cross-cultural Analysis.* London: Fortean Tomes, 1988.

"New York's Adirondack Coast: Champ History—From Ancient Times." Lake Champlain Visitors Center website. http://www.lakechamplainregion.com /content_pages/champhistory.cfm.

Nickell, Joe. "Legend of the Lake Champlain Monster—Investigative File." *Skeptical Inquirer,* July/August 2003. http://www.csicop.org/si/show /legend_of_the_lake_champlain_monster.

Novak, Sabrina (research coordinator, Tennessee Aquarium Research Institute, Cohutta, GA). Personal email, August 25, 2004.

Scott, Ed. Retired TVA aquatic biologist. Personal email. July 7, 2013.

Smith, Wendy (World Wildlife Fund). "News Advisory: Lake Sturgeon to Be Released into Tennessee River System." Posted on *Science Blog,* April 15, 2002. http://www3.scienceblog.com/community/older/archives/K/3/pub3590.html.

Wilson, Larry. "UT Institute of Agriculture Biologists Finding Good News in Restoring Sturgeon to Tennessee Waterways." Media release, November 20, 2012. https://ag.tennessee.edu/news/Pages/NR-2012-11-SturgeonStudies.aspx.

Whooping Crane

Allen, Arthur. "The Shore Birds, Cranes, and Rails: Willets, Plovers, Stilts, Phalaropes, Sandpipers, and Their Relatives Deserve Protection." *The Book of Birds.* Vol. 1. Washington: National Geographic Society, 1937. See p. 294.

Allen, Robert Porter. *On the Trail of Vanishing Birds.* New York: McGraw-Hill, 1957. See pp. 60–77.

Bodio, Stephen. "They Had Feathers." *Living Bird* 35, no. 2 (2016): 20–21.

Burns, Robert, and John R. Cannon. "Whooping Crane Recovery: A Case Study in Public and Private Cooperation in the Conservation of Endangered Species." *Conservation Biology* 10, no. 3 (1996): 813–18.

Doughty, Robin W. *Return of the Whooping Crane.* Austin: University of Texas Press, 1989.

In . . . Formation. Operation Migration Newsletter, Spring 2003.

International Crane Foundation website. https://www.savingcranes.org.

Johnsgard, Paul A. *Crane Music: A Natural History of American Cranes.* Washington, DC: Smithsonian Institution Press, 1991. See pp. 65–94.

Journey North website. https://www.learner.org/jnorth/.

Lishman, William. *Father Goose.* New York: Crown Publishers, 1996. See pp. 43–46.

Matthiessen, Peter. *The Birds of Heaven: Travels with Cranes.* New York: North Point Press, 2001. See pp. 274–300.

McCoy, J. J. *The Hunt for the Whooping Crane.* Forest Dale, VT: Paul S. Eriksson, 1966. See p. 153.

McNulty, Faith. *The Whooping Crane. The Bird That Defies Extinction.* New York: E. P. Dutton, 1966. See pp. 24–50.

Operation Migration website. www.operationmigration.org.

Owens, J. B. "For the Birds" column. *Knoxville Journal,* December 27, 1969.

Pearson, T. Gilbert. *Birds of America.* Reprint: Garden City, NY: Doubleday, 1936. See part 1, pp. 198–200.

Price, Alice Lindsay. *Cranes—The Noblest Flyers: In Natural History* and *Cultural Lore.* Albuquerque, NM: La Alameda Press. 2001. See p. 211.

Renne, Paul R., et al. "State Shift in Deccan Volcanism at the Cretaceous-Paleogene Boundary, Possibly Induced by Impact." *Science* 350, no. 6256 (2015): 76.

Romey, Kristen. "Rare Dinosaur-Era Bird Wings Found Trapped in Amber." *National Geographic* online, June 2016. http://news.nationalgeographic .com/2016/06/dinosaur-bird-feather-burma-amber-myanmar-flying -paleontology-enantiornithes/

"Whooping Crane." National Wildlife Federation website. http://www.nwf.org /Wildlife/Wildlife-Library/Birds/Whooping-Crane.aspx.

Coy-Wolf-Dog?

Darwin, Charles. *On the Origin of the Species: The Illustrated Edition.* New York: Sterling, 2008. See p. 513.

Denver, John. Song lyrics, "Rocky Mountain High." August 1972. RCA.

Faulkner, Charles. Personal conversation, June 9, 2016.

Flanagan, Siobhan. "Meet the Coywolf." *PBS Nature,* January 22, 2014. Produced and directed by Susan Fleming.

Hoffmeister, Donald F. *Mammals of Illinois.* Urbana: University of Illinois Press, 1989.

Kays, Roland. "Yes, Eastern Coyotes Are Hybrids, but the 'Coywolf' Is Not a Thing." *The Conversation,* November 13, 2015. http://theconversation.com /yes-eastern-coyotes-are-hybrids-but-the-coywolf-is-not-a-thing-50368.

Lantz, D. E. "Bounty Laws in Force in the United States, July 1, 1907." *The Yearbook of Agriculture.* Washington, DC: Government Printing Office. 1908. See pp. 560–65.

Morey, Darcy. "Burying Man's Best Friend." Archaeology Archive, Archaeological Institute of America website, November 8, 2006. http://archive.archaeology .org/online/interviews/morey.html.

Mussulman, Joseph. "Coyote," *Discovering Lewis & Clark* website, November 2004. http://www.lewis-clark.org/article/2177.

Plenke, Max. "The Cynarctus Wangi Made Those 'Game of Thrones' Dire Wolves Look Like Teddy Bears." *Science.Mic,* May 12, 2016. http://mic.com /articles/143330/cynarctus-wangi-bone-crushing-dog-game-of-thrones -direwolf#.aLoxQw9SO.

Ratliff, Evan. "The Forever Dog." *National Geographic,* February 2012, 53.

Wade, Nicholas. "From Wolf to Dog, Yes, but When?" *New York Times,* November 22, 2002. http://www.nytimes.com/2002/11/22/us/from-wolf-to-dog-yes -but-when.html?pagewanted=all.

Wang, Xiaoming, and Richard S. Tedford. *Dogs: Their Fossil Relatives and Evolutionary History.* New York: Columbia University Press, 2010. See pp. 66, 155–56.

Wayne, Robert K. *Canid Genetics* website. http://www2.fiu.edu/~milesk/Genetics .htm.

Wheeless, Casey. "Possible Coydogs Terrorizing Seymour Neighborhood." WVLT-TV website, October 7, 2014. http://www.local8now.com/home /headlines/Possible--278444161.html.

Wiens, John A. *Ecological Challenges and Conservation Conundrums: Essays and Reflections for a Changing World.* Hoboken, NJ: Wiley-Blackwell, 2016.

Southern Pine Beetle

Bales, Stephen Lyn. "Youth Rescues Water-logged Beetle." *Farragut Press.* June 27, 2002. See p. 27.

Caird, Ralph W. "Physiology of Pines Infested with Bark Beetles." *Botanical Gazette* 96, no. 4 (1935): 709–33.

Chadwick, Douglas H. "Plant of the Beetles." *National Geographic* 193, no. 3 (1998): 100–119.

Evans, Arthur V. and Charles L. Bellamy. *An Inordinate Fondness for Beetles.* New York: Henry Holt, 1996.

Evans, P. Jonathan. "The Southern Pink Bark Beetle and Forestry on the Cumberland Plateau in Tennessee: Uniformity and Vulnerability." *Distant Thunder: Journal of the Forest Stewards Guild* 16 (Fall 2003): 10–11. Available online at http://www.forestguild.org/publications/forest_wisdom/distant thunder16.pdf.

Frelich, Lee E. "Global Climate Change." *Distant Thunder: Journal of the Forest Stewards Guild* 16 (Fall 2003): 3. Available online at http://www.forestguild .org/publications/forest_wisdom/distantthunder16.pdf.

Lanting, Frans. "35 Who Made a Difference: David Attenborough." *Smithsonian* 36, no. 8 (2005): 74.

Löwith, Karl. *Nietzsche's Philosophy of the Eternal Recurrence of the Same.* Oakland: University of California Press, 1997. See p. 73.

Maser, Chris. "The Real Value of Healthy Forests." *Distant Thunder: Journal of the Forest Stewards Guild* 16 (Fall 2003): 1, 8–9. Available online at http://www .forestguild.org/publications/forest_wisdom/distantthunder16.pdf.

Payne, Thomas L. "The Southern Pine Beetle." University of Georgia Bugwood Network. www.barkbeetles.org/spb/spbbook/chapt2.html.

Rosner, Hillary. "The Bug That's Eating the West." *National Geographic,* April 2015, 102–15.

Savage, Henry, Jr., and Elizabeth Savage. *André and François André Michaux.* Charlottesville: University Press of Virginia, 1986. See pp. 249, 396.

Simmons, Morgan. "Pine Beetle Seen Declining in Areas." *Knoxville News Sentinel,* May 30, 2001.

"Species New to Science." *Discover Life in America* website. www.dlia.org/atbi/new _to_science.shtml.

Ungerer, Matthew J., Matthew P. Ayres and Maria J. Lombardero. "Climate and the Northern Distribution Limits of Dendroctonus frontalis Zimermann (Coleoptera: Scolytidae)." *Journal of Biogeography* 26, no. 6 (1999): 1133–45.

INDEX

From the day we arrive on the planet
And blinking, step into the sun
There's more to see than can ever be seen
More to do than can ever be done

—Lyricist Tim Rice, *The Lion King*

With you in mind, Darlene, sister dear,
you have always been there for me.